James H. Graff, Theodore Edward Hook

Passion and Principle

James H. Graff, Theodore Edward Hook

Passion and Principle

ISBN/EAN: 9783337812614

Printed in Europe, USA, Canada, Australia, Japan

Cover: Foto ©Thomas Meinert / pixelio.de

More available books at **www.hansebooks.com**

PASSION

AND

PRINCIPLE.

BY

THEODORE HOOK,

AUTHOR OF

"JACK BRAG;" "GURNEY MARRIED;" "PARSON'S DAUGHTER;"
ETC., ETC.

NEW EDITION.

LONDON:

CHARLES H. CLARKE, 13, PATERNOSTER ROW.

PASSION AND PRINCIPLE.

CHAPTER I.

Our labours you with sickly eyes behold,
And think them our dishonour, which indeed
Are the protractive trials of the gods
To prove heroic constancy in man.

DRYDEN.

AMONGST the laborious, honourable, and ill-paid professions to which men of ability devote their time and
talents, that of a schoolmaster is, perhaps, the most tiresome and worst rewarded. To expatiate here upon the
perpetual misery of hearing the same lessons repeated
daily, for the whole course of one's natural life, enlivened
only by the different occupations of correcting bad exercises or polishing nonsense verses, would be quite needless : first, because it would be impossible in terms
adequately strong to describe the horrors of such an existence ; and secondly, because it is not to the professional labours of Mr. Rodney, of Somerville House Academy, that I have any disposition particularly to call the
attention of my readers.

Suffice it to say, that in a country town (I hope it has
been observed how carefully I conceal the names of
places), not more than fifty miles from the metropolis, my
friend Mr. Rodney, had for many years governed the
school which, in compliance with the prevailing taste for
fine names and elegant definitions, had of late years been
dignified with the high-sounding title just mentioned; and

had, during his lengthened dominion theiein, whipped
into the world several pupils who had done him much
honour, and contributed, as well by their example as by
sending *their* children in turn to his "Academy," to raise
his reputation and increase his income.

His family, independently of the little boys, consisted of
a wife and daughter.—Heaven had blessed him with three
children, but one only survived; and, as is seldom the
case when a mortality occurs in the family, *she* that was
spared was the flower of the flock. She was perfectly
fascinating, and yet she was not what young novel readers
would call a *heroine;* for she had little pretension, although her talents and accomplishments would have
justified an abundance of airs, and a confidence in herself
to which she was a perfect stranger.

Mrs. Rodney, her mother, was a lady exemplary and
domestic, and as methodical and mechanical in all her
movements, as if she had been actually wound up at seven
o'clock in the morning to go through certain evolutions
until eleven o'clock in the evening. She was always at the
breakfast-table to see the boys fairly served with their
plank-like pieces of bread and butter, and jorums of milk.
She always carved their dinners; during which ceremony
she dressed herself in a peculiarly constructed apron with
a bib and sleeves. In the due execution of this office she
properly apportioned the fat and the lean, administered
with care the lumps of preparatory pudding, and produced
ninety-two cuts from every shoulder of full-grown mutton
which was sent to table.

She again presided at supper in the hall; and when
the little boys went to bed she did duty as mother to
them, and every evening received their parting kisses. In
short, never did she rest until ten o'clock; when Mr.
Rodney, relieved from the cares of the day, regularly
supped in his own parlour in the bosom of his family,
leaving to all his tender charges the delights of sleep, and
the smell of his evening repast, with which the air of the
great hall and staircase was always savourily scented.

One poor boy, indeed, fared differently from the rest of
Rodney's pupils, and when his son died, seemed, as it

were, in some measure, to repair the loss. This boy was called Francis Welsted ; he was the orphan child of an old friend of Rodney's, who had died in distressed circumstances, and Rodney brought the boy home, and reared him as if he had been his own, even while he had a son himself. Surely it was not unnatural when the pride of his heart was snatched from him, that he should love this little orphan better than he did before, and better than he loved any of his fellows; for he had been the favourite friend and constant companion of his own poor William, had shared with him the favours of the parlour and the delights of Mrs. Rodney's tea-table; and when his playmate died, Welsted still kept his place at the domestic board, although his co-mate had been taken away; and time rolled on, and Francis grew ; and, as it was but plain and natural that in time he would,—Francis became a man. From a first-form boy he rose to the sixth form ; and thence unconsciously, having no other pursuit, no other home, no other prospects, at length became usher to Mr. Rodney, at Somerville House ; in which capacity my reader is destined to find him on the day of his introduction, seated in his wonted place, enjoying the calm delights of the Rodney circle, and the prescribed tumbler of red wine negus, which was nocturnally swallowed by each of the gentlemen, Mrs. Rodney and Fanny dividing the third goblet between them :—all such goblets having been prepared with infinite care and regularity by the elder of the two ladies herself.

Mrs. Rodney was a pattern of excellence, but she had a few peculiarities ;—one consisted in always speaking the truth and the whole truth, regardless of circumstances or consequences ; and the other, in never permitting any human being to be happy or comfortable under any circumstances whatsoever, at the same time wishing them with all her heart to be both. As for Rodney himself, he was besides a schoolmaster, a poet, and had published a small volume of little ballads which had made a noise in certain circles. He was patronized by a great Lord resident in his neighbourhood, and what was much more important to a poet of *his* class, by a great Lady; but then he *talked poetry*, which, although it was thought very fine in company, was somewhat tiresome in private life. Of this failing his daughter Fanny and his usher Welsted were quite aware, and occasionally, when he was "off at score," their eyes would meet—eyes *will* meet sometimes—and Fanny felt conscious that she was doing wrong, and Welsted felt that he was occasionally very near laughing in a wrong place; and yet Rodney saw not, felt not the absolute uselessness of walking on stilts over dry ground, the trick to which he was so mightily addicted.

" There's a viridity of intellect," said Rodney one evening after supper, " about young Brashleigh, Mr. Welsted, which is highly refreshing; a single-mindedness truly touching, a newness of sentiment in all his sayings, strongly excitatory of that agreeable feeling which it is hardly within the scope of language adequately to define!"

" Yes, Sir," said Welsted, " he is a good, clever boy in his way."

" It is not so much the intrinsic power of his mind," said (or rather sang) Rodney, " as its characteristics, which force themselves, as it were, upon our attention. There is an originality about him which reminds one of that beautiful expression of Goethe when speaking of a *gurl* (so he pronounced it), fresh from the country, with all her rural recollections strong upon her, who .sees for the first time a great and populous city. The timid thing, instead of being surprised at the vastitude of the multifarious objects by which she, poor tender passive creature, is environed, turns to her anxious parent with an air of hesitation, and one of those soul-fraught looks which convey, as it were, direct to the mind the whole sentiment of those by whom they are reflected, and she says, with all the modest simplicity inherent in a creature so genuine and new—' Mother, I wish we were safe at home!' There's a delicacy in the turn of that thought, and a knowledge of human naturr" (so he pronounced it) " which are quite captivating : such is the intellectual originality of young Brashleigh !"

"He is a nice boy," said Mrs. Rodney; "but I'm sure something will happen to him; he'll never grow up to be a man."

"What reason, my dear Cordelia," said Rodney, "have you for so painful a supposition, wherewith to cloud the brightness of his dawning life?"

"Why, he is so clever;—those clever children never come to good," said Mrs. Rodney.

"His grandfather is devotedly attached to him," said Rodney.

Who this grandfather *was* time will show;—whoever he might be, no sooner was his name mentioned than Mr. Welsted became suddenly and violently embarrassed, and in his agitation knocked the tea-spoon out of his glass of negus.

"A very gallant officer is General Brashleigh," continued Rodney;—"Sir Frederick Brashleigh I should rather call him, since I see he has received the chivalrous distinction of the Bath, and an appointment to a high command abroad."

"Going abroad is he?" said Mrs. Rodney. "Poor dear old gentleman!—then I'm sure he'll never come back again."

"These are gloomy presentiments, Mrs. Rodney," said her husband; "I see no particular reason why a man hale, hearty, and vigorous, as *he is*, should necessarily die at fifty-six."

"Sixty-five, Papa, *I'm* sure," said Fanny;—and immediately Welsted, who had recovered his spoon, began stirring the last few drops of his negus most assiduously, having screwed up his mouth as if apprehensive of some burst of passion from the head of the house.

"Young ladies," said Rodney, calmly, and placidly, "are no judges of such things.—I know what I talk of—he is *under* fifty-seven, and as I before said, full of that nervous manhood which so beautifully characterizes the warrior chief."

"I don't know whether he is nervous, Mr. Rodney," said his lady, "but I know he is very bilious at times; and as for his health—"

" Look at his face, Mrs. Rodney," said the Pedagogue who for some reason best known to himself became quite animated in the discussion ; " the roseate hue of health suffuses his cheek."

" Yes," said Mrs. Rodney, " he has got a red face at times, to be sure, but that's not health, Mr. Rodney,—it is too purple to be wholesome. Take my word for it, some of these fine mornings he'll pop off suddenly."

Welsted's eyes rested for a moment on Fanny's countenance, but she saw not their expression. There was a mystery somewhere, which I believe it is my duty to unravel for the entertainment (it may be) of my readers; but perhaps time and patience will do that piece of service for us.

It should be known—for localities are most important things, and as absolutely necessary to the conduct of a tale, as painted scenery to the performance of a drama—that there was, lying contiguous to Somerville House Academy, a close, or field, containing eight acres, there or thereabouts, more or less, which close was bounded on its northern side by the wall of the church-yard,—one of the neatest and prettiest church-yards in Christendom. The path through this hallowed receptacle of earthly vanity was sheltered by thick umbrageous trees, and when the moon—for what is a grove without a moon ?—" threw her refulgent light" around, Fanny Rodney, whose taste did not lie among slices of bread-and-butter (though Werter's Charlotte's did), was accustomed to stroll through these lonely walks, while the rising generation in her father's house were preparing for bed by stuffing themselves with their substantial supper.

Unfortunately, perhaps, but as they then thought fortunately, the very hour at which this meal was partaken of by the boys, was that, at which Francis Welsted was first released from his scholastic duties ; for Mrs. Rodney was considered by all parties perfectly inadequate to the superintendence of the feeding, and Mr. Rodney, during the early part of the exhibition, always examined the sixth form exercises himself, in his parlour.

The force of habit is surprising. When mere boy and

girl, Frank and Fanny were accustomed to stroll round the close or in the church-yard during this brief period of relaxation, and so it went on, and they continued their rambles unconscious of the different circumstances in which they were placed by the flight of Time. In riper years they met and walked and talked, on other subjects, perhaps, from those which amused their minds in earlier days, but the alteration was so gradual, the change so imperceptible in its progress, that when Francis Welsted at length discovered that the lovely and amiable daughter of his patron and protector was the idol of his manly heart, he trembled at the consummation he so devoutly yet unconsciously wished.

It may be asked why?—It is true he had been received into Rodney's family an orphan, and his parents had died in distress; but then he had fitted himself to be the very prop which did sustain his patron's house, and even to be the successor to his honours and toils, when either inclination or nature should call him from the scene of his magisterial authority. But there *are* secrets they say in all families,—how they remain so, in this talkative world, if they ever do, I know not;—what the particular mystery was, which was apparently so important in the Rodney family, the following conversation may perhaps help to unravel.

Fanny and Francis were pursuing their accustomed walk the night subsequent to that on which the reader was introduced to them: the evening was mild and serene, not a sound was to be heard, save the distant barking of the village dogs, and as they approached the termination of their stroll, the young couple insensibly decreased the pace at which they had been proceeding and lingered near the stile which separates the close from the church-yard.

"Francis," said Fanny, " you are unusually out of spirits this evening. Has my father said any thing to vex you?"

" Not a syllable," said Welsted ; " I am oppressed by my own thoughts, my own apprehensions, my own suspicions ; and the very joy of this happy moment adds new bitterness to my presentiments."

"Have you had ill news from any one?" asked Fanny.

"News, Fanny!" said Welsted, "from whom should *I* hear news?—I am an orphan, an outcast, a beggar;—the creature of your father's bounty!"

"Why talk in this manner to me?" said the agitated girl, who felt that she would have given the world, had it been hers, that she had not touched upon the unlucky topic :—"do I not know all your history, Francis? have we not been brought up together? are we not like brother and sister?"

"Fanny!" said Welsted, "I was well born though ill provided for; my heart is pure and blameless, and, thanks to your excellent father, my principles have been strength-ened by the religious instruction, and moral education which he has given me. But it is because we are *not* brother and sister that my mind is disturbed, disordered, almost deranged."

"Dear Welsted," said Fanny, "what can you mean? — what *has* occurred to cast this gloom over your mind?"

"Fanny," said the devoted young man, "years have passed and I have known no home but this,—even the turf on which we tread is familiar to my eye. Those trees, that venerable tower seem identified with my exist-ence; I saw them as a child—here too I first saw you,— but years have passed away, and though all things around us remain the same, you have become a different being."

"Changed in age," said Fanny, "perhaps in figure, and in face,—but not in love for Francis!"

"Love, Fanny!" repeated Welsted in a tone of bitter anguish: "Did I hear it right,—you love?"

"As I should love my poor lost brother, William, whom *you* loved," said Fanny.

"This must not be," said Francis.—He pressed her hand fervently,—she felt him tremble:—"*We* cannot, must not, think of loving thus—do not delude yourself, Fanny, it is an impossibility!"

"Welsted, for pity's sake tell me what is it you mean!" said Fanny.—"You are ill?"

"No, no,—dearest, dearest girl," said he, "I shall be better in a moment. It has been all madness and folly, —I might have known what it must come to."

"Welsted," said the affectionate girl, "what have I said to vex and agitate you thus?"

"You love me, Fanny," sobbed Welsted, "and you have owned it!"

Her cheek sank upon his shoulder,—it was all too late to retreat—the doubt was over. Yet no responsive sigh re-echoed that, which heaved her snowy bosom,—no kiss of reciprocal affection pressed her cheek. He stood as if paralyzed, till after a pause he gently raised her burning forehead, and muttered in a deep and bitter tone of anguish, as she leant for support on his arm—

"God! what a situation!"

Those in whose hearts is not implanted the high principle by which the exemplary Welsted was at that moment actuated, will marvel at his difficulty and perhaps sneer at his distress. Even the unsophisticated Fanny herself felt surprise and something like disappointment, at the apparent apathy of him whom she had believed devotedly attached to her, and in whom (for disguise with my reader is useless) she always had considered (why, she hardly knew) she beheld her future husband. The disappointment and surprise which agitated her at the moment were not unmixed with dread, that she had committed herself by an avowal of unrequited passion; she trembled and sobbed violently: but the gentle pressure of her hand by Francis, and the sound of his voice mildly imploring her to be tranquil, smoothed and calmed her sorrow.

"For heaven's sake compose yourself, Fanny!" said Welsted. "I ought to have known all this; I ought to have seen the precipice upon the edge of which we stood; but the dreadful step was covered so with flowers that I was not conscious of my danger until too late."

"What danger, Francis?" said Fanny. "Am I despised by you?—Only say the word—"

"Despised!" exclaimed Welsted,—"adored! worshipped! No human being since earth has been **created** can have loved more fondly—more tenderly than I do.— Despise!—Oh, Fanny!"

"Why then this dreadful agitation?" said the sanguine girl.

"The crisis has arrived," said he, more ardently pressing her hand, "this is the last of it!—We must part."

"God forbid!" said Fanny.

"God forbid it should be otherwise," said Welsted.

"Explain," sobbed Fanny; "what have I said,—what have I done?—that I should lose the companion of my youth, the beloved of my heart?"

And again her cheek sank on his shoulder, and again did he more calmly than before raise her drooping head, and implore her to be composed.

'Stay a moment, Fanny," said he, "let the breeze blow on your face, your eyes are full of tears, your forehead burns and beats:—stay, stay, and I will speak."

In pity do!" said the unhappy girl.

"Fanny, idol of my heart!—for such you are," said he —and even *he* was moved to tears.—"you saw my gloom,—my wretchedness,—indeed I could not hide them. And why should I have any concealment from you?—Look round, my beloved, see those well-known fields, those walks, that river;—gaze on them with me this night, for never more must we behold them together."

"Why, why?" said Fanny.

"You shall be told," answered he, "since it must be so. I need not repeat the obligations I owe to your father, I cannot even enumerate them,—I owe him every thing;—he has allowed me the happiness of your society, and I have dared to feel myself your equal."

"Equal!" interrupted Fanny.

"Stay, dearest, stay," continued Francis; "in the course of our lengthened intimacy that feeling has been generated which might have been anticipated. I hoped— I feared;—I never knew till this night how blessed I was;—and what a night is this, in which to be convinced on such a point:"

' Why ?" said Fanny : " be assured my father will not disapprove the declaration of your affection for me. My mother, whom you know loves you as a son, has more than once spoken to me, half jestingly to be sure, of the time when you and I should fill their places here, and visit them in their retirement."

" It might have been," said Welsted ; " but the die is cast, you must never now be mine."

" Then Francis, I will vow—"

" You must not, shall not," interrupted Welsted ; " be calm, dearest;—listen :—As I have said before, I am bound by every tie of gratitude to your father, by every feeling of affection to *you.* I know my duty to both of ye too well, to stay another day beneath his roof,—to morrow's noon sees my departure."

" How can you speak thus ?" said Fanny; " what object can you have in such conduct, or what, indeed, in talking of it ?"

" Your welfare and prosperity, Fanny," replied her devoted Francis, " are the objects; if I stay and persevere in maintaining your affection, we shall marry, and not only will poverty be your lot, but worse, far worse, the curses of your parents will be upon your head."

" Why ; answer me, why ?"

" An alliance, honourable and noble, is at your command," said Welsted ; " I know more than you suppose, —I know more perhaps than even your father himself knows at this moment. Before the whole truth breaks upon him I will go ; never shall it be said that the orphan whom he cherished and supported, was the viper in his bosom to sting his fostering hand."

" Are you dreaming, Francis ?" said Fanny. " What alliance ?"

" You will know all in time," said Welsted ; " the offer is at hand, and you must accept it ; because the acceptance of it will raise you to a rank and station in society which you are well qualified to fill ; you must accept it, because it will be the ardent desire of your parents that you should accept it ; and, above all other reasons, you must accept it, because your disobedience will not only entail poverty and wretchedness, but sin itself upon your head."

" I cannot—will not—"

" Stay, Fanny," continued he; " I am firm, nay more, I am desperate ;—your refusal would kill your father ; recollect his death would rest on me,—that I, like a base, insidious, ingrate, nurtured in his heart and house, had stolen his child's affections, and wedded her to wretchedness and woe."

" Oh, but Welsted," said Fanny, " a cottage with you—"

" I will not hear it, dearest," replied her maddened lover : " the world, if they knew of this, would set me down either for a fool or a dullard, unable to appreciate a lovely, amiable creature, like my adored Fanny. Believe me, dearest, best of girls, in my very heart of hearts I love you, and therefore will I *not* subject you to the precarious life which I am doomed to lead ; therefore will I *not* bring down upon your head the malediction of your parents ; therefore will I *not* interfere with the bright prospects which await you."

" What earthly offer can be made to me," said Fanny, " to compensate for the loss of one I so tenderly love ?"—

" —As a brother?" interrupted Francis.

" As a brother, if you will have it so," cried she eagerly.

" *Then* we must part, indeed," replied he ; " never believe the insidious trash of any man who talks of loving like a brother : after what has passed this night, the deception would not avail us long. Avoid deceit and temporizing, avoid all qualification with yourself ; be assured, Fanny, we *cannot* love like brother and sister : we *must not* be husband and wife,—therefore must we part."

"Surely it will be time to take this measure," said she more mildly, " when this proposal comes. But why am I to accept—"

" I have already said why, Fanny," said Francis,—" it is for your good, your advancement, the advancement of your family."

" Hear me, then," said Fanny—

And he would have listened, perhaps, not to be shaken
in his determination, but to have soothed her anguish, had
not the well-known bell which summoned the establishment to prayers, pealed through the stillness of the night,
and warned them of the necessity to hasten towards the
accustomed parlour, where the evening's meal would soon
be waiting.

" Dry those tears, my best beloved," said Welsted, " we
have no time to spare."

" How can I appear?" said Fanny—" it will be seen
that I have been crying."

" No matter, no matter," said Francis, " to-morrow will
set all to rights ! and God be merciful to me under the
trial ! Hush, hush!" he added, as he felt her bosom
heave rapidly ; " be calm, be calm, my dearest, dearest
love." And when they reached the side gate, he drew her
closer to his heart, and uttering a short and fervent prayer
to Heaven for her happiness, impressed one burning kiss
upon her trembling lips. It was the first,—the LAST !

CHAPTER II.

—— What though the hunter fly,
The stricken stag bleeds on ;
Th' impression that thou leav'st upon my soul
Lies there so deep, so lively, and so full,
That memory recalls no other thought
But only love, and only love of thee.

LANSDOWN.

FANNY, as it might be imagined, was unable to
appear at the supper-table ; she could not rally her spirits
—she felt abashed, miserable, half guilty. There was
something so extraordinary in Welsted's conduct —
something so unaccountable, that she was distracted, tormented, fevered ; in vain she essayed to rouse herself from
the weight of her contending feelings, and hastily undress-
ing, threw herself into bed, and hid her face in her pillow,

w ich was for the first time bedewed with tears of LOVE—
of avowed, and as she then believed, unrequited LOVE.

The servant had no sooner announced to the party assembled, that Miss Fanny was not well, and had gone to
bed, than Mrs Rodney bustled up to her room, and began
Pinnockizing her with the most scrupulous exactitude.
" Quite sure you did not get your feet damp, my dear?"
—" Sit in a draught, my love?"—" Read too long, perhaps?"—" Eat any thing that disagreed with you?"—
" Those mushrooms at dinner, couldn't be toadstools?"
—" Do you think sherry makes you ill?"—these and ten
thousand similar questions did Mrs. Rodney ask, of which
the repetition may be well spared. They indicated that
tenderness which is inherent in mothers, but under the
circumstances, tortured the afflicted girl more than any
bodily ill she had ever endured.

She got off, eventually, upon condition of swallowing
at least half a pint of hot white-wine-whey, and being covered up with four layers of blankets and quilts: Mrs.
Rodney, having decided in the most peremptory mannei,
that the whole of Fanny's disorder proceeded from sudden
and violent cold ; which, " she had no doubt, if not taken
care of in time, would turn to an inflammation of the
lungs, and then there would be an end of their poor
daughter in three days."   Indeed it was with the greatest
difficulty the suffering girl escaped immediate venesection,
which was twice threatened during the course of her
anxious mother's consolatory conversation.

All the attentions paid, all the remedies administered,
Mrs. Rodney returned to the supper-table, which was covered as usual with substantial fare. A new and unusual
visiter, however, graced the board. Master Brashleigh
had been allowed to sit up to supper—he had evinced such
extraordinary originality of idea in the composition of a
theme in the course of the afternoon, that his delighted
preceptor could not refrain from bestowing upon him the
signal and singular distinction of an invitation to eat
roasted fowl and egg sauce with the family, as a reward
for the almost supernatural precocity of genius which he
had displayed in his exercise.

This was what Mr. Rodney *said*—and he said it in his most figurative style, and in the most florid language; and Welsted never was more convinced of the *poetical* talent of his superior, than at the moment when his eulogy upon Master Brashleigh's merits was concluded. Indeed the sudden patronage and indulgence of the wayward urchin were intimately connected in Welsted's mind, with the subject of his present sorrow and determination

"Have you relished your supper, Brashleigh?" said Mrs. Rodney.

"Yes Ma'am, thank you," said the boy.

"Well, I hope you won't be ill in the morning," said Mrs. Rodney; "if you are, we must send for Mr. Dawson to give you some physic."

"I trust there will be no occasion for that, Cordelia," said Mr. Rodney, patting Master Brashleigh on the head paternally; but if there be, Brashleigh has a sufficient sense of moral obligations to take whatever may be prescribed for him by a superior in age and authority, without murmuring or hesitation."

"Oh yes, Sir," said Brashleigh; and after a small glass of negus with a very little wine in it, the bell was rung for Mrs. Enoch, and the young gentleman retired. Welsted's insuperable dulness at supper was seen by the master of the house, and after the departure of his pupil the poet rallied him somewhat inopportunely about love, in a strain worthy, however, of his muse in one of her happiest flights, and concluded by charging him with a sly *penchant* for Miss Ann Tucker, one of the bouncing, rosy-cheeked daughters of the farmer, whose premises adjoined the school.

This was striking the master-chord, and it was with difficulty Welsted preserved sufficient calmness under the accusation, to conduct himself as an usher *should* conduct himself to the principal of such an establishment as Somerville House Academy. Of one thing it convinced him, that no suspicion had been excited in the old gentleman's mind of any attachment in the quarter where it really existed, and he felt grateful for it, however much surprised that the intimacy should so long have subsisted without giving

2

. rise to a supposition in the mind of Fanny's parents, that
it might terminate as in fact it had terminated. He would
not have marvelled at this had he known the world: such
things are going on before our eyes every day in the week,
and will go on, I suppose, " till time shall be no more."

The morning came, and Fanny still remained unwell—
so unwell indeed, that Mr. Dawson the apothecary, who
generally made his tour of the school, and his two or three
shillings every day (Sundays not excepted), by ordering
little boys to swallow small quantities of *Pulv: rad: Ja-
lapi:* and *Supertart: Potassæ*, liquified by large quantities of *Aqua pura*, was called in, and pronounced Miss
Rodney feverish ; " he would, however, send a draught or
two which would infallibly set all to rights, provided she
was kept perfectly quiet : she seemed weak and nervous,
and any thing likely to agitate her would be extremely
improper, if not absolutely dangerous."

Things continued thus until after school broke up at
twelve o'clock, when one of the boys came with a message
from the master to Welsted, begging to see him immediately, in the library. Welsted, whose mind had been
prepared by sundry little events that way tending, anticipated too truly the object of Mr. Rodney's communication, and proceeded to the presence of the head of the
house with a feeling hardly describable, of mingled dread
and doubt. ˙He calmed his agitation as well as he was
able, and upon opening the door of the *sanctum*, found
Rodney in the act of reading (how many times read before
he knew not) a letter, which had arrived by post.

" Welsted," said the old gentleman, and his eyes sparkled with joy, while even dimmed with a tear ; " come
hither, my good boy, Francis, come hither ;—sit you down
—shut the door—there—sit down," and the old gentleman was visibly moved by some strong feeling.

" It is extremely provoking," said he, " that trivial circumstances of bodily indisposition should have combined
at the moment, like gathering clouds about the sun, to
mar the brightness of my daughter's prospects. Fanny
must not be trusted with the important news I have just
received from London, because she is too unwell; and

Mrs. Rodney is equally disqualified from hearing them, inasmuch as they would be forthwith conveyed to her child ; such is the inherent communicativeness of her disposition, such the ever-springing green-leafiness of her character; but to you, Francis, who regard every incident however minute in which our welfare is concerned, with interest and affection, to you I can,—I *must* confide the astonishing intelligence."

" I think, Sir," said Welsted, looking as pale as death, " I could almost guess the nature of your intelligence."

" I think not," said Rodney : " had I been told that I should be enthroned monarch of the Indies, or doomed to die the death of the hardened murderer, I should have listened to the prophecy with not more incredulity than to a prediction made last night of what has been announced to me to-day."

" It relates," said Welsted, in a tremulous voice, which he intended to sound particularly firm, " to Sir Frederick Brashleigh."

" It does," said Rodney, elevating his eyebrows, and looking with a sort of vacant stare at his companion ; " but the purport, Francis, the purport."

" Your daughter is deeply concerned in it, Sir," said Welsted.

" Extraordinary !" exclaimed the astonished schoolmaster ; " have *you* had any communication with Sir Frederick ?"

" I !" said Francis, " not I, Sir; but common observation upon his conduct towards Miss Rodney, when he last came to leave his grandchild here, led me to anticipate an offer of his hand for her, ere long,—indeed I would have staked my life on the event."

" That is very surprising," said Rodney. " The truth, however, had flashed upon your mind, although, perhaps, a little prematurely,—the thing is now confessed, he actually announces his intentions seriously, and purposes shortly paying us a visit to demand her hand, in due form."

" I could have sworn it," said Welsted.

" It is indeed the bright dawning of a glorious day for her, poor child," said Rodney. " What brilliant prospects open upon her young senses—what anticipations of splendour—what anxious hopes of happiness glow in my heart—how little did I expect, and how much less have I deserved this kindness of Providence!"

"I am apprehensive," said Welsted, with as little emotion as possible, "that Fanny will not equally value the conquest with yourself— she has expressed opinions of Sir Frederick——"

"Opinions!" interrupted Rodney, "what are the opinions of a child, compared with the results of such an alliance?—rank, fortune, title, are all at her command—and more than all,—absolute control, where she is going to share the honours of her future husband's elevated command."

"I trust," said Francis, "that it may be for her happiness eventually, and I trust still more anxiously, that she may feel it so."

"There can be no doubt," said Rodney; "the only impediment to an unconditional and eager acceptance of such an offer, would be a prior attachment—of that I have no fear. We have no connexions, no acquaintance, no visiter likely to insnare her heart, or captivate her affections: he is older, to be sure, than Fanny, by some forty or perhaps five-and-forty years—but what of that?"

"There exists a prejudice against such a disparity," said Francis.

"I know it," said Rodney, "and I know, my excellent boy, that Fanny has at times expressed her opinion of the veteran warrior, in language bordering upon the satirical; but the flattering unction of adulation will sooth away any little asperity which she might have felt before she knew his high opinion of her, and I doubt not we shall be able to smooth all difficulties before his appearance in person."

"We," repeated Welsted.

"We," said Rodney; "one of my motives, Francis, for thus early unburdening my mind and making you the partner of my precious secret, is the knowledge that you have a powerful influence over her: you supplied, as it were, the place of her lost and affectionate brother; she

considers you in the light of a near relation, and I am
sure, whatever you say, she will attend to, with cordiality
and readiness; and, as it will be unchilled by the apprehension of paternal advice or influential control, she will
receive it as the genuine tribute of friendship and fraternal affection from one whom she highly regards."

" I fear, Sir," said Welsted, " I should ill support the
character of advocate in such a cause ; indeed the moment has arrived which I have anticipated with dread for
months, and in which I am doomed to undergo certainly
the severest trial of my life. I entreat your patience till
you have heard me out, and I can safely assure you, that
you shall have no cause to condemn the determination at
which I have arrived."

" I do not understand this," said Rodney, " there is as
it were a mist of obscurity (if I may be allowed the expression) before my mind's eye, which involves the whole
plain of circumstances by which we are surrounded."

" First then," said Welsted, " I must confess my faults,
and, secondly, repair them : I love your daughter Fanny,
better than the wholesome air of heaven which I breathe :
—ay, Sir, dearer than the blood which flows in my veins ;
educated, trained up, domesticated with her, was it not
natural that it should be so ?"

' Francis !" said Rodney, and the expression of his
countenance changed from the bright confidence of elated
hope to a look of mingled anger and despair,— " remember———"

" Stay, Sir," said Welsted, " hear me out ; for months
and years Fanny and I have been constant companions,
our thoughts and tastes assimilated, our pursuits and
pleasures have been the same ;—the result is inevitable."

" Recollect," interrupted Rodney.

" Stay, I implore you," said Francis, " let not the
words of reproach which you may think I merit, pass
those lips. I know what you have done for me, I know
what I am, and I know that if I permitted my passion for
your daughter to interfere with her future welfare and
happiness, I should deserve what I entreat you not yet to
bestow upon me—your bitterest curses."

" I should indeed be sorry to think you deserved them," said Rodney.

" I anticipated this offer," continued Welsted, " as I before told you ; you may have observed, perhaps, how cautiously I spoke of the General whenever his name cr merits were discussed.   I saw the advantages which the proposal promised, but I determined whenever the blow should fall, to withdraw myself from your house and all communication with your family.   I have candidly told you how I love your child ; with purity, and honour, and enthusiasm : I have confessed my innocent fault, you shall now find, Sir, that I know my duty.   Thanks to that education which your liberality and kindness have given me, I am enabled, through the support of Him who made me, to prove to my benefactor the triumph of Principle over Passion."

" I had no idea," said Rodney, still lost as it seemed in wonder, " that the affection of fraternity had been thus transmuted, as it were, by time into a more ardent, and differently characterized feeling.   I might too have anticipated it, yet I had a reliance on you."

" Which shall not deceive you," said Francis : " to argue with Fanny upon the merits of this marriage, to persuade her to take the step which kills my hopes of worldly hap- piness, I will not undertake ; but since circumstances fa vour, and her indisposition prevents the immediate com munication to herself of Sir Frederick's letter, let me avail myself of them ; conceal the fact till the morning, and before sunset this evening I will be far away from the home that has sheltered and the hand that has fed me."

" Welsted, I am *not* deceived in you," said Rodney ; " your conduct is such as I might have expected.   It was incautious on my part, I am free to admit, to have suffered this passion thus gradually and imperceptibly to grow with your growth and strengthen with your strength ; but whither are you to go, my dear Francis ? what are you to do ?   That must be considered "

" Thanks to your care," said Welsted, " I am qualified for many stations, the humblest will serve my turn ; any

thing, Sir, so that I can live honourably, and reflect with
satisfaction that I have done my duty."

" Let your absence be but temporary, Francis," said
Rodney; " return to us when the ceremony is over and
the bride departed."

" Return !" exclaimed Welsted in a tone of bitter anguish. " Return, Sir! my duty bids me go, but worlds
should never tempt me back. Every object I saw, every
being I met, every sound I heard, would recal my Fanny
and remind me of her loss; no, Sir, in such a case the
measures must be prompt, decisive, and permanent—we
must part eternally."

" How I lament," said Rodney, "that——"

" Lament not," said Welsted; "rejoice at the prospects which would open on your child; it would be madness to temporize—the connexion with Sir Frederick is
honourable to *her* and *you*. I alone am to blame; perhaps she will start difficulties, raise objections, you are
welcome to allude to my defection in any way you please;
teach her to hate, instruct her to forget me,—I know it is
for *her* advantage, I know it is essential to your happiness that she should do so. All I ask is, keep you
secret this evening, and I will be gone; the pain of separation must be spared us: *you*, Sir," said Francis, deeply
affected, " *you* shall hear from me sometimes."

" You must allow me," said Rodney, who for once
laid aside his stilts, to furnish you with funds which
may ——"

" Not a shilling, Sir," interrupted Welsted, " not a
farthing; I have economised sufficiently since you thought
my labours worth remunerating to spare me that pang.
Upon the amount of my savings I can support myself
well enough until my own hands shall again earn me a
subsistence; you have given me the *means* of gaining a
livelihood, and I am grateful, and as long as I have life,
so long shall I bless your name and that of my kind and
excellent Mrs. Rodney, who has been a second mother to
me. You had better say nothing of this," continued
Francis, " to poor Fanny, Sir ; it may agitate and worry
her—it *can* do no good : say, if a falsehood be allowable,

that we parted in consequence of some misconduct of mine, and of some hasty observation of yours upon it. Say any thing, in short, to avoid discussion, and let my name be interdicted in the family—it will be better."

"No, Francis," said Rodney, "in your conduct upon this trying occasion you have taught me better than ever, how to estimate your honour and vitue. I cannot consent to such measures as those which you propose, yet can I not, such is the strength of paternal feeling, object to the generous course you have marked out for yourself; but I appreciate your excellence, and although professedly we part, not to meet again, I shall cherish the fond hope that circumstances may occur, which will induce you hereafter to join our circle."

"God send my Fanny happy!" said Welsted, "that will be my constant prayer.—And now, Sir," continued he, "I will leave you, to make the few preparations necessary to my departure. I require but little;—it may be ——all I implore is—for with the best intentions I tremble for myself—do not subject me to a parting interview."

"I am going over to Lord Springfield's," said Rodney.

"Then God bless you, Sir," said Welsted, "I shall see you when you return;—the hall bell is just ringing, you will be late.

"I shall be back at three," said Rodney.

"That's well, Sir," said Francis, "that will suit well:" and he hurried abruptly from his protector's presence, rushed to his room, threw himself on the bed, and shed a flood of tears. This was momentary—he roused himself —sat up—listened—the rattling of plates and clattering of knives and forks announced that dinner was served to the boys. Mrs. Rodney would be with them superintending. Fanny was still in her room—Welsted saw the master mount his iron-gray horse at the gate, to depart for Lord Springfield's—he descended the stairs—crossed the entrance-hall—entered the well-known parlour where hung, amidst a dozen others, a paltry silhouette of Fanny; this he detached from its accustomed nail, and thrusting it into the bosom of his waistcoat, fled again to his room. He hastily packed up his linen and the few books he could call his own, in his solitary portmanteau, carried it himself down stairs to the side-door of the house which opens into Farmer Tucker's lane.—One of the farmer's boys stood at the gate, who volunteered to carry the trunk wherever directed. Welsted ordered him to take it to the Crown-inn in the village, and saw him depart: then slackening his pace, composing his spirits and changing the direction of his steps, he passed up the lane into the high road upon which the front of the house stands. He lifted his eyes towards the window of Fanny's room—she was there—looking pale and ill, wrapped in her shawl, standing at the window which was open :—to speak to her was inevitable.

" Isn't the air too cold for you ?" said Francis.

" No," said Fanny, " I am pronounced quite well, and shall be down stairs at tea."

To think that a simple observation, couched in common homely language such as this, should cut a man to the very heart of hearts !—the struggle was renewed—his bosom heaved—his knees trembled.

" I hope," said Fanny, leaning forward and speaking more softly, " your spirits are better than they were last night, Francis ?"

He made no answer.

" Where are you going now ?"

" Going," said Welsted, and he was as pale as death " I'm going—to—call——"

" *You* don't look well to-day," said Fanny somewhat impressively.

" No, indeed !—I—I—am pretty well," said he.

" Well, make haste back, Francis," said Fanny, " perhaps Mamma will let me out of prison before tea-time, and then——"

" Yes, I will," exclaimed Francis, interrupting her in a tone of affected gaiety ; and after gazing one moment longer upon her lovely countenance, after beholding one of her sweetest smiles and an affectionate wave of her hand, he hurried along the street of the village, and reached the inn just at the moment the London coach arrived, to change horses. he spoke to the coachman,

gave the portmanteau into his charge, and walked onwards, desiring to be taken up at the outside of the
town.

And all this was the operation of a few minutes; in a
few minutes more he had passed the last house on the
London road ; and in less than a quarter of an hour he was
seated on the roof of the stage, travelling towards the metropolis at the rate of ten miles an hour.

CHAPTER III.

Thou canst fight well and bravely ; thou canst
Endure all dangers, heats, colds, hungers ;
Heaven's angry flames are not suddener
Than I have seen thee execute ; nor more mortal.
The winged feet of flying enemies
I've stood and seen thee mow away like rushes,
And still kill the killer !   Oh were thy mind
But half so sweet in peace, as rough in dangers !

ROCHESTER.

MAJOR-GENERAL Sir Frederick Brashleigh, K.C.B.,
recently appointed Commander-in-chief at Bombay (who
is destined to make a conspicuous figure in this narrative),
was born in the year 1760 : his parents were highly respectable persons in the North of England, who intended
their son Frederick for the church ; not that his personal
qualifications or intellectual endowments were particularly
adapted to the sacred functions of the priesthood, but because an aunt of his, had in her gift, the valuable living
of Glebeland, in the immediate vicinity of his father's
place.

Accordingly, Mr. Brashleigh, after an education at
Rugby, was entered at Exeter College, Oxford, and kept
some two or three terms, when, in consequence of a most
unexpected event, his views and intentions for after-life
underwent a sudden and singular alteration.   His maiden
aunt, whose heart had remained unthawed for upwards of
sixty winters, fell a victim to the devoted attentions and

unremitting assiduities of the Reverend Mr. Huggin, a man of unquestionable piety and devotion ; sanctified in his manner and conversation, of unimpeachable purity of conduct and excellence of temper, and who, after a lengthened service as curate to the then incumbent, the Reverend Arthur Brashleigh, induced the patroness of the living to surrender, not only her ancient person and matured heart, but the valuable bit of preferment into the bargain, to his possession ; an act which was set down in the Brashleigh family as indicative of insanity on the part of the antiquated relation, although not sufficiently conclusive for the attainment of a statute of lunacy.

Cut short in his career towards the dexter bench of the Upper House of Parliament, the young Oxonian applied to his father to know what course he would advise him to pursue. Mr. Huggin was young and healthy, the air and neighbourhood of Glebeland particularly salubrious, and therefore any thing like waiting for the next vacancy appeared wholly out of the question. For the bar, Frederick was convinced that he had neither talent nor application ; for the navy, he was considerably too old, it being quite clear that it is a mistake for gentlemen with beards to assume the character of midshipmen, and try trips to the main-top-gallant truck, after their legs have grown long and awkward, and themselves heavy and unwieldy.

The army, therefore, seemed the only chance left ; and accordingly in the year 1781, and not before, Mr. Frederick Brashleigh procured upon the interest of his family, which in those days had some weight in the county, an ensigncy in a regiment of the line, the number of which I shall most carefully keep secret.

Brashleigh was an ill-favoured, hard-featured young man ; his hair was white, and his eyelashes white, and his eyebrows white, and his complexion cowslip yellow, covered with a profusion of freckles ; a strong sympathy between a pair of grayish-greenish eyes, induced them to ogle at each other across a nose, which though of the aquiline order, had received considerable damage when its proprietor was a boy, by a blow it received from a falling folio of voyages, which, while the adventurous youth was dragging down some more interesting work from a shelf in his father's library, pitched directly upon that part of the projecting feature vulgarly called the bridge, and gave it such a twist that it never after recovered the much-desired mediocrity of his face.

He was perhaps one of the worst tempered, violent, and uncivilized youths ever bred in a decent family; self-willed, vindictive, suspicious, overbearing to his inferiors, obsequious to those above him, illiberal in all his thoughts and views, and, in short, held to be so disagreeable at Oxford, that if he had not voluntarily removed himself from Exeter, the whole stock of ingenuity of that ingenious College, would very soon have been exerted to compel him to retire.

The regiment to which he was appointed was in India, when he received his orders to join it ; and accordingly he proceeded to Fort William by the earliest opportunity, having quarrelled during the voyage with every passenger in the ship, except a brother subaltern, his junior, who kept terms with him more from awe than affection.

Arrived safe at the end of his salt-water progress, he commenced a fresh-water one, and after four months *budgerowing* up the Ganges, reached the head-quarters of his corps, which, at that time, was stationed, I believe, at Futtyghur, or some such place.

Before nine months had elapsed he had fought three duels, been once tried by a court martial, and sent to Coventry by the regiment half a dozen times for churlish conduct ; tired therefore of the round of tiffing, dining, and supping, with a set of men by whom he clearly saw he was hated, and for whom he entertained the most sovereign contempt, he availed himself of the removal of the regiment to the city of palaces (as Calcutta is called in India), to unite himself to one of those young ladies who are annually sent out to the white flesh market of the East, like unstamped cards, which are made for exportation, the return of which, to England to be played with, incurs a heavy penalty. Of the lady's family, friends, connexions, or circumstances, he of course knew as little as she knew of his ; but, nevertheless, she accepted his offer immediately upon its being made, in obedience to the directions of her female friend and *consignee*, who gave her to understand that it was a rule in the carnal bazaar of Bengal, for Venture-Misses to take the first man who proposed ; and accordingly Miss Amelia Fossdyke became Mrs. Brashleigh in about three weeks after her first interview with her future husband.

As I was at no period of their residence there, either in their Bungalow, or indeed, in India itself, it is impossible for me to say how they passed their time. I have heard that he was chiefly addicted to cock-fighting, in which humane diversion, and all its concomitant pleasures of training, feeding, matching, weighing, and heeling, he took great delight, and consumed much of his time ; she was amiable, placid, and contented, and became a mother during the first year of her marriage, and, occupied with her Ayah and baby, went on pretty well, until, as the novelty of matrimony wore off, and her laudable determination to be pleased with India and her husband a little abated, she began to discover, as all his acquaintance had discovered long before, that there never exist d upon earth a more uncivilized disagreeable animal in human shape than her " dear Frederick Brashleigh."

It so happened, and such things will happen, that Mrs. Brashleigh, who was extremely pretty, and graceful beyond the general average of exportation girls, was at a public entertainment at Calcutta, and most particularly attracted the notice of his Excellency the then commander of the forces :—who his Excellency was, I shall keep religiously secret, for more reasons than one : no matter, he saw, and admired her, discovered her name, inquired of his aide-de-camp the regiment and rank of her husband,—whether a King's officer or a Company's? to all of which he received (as generals do, when they ask such questions of their staff) answers clear and succinct, which appeared extremely satisfactory ; the character of the lieutenant was sketchily given, and upon reference to a gay lady of a certain time of life, high in favour at the Presidency, his Excellency was satisfied that the plaintive expression which Mrs. Brashleigh's features occasionally wore during the evening, resulted from some secret sorrow, some silent grief connected with domestic events, and, in short, that she was what is colloquially called " *not* happy with her husband."

His Excellency the commander of the forces caused himself forthwith to be introduced to the fair mourner ; and although no places in the world are so ridiculously ceremonious as our oriental settlements of tea-dealers and cotton-pickers, his Excellency waved all the usual forms which are so jealously adhered to, in order to give the money-making exiles who reside there, something like importance in their banishment, and made the amiable during the evening most charmingly and successfully.

Poor Mrs. Brashleigh, who had been long enough married to value her charms and attractions by the way in which her husband seemed to appreciate them, held them in no great estimation, and never dreamt that she had that evening captivated the gay and gallant general who ruled and reigned over his Majesty's forces and those of John Company with undivided power and control.

Poor unsuspecting thing ! she was doomed very soon to be undeceived upon this important point. Early the next day, as she and her loving spouse, who had just returned from cock-feeding, were seated at tiffin in their Bungalow (some fish and rice, a tureen of Mulicatauny, and a bottle of Hodson's pale ale, on the clothless table), when, to their surprise and amazement, one of the aides-de-camp of his Excellency the commander-in-chief made his unexpected appearance. The glittering visiter was received by the lady with her usual good-nature and kindness, and by her husband with a sort of sullen impatience not unmingled with mortification, that one of his Excellency's staff should have detected the irregularity with which the repast had been put down.

" I hope," said the aide-de-camp, " you caught no cold last night, Mrs. Brashleigh ?"

" I don't *think* I have," said Mrs. Brashleigh, for she was afraid to state distinctly whether she had or had not, until her husband had signified his will and pleasure whether she should disclaim or admit the apprehended indisposition.

" Not *she*," said Brashleigh ; " she is as hard as iron, Walford, and takes more killing than a badger. I'm afraid you won't like our tiffin, Walford, coming from head-quarters ; but I can't help it. I have no regular cook, and as for Amelia, she can't manage any thing in our way."

" I *have* tiffed," said Walford, " and have not a moment to spare—I have called on business."

" Oh," said Brashleigh, " about that infernal fellow, Magann, I suppose—another court of inquiry ?"

" No," said the aide-de-camp, " I really don't know exactly what the bus'ness *is*, but I am directed by his Excellency to beg you will call on his military secretary to-morrow, as early as you conveniently can, after morning parade."

" Not regimental business then ?" said Brashleigh, who had just involved himself in a serious quarrel with a bro-ther-officer, who happened unfortunately to be decidedly in the right.

" I fancy not," said Walford, who appeared during the conversation to treat *Mrs.* Brashleigh with the most marked deference and respect ; but I know nothing more than I am bid to know."

" That's the case with you, grandees," said Brashleigh : " thank God I'm independent of every body. I do my duty, and don't care three cowries either for the general or my own commanding officer ; and how you *can* live the life of an aide-de-camp, always bowing and cringing, and smirking and smiling, and carrying hats and messages, and carving at dinner, and playing at cards, and trying horses, and riding backwards in coaches, I don't in the least comprehend : for *my* part, I'd starve first."

" Your satire upon dependants falls harmless to-day, Brashlegh, as far as I am concerned," said Walford : " for I join my regiment, which is ordered on service, and quit his Excellency's staff to-morrow."

" You are right, Walford, you are right," said the ant-

mated subaltern ; free and easy, bread and cheese and
liberty, is my motto ; how happy you'll feel when once
you are out of harness."

" I have had every reason to be grateful to the general,"
said Walford ; " he has been kindest of the kind to me,
and has never exacted half the duties which he had a right
to claim."

" His Excellency seems an extremely pleasant man,"
said Mrs. Brashleigh.

" His Excellency," said Walford, " would be extremely
well pleased to hear that you think so, Mrs. Brashleigh."

" *She!*" said Brashleigh ; " how should *she* know any
thing about generals ?—why her father was a hatter in the
Poultry, or some such place. She'd call any thing gentlemanly and pleasant that was a cut above the counter."

" Well, my dear," said Amelia, " I only observed—"

" Keep your observations to yourself, then, Ma'am,"
said Brashleigh, " and go and nurse your little child—
I hear it squalling again. There never was so peevish a
brat in Bengal as your pet lamb. Come, go, Ma'am, and
make them keep it still."

The tears stood in the poor young creature's eyes, and
casting a glance at Walford, she pushed her plate away
from her, hastily rose and left the room.

" Now that's what she calls fine ; she'd have made a capital actress," said her husband. " She thinks you'll pity
her, and set me down for a brute and a tyrant—that's just
her way."

" Well," said Walford, anxious to get away, " I will
not intrude any longer ; you will call on Mansel to-morrow as soon as you can."

" Can ?—must, you mean," said Brashleigh. " I must
go full fig, I suppose, to the military secretary ; no mufti
—no white jacket—no being comfortable "

" I think you had better be dressed," said Walford,
" for I rather believe—I don't know—that his Excellency
wishes to speak to you himself."

" Oh, then," said Brashleigh, " I'd bet fifty rupees I
know what he is after."

" The deuce you do," *thought* Walford.

'Great men always want something when they are so devilish civil to little ones," said Brashleigh.

Walford was startled by this observation, and somewhat apprehensive that his *friend* might suspect the real object of his Excellency's desire to see him, inasmuch as there are but few things in the world which a commander of the forces can possibly want from a lieutenant.

" Indeed," said Walford, " I can't assist you in your surmises."

" He's going to ask me to give him some of my Malay cocks," said Brashleigh ; "that's it, you may depend upon it—he wants to mend the breed."

An irresistible smile played over Walford's countenance at this announcement of the lieutenant's suspicions, and after again assuring him that he really did not know what his Excellency's object was, the gallant aide-de-camp mounted his little Arabian, and followed by his sice at full speed, galloped away to head-quarters to report progress.

When he departed, Brashleigh returned to the room where tiffin was still on the table, and having regaled himself with all the different degrees of the then favourite Indian beverage, in as many distinct tumblers, from Sangaree the first to Sangrorum the last, proceeded half asleep and half stupid, with the aid of his servant, to buckle on his accoutrements and betake himself to afternoon parade.

His poor wife remained with her hapless child until his return, which occurred at a late hour, just in time to announce that he should dine at the mess, a measure he often adopted, not because he liked the society of his brother officers, or received the smallest gratification from visiting them, but because he knew they were always happier and more comfortable when he was absent. This, and the desire to show that he had a right (for he had a great notion of his *rights*) to be there, ordinarily led him into their company about twice or three times in each week, upon which occasions he generally involved himself in some new scrape, and excited some new disgust.

On the particular occasion under discussion, he sig himself by the display of his independent indigna-

tion at the conduct of the commander of the forces, whom
he denounced in terms hardly decent, and not quite safe,
even at a mess-table, for having tyrannized over some poor
fellow of his acquaintance and stopped his promotion to
favour a *protegé* of his own ; and swore that if *he* were
Jackson, he would do *this*, and he would say *that*, and
he would write home to the Horse Guards, and he would
never submit to be made a fool of, nor a tool of ; *he* would
have justice, the birthright of a British soldier; and thus
the conversation was engrossed, and the evening's harmony destroyed, by one of Lieutenant Brashleigh's edifying
exhibitions of military independence, good taste, and good
sense.

The morning came ; and with it parade.—" Halt, left
wheel—front—dress," as usual ; then breakfast and more
quarrelling with poor Mrs. Brashleigh, to whom for the
fifty-third time he mentioned how bitterly he repented
having married her, upbraided her with low birth, swore
that he had been tricked and deceived, and wished himself
dead, which, being calmly interpreted by his better half,
was translated into a wish that *she* were dead and he rid
of her.

After parade, however, Lieutenant Brashleigh betook
himself to the office of Major Mansel, the Military Secretary, where he remained for upwards of an hour. When
he returned home, he appeared to be in an extraordinary
humour ; he seemed nearly good-tempered, spoke almost
kindly to his poor wife, whose beautiful eyes were actually
reddened and swollen with tears. Something very strange
had evidently occurred, he was an altered man, and she
an astonished woman ; he dined, however, at the mess,
and there, when reminded of what he had said the night
before, seemed particularly anxious to bury all recollection of his former conduct and conversation in oblivion ;
his brother officers wondered at the subdued and softened
tone of the boisterous lieutenant, and were marvelling at
the strange alteration so suddenly effected in his manner,
and the tone of his observations upon his superiors, heretofore the constant objects of his vituperation, when the
orderly-book was brought to one of the captains at table

by his sergeant. He opened it, and the exclamation which escaped him as he read the order of the day, excited a sudden feeling of surprise in all around him.

" I wish you joy, Brashleigh," said Captain Osborne, returning the book to the sergeant. " Why this *is* a surprise."

" What—promotion?" exclaimed the president.

" Read—read!" was the general cry.

Osborne took back the orderly-book and read with an audible voice

Head Quarters, Fort William, Feb. 8, 1786.
G. O. His Excellency the Commander-in-chief has been pleased to appoint Lieutenant Brashleigh, of the —— regiment, to be his Excellency's Aide-de-camp, *vice* Walford, who joins his regiment.
(Signed) W. MANSEL, Mil. Sec.

A thunder-bolt, an apparition, Old Nick himself, had he made his appearance, in the full uniform of the corps, could not have more completely surprised the assembled party than this announcement; indeed, in Brashleigh's presence, it was almost impossible to do justice to their astonishment! That so accomplished a person and so distinguished an officer as the Commander-in-chief should have selected from amongst all his Majesty's regiments then at Fort William, a man hardly two removes from downright boorishness for one of his personal staff, seemed like a miracle, or a proof of sudden and violent insanity; they looked and winked, and stared, but finally drank the health of the new aide-de-camp by unanimous consent; consoling themselves, in the midst of their contending feelings upon the subject, with the reflection, that let what might happen, at all events *they* should get rid of him.

As I do not profess to detail the history of Mr. Brashleigh's early life, and as our concerns with him are of much more recent date, I shall merely observe, that in the course of the following week the new aide-de-camp shifted his quarters to the general's house, where, with the urbanity and consideration which always marked his

Excellency's conduct, his Excellency caused rooms to be
fitted up for Mrs. Brashleigh and her *dear* infant. That
after nine or ten months had elapsed Lieutenant Brashleigh became the most abject sycophant that ever crawled,
devoted his days to tattling, and his evenings to eaves-
dropping, to collect anecdotes, scandal, or even more
serious matter of information for his Excellency; that he
was the warmest advocate of all his Excellency's military
measures, and the constant eulogist of his Excellency's
domestic virtues. That Mrs. Brashleigh, shortly after the
appointment, recovered her health and good looks sur-
prisingly; that whenever she took her airings, it was in
the lofty phaeton of his Excellency (at that time the
fashionable carriage); that whenever she went to parties,
his Excellency's palanquin attended her; that her control
over her husband, and her sovereign contempt for him,
were as evident to all beholders as her influence over, and
her high consideration for, the General; and that at the
end of some ten months she presented Lieutenant Brashleigh with a fine boy, which, though pronounced by the
lady's female friends to be the " very image of his father,"
did not in the smallest degree resemble her former child,
who was, at the time it was born, declared, by the same
competent authorities, to be the lieutenant's counterpart.

Were I to go into details, or recount the various
reasons assigned for the lieutenant's getting a company by purchase, when it was notorious that he had
not five rupees at his command, or for the entire revolution worked in his habits and principles, I should unne-
cessarily swell the bulk of my narrative. Suffice it to
say, that his elder child died, that his wife shortly after
became an invalid, and that his Excellency the commander of the forces, having continued in Calcutta even
beyond the usual period of commands, was at length recalled, and his successor arrived in India. To *him*, as a
treasure, his Excellency recommended Captain Brashleigh as military secretary, and succeeded, to the great
joy of the said captain, in fixing him in that respectable
situation. Mrs. Brashleigh's health, according to the *fiat*
of her physician (a particular friend of his Excellency) at

this particular juncture required her immediate removal to Europe with her surviving boy, of whom she was dotingly fond ; and accordingly, as his Excellency was returning to England at the same time, nothing could be more convenient for Mrs. Brashleigh than taking a passage in the same ship with his Excellency, where she would enjoy every comfort which the exalted rank of her husband's patron would command, and be sure of society to which she was accustomed, and in which she was always extremely well pleased to be.

These preliminaries arranged, time glided insensibly on, and on the 14th of February, 1789, his Excellency proceeded in his budgerow, attended by several of his friends, and accompanied by Mrs. Brashleigh and her son, an Ayah, and several domestics, down the Hoogly to Fultah ; where, his Excellency having taken an affectionate leave of his staff and friends, and the lady having bade a tender adieu to her husband, the party embarked on board the Honourable Company's Ship Horncastle, of nine hundred and fifty tons, which, after firing a salute in honour of his Excellency (by which attempt at a nautical manœuvre she burst two of her guns, killed four of her men, and wounded seven others), let fall and sheeted home her topsails gradually and deliberately, one by one; shook out her three topgallant sails in the course of the next three quarters of an hour ; and, having in forty-eight minutes more, got way upon her, began to bore her great round bows through the foaming waves on her voyage to England.

And thus parted Captain and Mrs. Brashleigh, as it turned out, never to meet again. The captain, habituated to India, " held on," with staff appointments, as long as he could, until his regiment, in the course of service, was ordered home ; he then exchanged into another, the exchange lost him much of his army rank, and he found himself in the year 1801, a widower, an invalid, and second captain of his regiment. Pains in his side, yellow cheeks, constant fever, and insatiable thirst, warned him to shift his quarters ; and early in the Spring

of 1802 he reached his native country, shattered in constitution, and, as it may easily be imagined, not particularly improved in looks.

Cheltenham, however, in time resuscitated him, and a
tour made with Mrs. Brashleigh's favourite son (then in
his fifteenth year) sufficiently re-established him to feel
anxious again for active life. His regiment shortly after
returned to England, his friends purchased a majority in
it for him; he was now in the path of preferment, and
having risen progressively through the different grades of
the army, served with much honour and credit to himself
during the Peninsular war, and consummated his military
fame by most gallant conduct on the immortal field of
WATERLOO; on that plain fell by his side, covered with
wounds and glory, the son bequeathed to him by his
departed wife, who in the previous year, and when a
prospect of peace was temporarily held out to the world,
had married happily and advantageously : the offspring of
that marriage was the boy now at Mr. Rodney's school,
and his grandfather, as I have traced him up to the
present moment, the intended husband of Mr. Rodney's
daughter.

His Excellency, the anonymous commander of the
forces of Calcutta, died in the year 1798, or 1799; and
Mrs. Brashleigh, after a short illness, contracted by eating ice while over-heated with dancing, shuffled off this
mortal coil about two years before him ; and thus for five
or six and twenty years had the veteran lover, Sir Frederick Brashleigh, solaced himself in widowed singleness;
if report speaks truth, however, not voluntarily,—he had
proffered his honours, and the temptation of a title, to
more than one unwilling fair, but his person and manners,
not improved by age, were such terrible drawbacks to the
advantages which he submitted. that none were found so
silly or so base as to sacrifice themselves at the shrine of
avarice or ambition for the sake of what *he* could give.
Disgusted with the obduracy or insensibility of town-bred
belles and fine ladies, Sir Frederick, unfortunately, transferred his affections to our poor Fanny, and divulged his

serious intention of laying his fortunes at her feet in the letter to Rodney, which that gentleman received on the memorable morning of Welsted's departure.

I sincerely apologize to my reader for the digression into which I have been inevitably led : it was absolutely necessary to an understanding of the following narrative, and I trust I have fulfilled that, which I admit to be an unpleasant duty, as briefly and succinctly as possible; the state of things at the end of this chapter, as far as relates to our present position, is as nearly as possible the same as that with which we concluded the last, except that Rodney has returned from Lord Springfield's, Fanny has been allowed to come down into the parlour, Mrs. Rodney is preparing to make tea, and Welsted is thirty-three miles on his road to London.

CHAPTER IV.

—— See, I am all obedience :
Did ever daughter yet obey like me ?
Not she who in the dungeon fed her father
With her own milk, and by her piety
Saved him from death, can match my rig'rous virtue :
For I have done much more.
LEE.

WHEN Rodney returned home from Lord Springfield's, his first inquiries were for Welsted : he had been asked where Mr. Welsted was going, by a neighbour who had seen that young gentleman on the top of the stage passing the second milestone on the London road. This inquiry assured Rodney that his young *élève* was actually gone ; but to make this " assurance doubly sure," he questioned Monsieur Louvel, the French master, and two or three of the elder boys, whether they had recently seen Mr. Welsted ? The unanimous negative returned to his question induced him to proceed to the young man's apartment ;—it was deserted. A few books belonging to Mr. Rodney's library were deposited on the table, a drawing-book and pencil-case of Fanny's lay beside them, but of the little property poor Welsted could call his own, there was not a vestige left.

It was clear that he had adopted the bold measure, upon which alone he relied to terminate, honourably and decidedly, his long and affectionate intercourse with the daughter of his benefactor. Rodney's heart was pained as he gazed round the vacant room, and he felt a shuddering regret that his almost son had been driven from him by feelings which, at his time of life, he could scarcely appreciate. He opened the books—turned over their leaves, mechanically gazing on them, but seeing nothing; he put them down as if it were almost sacrilege to move them from the place where they had been deposited by Francis; and satisfied, by the appearance of things, of the correctness of the information he had received, left the apartment, and closing the door quietly, and as it were respectfully, descended to his sanctum, the retreat so often shared with the poor fugitive, whose desired flight was the cause of his present uneasiness.

A few minutes' consideration of the subject brought with it composure, and even satisfaction at the course which things had taken. He drew Sir Frederick's letter from his pocket, and re-read it carefully; then weighed in his mind the various events of the past lives of Welsted and Fanny, by which he thought he could form an estimate of their attachment; for now that the clue had been given, and his suspicions excited, he felt assured that an attachment on *his* part did actually exist. He reflected upon the sorrows which awaited the young couple, if his apprehensions were correct; but he put into the opposite scale the advantages which the unexpected alliance of his child with a Major-General, Knight Commander of the Bath, and Commander-in-chief of an East Indian settlement, would necessarily produce; advantages which he felt to be more important than we can well imagine them: and in addition to an eventual retirement from his scholastic toils, anticipated with all the ardour of a poet (who is as vain and foolish when old, as he is when young) the additional *éclat* which would await his " lines," in her

ladyship's azure circle, when it should be known that their
author, instead of being old Rodney the schoolmaster,
was Rodney, Lady Brashleigh's father, until all pity for
Fanny, all commiseration for Welsted retired from his
heart, and gave place to the palpitations of expected son-
net celebrity, and the throbbings of a very small ambition.

At this juncture Mrs. Rodney, his " better half," op-
portunely made her appearance in the study, and informed
the head of the house that Fanny was so much better, that
she was to come down to tea.

" Cordelia," said Rodney, "sit down, my love."

" Me! Mr. Rodney—what here?"

" Yes, dearest," said her husband.   " The mind when
overcharged, droops, as it were ; and like the rose suffused with evening dew, seeks, if I may be allowed the
expression, support from its kindred branches.   I have
much to tell, and much to ask of you."

" Well, I'm sure I shall be very glad to hear what you
have to say ; but—" said Mrs. Rodney, "while I think
of it, I'd better tell you that Evans charges sevenpence-
halfpenny a pound for that mutton which we had last
week, and Mrs. Fisher tells me, they get theirs at Miller's
for sevenpence."

" Mutton, my angel," said the poet, throwing his eyes
heavenwards, " mutton as nutriment is wholesome, nay
needful ; and there is a charm to me, a winning charm,
in that single-mindedness which you so eminently possess, and which is so beautifully and singularly your characteristic.   There is something highly refreshing in that
constant carefulness of a husband's worldly interests,
which marks the conduct of the excellent wife ; and I
duly appreciate, nay, perhaps I may be allowed to say
venerate, the motives by which, in the true spirit of unsophisticated housewifery, you communicate the relative
prices of the same article purchaseable of different persons in the same village ; but at this moment, Cordelia,
I am too much engaged in matters where hearts are concerned, to lend myself to other topics."

" The hearts, my dear," said Mrs. Rodney, " are only

fourpence-halfpenny any where,—that *is*, if you take the livers with them."

"Dearest Cordelia," said Rodney, whose fat flat face and swimming blue eye were animated with something like expression, "abstract your ideas for a moment from meaner things, and let me question you upon a subject more important, more heart-stirring, more intensely interesting, if I may be allowed the expression, than those to which you are at present directing your attention, I want to ask you something concerning Fanny."

"Why, she is a great deal better," said Mrs. Rodney; "and Mr. Dawson says she will do very well, only she must keep her——"

"My dear Cordelia," said Rodney, "still we are at issue—it is not of her present bodily complaints I speak : I would consult you upon an event of the greatest importance which has ever occurred to us, and which is on the eve of happening. Let me prepare your mind for the reception of the welcome intelligence, which is at once cheering and astounding, animating and overpowering ; but before I do so, that I may the more readily and dispassionately fit myself for the duty I have to perform, I would, as I have before expressed myself, ask you a few questions."

"Well, make haste, Mr. Rodney," said his lady, "because Evans's boy is waiting about the mutton."

"My love," said Rodney, somewhat impatiently, "during the long intercourse of our daughter with Frank Welsted, has it ever occurred to you that any tender feeling of affection, of that beaming glowing passion which baffles all attempts to paint its force, existed between them,—that their young hearts were insensibly, as it were, attracted towards each other, or that even if one of the young creatures felt the powerful influence of the tender all-subduing passion, it was at any time reciprocated by the other?"

"If you mean to ask whether Frank is fond of Fanny, and Fanny of Frank, I'm as sure of it as that I am sitting here," said Mrs. Rodney.

" And how long has that conviction beamed upon your mind ?" asked Mr. Rodney.

" Conviction !" repeated his lady, " why I've thought so these two years : I always knew what it would come to at last, and so has every body in the place, only I stopped them whenever I heard them, and said I was afraid it would not end so well as they thought."

" To every body, you say, this partiality has been evident," said her husband.

" Every body," answered Mrs. Rodney : " and now, I suppose, Frank has told you the whole story."

" Frank is gone," said Rodney.

" Gone ! Mr. Rodney," exclaimed his wife, " Francis Welsted gone away from *us !*—where to—to whom—how —when does he come back——?"

" Stay, love," said Rodney, thinking it best in her present humour to temporize with his lady ; " he is gone to London."

" He'll be ruined," said Mrs. Rodney ; " but how is he gone ?"

" On the top of the stage-coach," said Rodney.

" He'll be overturned and killed," said Mrs. Rodney, —" When does he come back ?"

" Why, judging by the spirit of your unseasonable prophecy, Cordelia," said Rodney, " never."

" Poor boy !" said the kind-hearted lady.

" But it is *not* of him I am anxious to speak just now," said Rodney ; " I have a letter here, which I wish you to read carefully and attentively;" saying which, he put Sir Frederick Brashleigh's formal offer of marriage into his wife's hands.

" Think the contents of this well over—examine all its points and bearings, bring to the task of its consideration all the energies of your able mind, and all that pure intellect with which the cheering power of Providence has so benignly gifted you ;—read it, I charge you, with care, and, till I see you again, keep its contents secret from Fanny. I repeat, Cordelia, it relates to matters of high importance to us and to our interests ; and upon the decision to be formed upon it, hangs the good or evil fortune of our future lives."

Mrs. Rodney took the letter and looked at it. " This comes from old General Brashleigh," said Mrs. Rodney.

" It is immaterial, at the present moment, whence it comes," said Rodney ; " I wish you to peruse it alone, and unacted upon by any extraneous influence."

" Very well, love," said Mrs. Rodney, putting it into her pocket ;—I'll read it all through, you may depend upon it ; but I must just step and tell Evans's lad he need not wait any longer about the mutton, because we can send Jem down in the evening, after the boys have had their supper."

Saying which, his amiable helpmate retired ; his eye followed her ; and as the door closed, and excluded her from his sight, he involuntarily exclaimed in his peculiar tone and twang,

' What intellectual viridity that exemplary creature possesses !"

Hardly had the ingenuous, single-hearted, green-minded lady, as he called her, quitted the apartment, before Fanny, who in truth was searching all over the habitable part of the house for Frank, gently opened the study door, but on seeing her father, started back, half alarmed, and more than half disappointed : it was, however, too late, she was insnared, for the old gentleman thought the opportunity, having offered itself accidentally, by no means an unfavourable one to make her acquainted with Welsted's departure.

He accordingly called the poor creature back to receive the cruelest piece of intelligence she had heard, since her poor brother's death.—When her father bade her stay, her eye wandered round the room in hopes that Welsted might be there—in an instant she coupled the cold command of her parent to sit down and listen, with the wild, and *then* to her, inexplicable conduct and conversation of Frank on the preceding evening ; she trembled, and turned as pale as death.

" Fanny, my love," said her father, " I am going to

communicate something that will, I dare say, surprise you greatly; but you must prepare your mind for it, and assure yourself beforehand that whatever is, is right—and that under the circumstances, painful as may be the first struggles of strong feeling, your duty demands the sacrifice, and——"

" I know—I know it all," cried the poor girl ; " I see it—don't speak to me, father—it *is* right—I'm sure it is —he's gone. I thought so—Francis——"

Words more than these she uttered not : in a moment all that he had said flashed into her mind—the first, the last sacred kiss of love, which but the night before he had given, seemed again to press her parched and burning lips ; her eyes grew dim, her head whirled, and she fell, as if dead, before her afflicted father.

Rodney instantly rang the bell to summon aid to his afflicted child ; he saw the mischief which had been done ; he was at once convinced of his thoughtlessness and imprudence in suffering the uninterrupted intercourse of these young people if he had not predetermined how their constant association should terminate. Immediate assistance the senseless girl required, and received ; her mother and the servants raised her from the ground, and the fond parent bathed her temples and pale cheeks with water.

" Poor child !" said Rodney.

" I'm sure it's the mushrooms," said Mrs. Rodney. " I remember my aunt Chisholme used to be this way for a week sometimes after eating them "

" Dearest love, never mind what it *is*," said Rodney ; " remove the poor child carefully to her room, and see that she be not disturbed or agitated."

Accordingly the fainting Fanny was lifted unconsciously from the sofa on which she had been placed, and re-conveyed to the chamber, which but a few minutes before, she had quitted, full of the hope of seeing Welsted, and of obtaining a further explanation of his ambiguous hints and mysterious conduct of the preceding evening.

As soon as she was removed from the study, the mortification and sorrow of Rodney seemed powerfully to in-

crease; at one glance not only did he perceive the cruelty
of which he had been innocently guilty, in suffering the
intimacy to exist between his child and Francis; not
only did he bitterly lament the absolute necessity which
justified the removal of the young man (who was as dear
to him as a son) from his house and society; but he was,
moreover, filled with serious apprehensions of the difficulty to be encountered in carrying the ulterior point, of
inducing his daughter to accept Sir Frederick's offer. If
he could at once decide upon abandoning this object,
then the necessity for Welsted's absence would be removed, and he might again receive his favourite into the
bosom of his family—and might (as indeed there was
apparently no reason why he should not) consummate
his daughter's happiness, and that of his adopted son,
by uniting them for life, establishing them in the school,
and retiring with his exemplary Cordelia to the enjoyment of privacy and poem-writing—but, alas! not only
had ambition taken hold of him, not only did he anticipate the elevation of his daughter to be the great " Captain's Captain," but he looked with dread and apprehension to the hidden consequences of her refusal—consequences of which, at present, we have no just idea, but
which we shall learn in time, perhaps properly to appreciate. Amidst all these contending feelings, he satisfied
himself that it was now at all events too late to revoke
his intentions with respect to Sir Frederick; besides, he
did not know where to address a letter to Welsted.
The way in which he allowed such a circumstance as *this*
to influence his decision in a matter of such importance,
proved more than any thing yet cited, the immovability
of his first determination.

After waiting some time in anxious suspense about
Fanny, and not daring to show himself to her, lest his
appearance should cause a recurrence of the dreadful
agitation in which his last communication had plunged
her, he became alarmed at the protracted absence of his
wife and rang the bell gently.

When the servant appeared, he inquired where Mrs
Rodney was.

" Making the boys' milk-and-water, Sir, in the hall,'
said the servant.

" What! is she down stairs?" said Rodney.

" Oh yes, Sir; *Missus* came down from Miss Fanny
the minute the boys' bell rang," said the servant.

" Happy equanimity!" muttered Rodney; " tell your
mistress I would be glad to speak to her."

The servant disappeared, and Mrs. Rodney entered
the apartment almost immediately.—In her hand was the
letter of Sir Frederick.

" Well!" said Rodney, " how is the child?"

" Fanny?" said Mrs. Rodney; " oh, she is a good deal
better. Do you know, Mr. Rodney, I begin to think it is
not the mushrooms; I believe it is something on her
mind."

" Too surely, my Cordelia," said Rodney; " but is she
calm?"

" Oh, yes, nice and quiet just now," said her mother;
but I hope she won't fret herself into a decline, Mr.
Rodney. I told her that Frank was gone to London,
and I thought somehow or other we should never see him
again; and, do you know, I think she has been better
since she heard the worst, for she has not spoken a word
since."

" You should have been careful not to agitate her,"
said Rodney.

" That can't agitate her," said his lady; " if the poor
boy isn't to marry her, what's the use of keeping her in
suspense, hoping and moping about it."

" I presume you have read the General's letter, my
love?" said Rodney.

" Yes," replied Mrs. Rodney, " I have."

" And what do you think of his proposal?" asked the
anxious parent.

" Why it's all very well," said Mrs. Rodney; " only he
talks of coming next Friday — and next week is our
washing-week. And I—"

" Oh reject, let me pray you, such trifling considerations as these," said Rodney. Come to the point—is the
offer acceptable?"

"I think it will be a good thing for Fan," said Mrs,
Rodney. "She has no fortune, you know, and if Frank
were to marry her—"

"They would be as well off as *we* w. re when *we* married," said Rodney with a sigh—regretting that the pressure of circumstances had induced him to suffer Welsted
to depart; or rather that he had not, at all hazards, for-
bidden his going.

"I told young Brashleigh, when he had tea, that his
grandfather was coming," said Mrs. Rodney.

"Told the boy!" said Rodney.

"Yes—"

"What did you tell him?"

"Indeed, Mr. Rodney, I only said that his grandfather
was coming," repeated Mrs. Rodney.

"Then the thing is settled," said Rodney, convinced by his wife's manner that she had said more to the
brat than she confessed. Whether this were actually
the case or not, it is impossible for me to decide; certain
it is, that young Brashleigh was most especially petted
by his dame during the following week, as if she had
some object to gain; it might be to bind him to secrecy;
it might be merely in anticipation of their closer connexion.

Meanwhile poor Fanny, who until her mother's undisguised communication had convinced her to the contrary,
imagined that the absence of her beloved (for he *was*
beloved) was merely temporary; lay suffering tortures,
wholly beyond the imagination of those who have never
endured such afflictions. Now that the playmate of her
infancy, the friend and companion of her youth was gone,
she felt conscious how dearly, how fondly she loved him.
They had never before been parted:—the shock of separation, and such a separation, would of itself have been
sufficiently agonizing; but when she recalled his wild incoherent language, the coldness of his manner, and the
apathy with which he received, nay, almost repulsed the
spontaneous marks of her affection, then the fever of her
brain was maddening; she had loved hopelessly, and her
love was unrequited; she had made advances of a warmer

passion than Welsted owned—she had betrayed the secrets of her heart—had committed herself to him whom
she loved—had incurred his scorn and contempt, and he
had fled from her with disgust.

Had he parted from her in friendship would he not
have left one line?—one word, from his loved hand, would
have been consolation;—but no—not even did he *say*
farewell.

She rose from her bed, and silently and carefully stole
to his vacant room :—the door stood open—she entered;
—all was hushed; she saw the books—the sketches which
belonged to her:—the prints—the pencil—he had left
them all silently and sullenly;—she opened the drawing-
book—turned over each leaf,—each marginal mark reminded her of some foregone happiness—each view—
each portrait as it passed under her eye, recalled some remark of his—but not a word of his writing was there for
her. She turned to the fireplace; on the chimneypiece
stood a small china vase filled with flowers; she had gathered them the preceding day—they were yet fresh and
blooming; but *he* that had tied them—*he* that had placed
them in the vase was gone—whither she knew not—and
never to return: she drew one of the flowers from the
bunch—hid it carefully in her bosom—she trembled with
cold as she pressed it to her heart, while her eyes burned
like fire, and awaking, as it were, from a stupor of grief,
in a flood of tears, hastily retraced the way to her apartment, and threw herself again upon her bed in an agony
of sorrow.

Little did she know the heart with which she had to
deal;—little did she think at the moment in which she
reproached herself, not less than Francis, that he was suffering tortures equal to her own:—little did she know
that his adoration of her was unqualified, and wrongly
did she estimate the vastness of the sacrifice which he had
made, because as yet she knew neither the motive which
induced his abrupt departure, nor the nature of the dreadful proposal about to be made to her.

He, full of ardour and enthusiasm, found himself beloved by *her*, to whom his heart was devoted; he knew

that a marriage with her, at any time disadvantageous to
her (in a worldly point of view), would at the moment
when a more desirable offer was at hand, not only do her
manifest injustice by interfering with brighter prospects,
but by exciting her to disobedience towards her parents
and incurring their anger and malediction. In truth, he
had determined upon the course to be pursued, the instant he assured himself of the probable intentions of Sir
Frederick; deeply did he desire to be enabled to absent
himself before any thing like a disclosure of her feelings
for him had been made; but he was foiled; circumstances
had extracted a direct confession of her love at the very
hour in which the certainty of its unhappy fate was to be
established.

Having taken his resolution, having obeyed the stern
voice of duty which called on him to relinquish the dearest
object of his life, Francis assiduously laboured to leave no
trace or remembrance of himself behind ; he darted, as it
were, from the sight of his adored Fanny, and rushed with
desperation into an eternity of wretchedness : he had a
double object in view ; he rescued himself from the possibility of relaxing in his decision, and by doing so, seemed
to outrage the feelings of his beloved, purposely to induce
her to discard him from her thoughts; and lest surround-
ng objects should needlessly recal him to her recollec-
ion, he carefully destroyed every thing before his departure, which might, even by implication, appear to bear
the character of a "remembrance;" but vain, vain were
all his efforts, fruitless all his best intentions. *There*
stood the well-known elms, there ran the rapid river, there
bloomed the verdant fields,—these were associated in the
mind of his devoted Fanny with the happiest hours of her
life, nor did she need such objects to remind her of her
past enjoyments—her present misery.

Still, however, she had not reached the climax of distress. Still was she ignorant that the proud, the petulant,
the ill-tempered, violent, morose, ungracious, and tyrannical Brashleigh had declared her to possess the unalter-
able affections of his aged heart; little did she anticipate
the trials she had to undergo, little did she calculate the

difficulties she had to encounter. Rodney had already announced the offer of Sir Frederick to his noble patron Lord Springfield; much had he dilated, in language the most flowery, on the advantages derivable from the connexion; in which pleasing anticipation his Lordship complacently joined, although upon a person of his Lordship's rank and influence, the benefit likely to accrue from an alliance with a soldier of fortune, who derived his fleeting title from a commandery of knighthood, and the *ultima Thule* of whose dignity and importance was the military command in an Indian presidency, did not produce so powerful an impression as that which they evidently had made upon the mind of the village schoolmaster.

It would be useless to detail the various schemes and stratagems which were formed in the inventive and poetical mind of Mr. Rodney as to the best and safest mood of imparting the important intelligence which he had to communicate to his daughter; first, because they varied with each coming hour and took their colours from each changing circumstance, and were, moreover, so numerous and contradictory in their character and arrangement, that it would fill a volume even to recapitulate them; and secondly, because all the plans and contrivances of the anxious father were absolutely nullified by the candid communicativeness of his lady, who saw no use in "going about the bush," nor any kind of good in keeping up the farce of secrecy, while she was sure that Fanny was "a good girl, and would marry any body they chose to select;" and thus preconvinced of her daughter's pliability and obedience, she seized the earliest opportunity of imparting to the unhappy girl, without any preface or ceremony whatever, the full extent of her affliction.

Then it was that Fanny for the first time rightly understood the meaning of Welsted's mysterious hints; then it was that she felt most bitterly the rashness and imprudence of her conduct in confiding the state of her heart to him; then only did she appreciate the real motives of his sudden flight; but were all these feelings likely, by the force of any human power, to create in their combination a passion like that of love for Sir Frederick Brashleigh? or did Mrs. Rodney *really* believe that the inclinations and passions of her child could be so perverted as to receive into her heart the ill-favoured, ill-tempered veteran, and discard the fond and affectionate companion of her youth and childhood at the command of a parent? What Mrs. Rodney might have expected I cannot say, further than as she spake herself. What occurred—we shall see presently.

It must be evident, that to a letter of such import as that of Sir Frederick Brashleigh, an answer as soon as it conveniently might, must be returned; and as Rodney justly calculated that any appeal to Fanny herself at the moment would be attended with consequences highly prejudicial, if not seriously injurious to her health, he communed with his better half upon the propriety of accepting Sir Frederick's offer without consulting her, and afterwards citing their acceptance as an act positively binding upon *her*, whose consent had been given by her parents and representatives. This line of proceeding, therefore, was adopted; for Rodney was quite assured by his wife's description of Fanny's character, disposition, and present conduct, that she would make no resistance after the offer had actually been accepted, whatever previous effort she might have been disposed to try in order to prevent such a measure. Mrs. Rodney dilated too upon her belief in the non-existence of any affection on Fanny's part for Welsted; and, in short, by what she said (which was not a little), at length confirmed her husband in his first determination of closing with the General at once.

Accordingly he sat down, and, in his most florid and figurative style, acknowledged the receipt of Sir Frederick's letter, as well as the honour done his daughter and himself, by the favourable opinion of a personage so exalted in rank, and a judge of human nature so discriminating as Sir Frederick Brashleigh; assured his correspondent that there never was a better-tempered " sweeter-dispositioned" creature upon earth, than his unsophisticated Fanny; and concluded the high-flown low-toned epistle, with praying God to give his child humility.

grace, and gratitude to bear her coming honours meekly
and amiably; and entreating Sir Frederick to make his
visit whenever it was most agreeable and convenient.

This letter was despatched per post, and when gone,
Rodney experienced a return of the pangs which he had
felt in the earlier part of the day, at the eternal separation
of his daughter and Welsted, for whom it must be always
recollected, he was truly and tenderly anxious; but when
Mrs. Rodney came to him, and surprised him, by telling
him that she had developed the whole history to Fanny:
he was, although at first alarmed by the old gentlewoman's abruptness, not a little consoled; and when the
tender mother added that Fanny had received the intelligence not only without much surprise, but with apparent
calmness, he actually rejoiced in the step which he had
taken; and judging the merits of the measure by the
result, applauded his wife's firmness, convinced at once
that Fanny's love for Welsted was not equal to *his* for
her, and that she had sufficient good sense to prefer the
comforts and advantages of an union with such a person
as Sir Frederick Brashleigh, to the embarrassments of a
precarious life with a young man, whose only means of
existence were derivable from a toilsome profession, to
which constant and undivided attention was absolutely
necessary.

But, alas! little did Mr. Rodney know of human nature,
or female hearts; all the energies of his mind had been
applied to the learning necessary to his calling: a pursuit
ill calculated to give a man an insight into the ways of
the world, or practical knowledge of every-day life; and
thus, good classical scholar and able mathematician as he
was (and poet into the bargain), his ideas were bounded
by the walls of his academy, and his skill in the development of human character, confined to the detection of
juvenile nest stealers, or youthful orchard-robbers. Had
woman's fear fallen under his serious consideration, perhaps he might have formed a different estimate of Fanny's
feelings from that made by his amiable partner: but he
had never studied from nature, and knew nothing more of
the sex than he had been able to attain from a six-and-

twenty years' intercourse with his Cordelia, of whom the
reader has perhaps already seen enough to be convinced
that her sentiments formed not a good criterion, whereon
to found an opinion of females generally; and therefore,
coinciding in all his lady's notions of the case, and mis-
taking the silence of his child for consent, he sat down to
his tea and toast, perfectly contented with what he had
done in the affair, and thoroughly satisfied that every
thing was going on well.

Different indeed, however, from the view which Mrs.
Rodney had taken of it, was the case in reality; never
had poor creature received a wound so deep, so bitterly
agonizing, who was at the same time so desolate and
wretched as Fanny; the course of her life had been such,
and her seclusion so uninterrupted, that she actually had
no friend to sympathize with her, no human being to
whom she could breathe her sorrows. Her only friend and
companion had been Welsted, and *him* she had lost—and
how? To describe the agonies of mind which she suffered,
when she became acquainted with the full extent of her
miseries, is a task beyond my feeble power; indeed, it
seems almost impossible to depict, with any hope of success, a combination of such feelings as those which
assailed her; not only was she threatened with a calamity,
abstractedly overpowering, in the dreaded marriage which
was proposed to her, but *he*, to whom she would have
turned for counsel, and from whom she would have
sought support, was gone—gone, too, voluntarily; and if
she might fairly interpret his conduct and language of the
preceding evening, gone purposely to leave her to the horrible fate which awaited her.

Even this was not all; at the moment of his departure
her feelings had overpowered her, and she had confessed
her love for him! She had before, as we have seen,
trembled to think what his opinion of her forward bold-
ness must have been: aggravated all her sorrows, by continually reflecting on her own conduct, in making un-
sought, and as it should seem, undesired, a bold and
indelicate declaration; yet now it became still more fearful for her to anticipate his future opinion of her when,

having made such an avowal, he should hear that she had
consented to ratify the hateful engagement submitted to
her so shortly after, (for she even then did not know it had
been actually accepted in her name,) the fulfilment of
which, she had been told in plain terms by her mother,
could alone save her from the malediction of her parents,
or preserve them from the deepest sorrow and distress.

If Fanny could have satisfied herself as to the real
state of Welsted's feelings towards her, she would have
been, in some degree, reconciled to her dreadful destiny.
It was true his manner on that fatal evening had been
cold, yet it was tender and affectionate. That he was
terribly agitated she saw; that the kiss which he had given
(or taken) was full of ardour and affection, she (innocent
as she was) felt conscious; yet, if he loved her, why leave
her to be sacrificed to one whose name and character were
alike odious to her, and of whom her opinion was perfectly
well known to him?

It was clear that to *this* offer, Francis had alluded in his
observations; but Fanny, consider as she might, could
not comprehend why, upon what pretext, or with what
intention Francis could quit her at such a time if he cared
for her; if he did *not*, she little cared what became of her;
and could she have decided against herself on this point,
she would have implicitly obeyed the mandate of her
parents, and accompanied Sir Frederick to the altar indifferent to all feelings except those of filial duty and
obedience.

The effect produced upon her, by the development of
Sir Frederick's proposal, and the decree of her father that
she should accept it, was wholly different from what he
had anticipated; and, although correctly described in its
external symptoms by her mother, equally dissimilar to
what she believed it. Fanny's grief and sorrow were in
the heart, not on the tongue; and instead of venting her
wretchedness in groans and sighs, or indulging in those
extravagant demonstrations of violent passion, which give
relief to weaker minds, she called to her aid the soothing
influence of our holy religion and from her Maker sought
consolation and support; she prayed that he would direct

her mind, and strengthen her good intentions, that thus armed by his Almighty power, she might honour her parents according to his sacred commandment, and righteously fulfil the duties which were demanded of her.

When she came down stairs in the evening, she was pale as death, and her eyes gave evidence that she had been unable to restrain " some natural tears ;" but her manner was calm and placid ; she trembled as her father kindly took her hand and pressed it to his bosom with a fervour which could not be misunderstood ; it was the pressure of approving fondness, and implied his satisfaction at her acceptance of Sir Frederick's offer ; for, from her mother's account of the scene which had passed between them, Rodney chose to be convinced that his daughter had tacitly, if not expressly, consented to admit his pretensions.

The subject, however, was one to which neither the parent nor the child thought it advisable to recur ; yet Rodney considered that a fair opportunity offered itself to allude to Welsted's absence, of which he proposed to avail himself, in order to ascertain whether his wife's strong but homely assertion, that " Fanny did not care a button about him in the way of a sweetheart," was quite well grounded.

" I have an extra share of labour, Fanny," said Rodney, " now Welsted has left me, or I should certainly have gone to your room and sat with you."

" Yes," replied Fanny, " it must—have—given you considerable inconvenience;" and so saying, burst into tears.

Rodney by no means admired this equivocal evidence of his daughter's indifference to Welsted ; nor did he consider it at all symptomatic of that philosophical equanimity upon the subject which Mrs. Rodney had described in such extremely forcible language.

" Why those tears, my child ?" said the parent.

" Don't ask me, Sir," said Fanny. " Is it not natural that a separation so sudden and unlooked for, from a being who has been my constant companion since my childhood should affect me ?" If I could have seen him once ; have only bid him farewell, I could have borne it; but it was cruel in him to abandon me without one word."

" Abandon you, Fanny!" repeated her father, elevating his brows. " What language is this, child ? Mr. Welsted was *my* assistant, fitted for that office by *my* care and attention, appointed to it by my favour, and I have now dismissed him for reasons known to myself. How are *my* arrangements connected with your casual intercourse with the young man ?"

" Oh ! Sir," said Fanny, " do not speak thus of Francis ; do not yourself so much injustice as either to misrepresent your kindness to *him*, or his gratitude to *you*, you have had no dispute, no disagreement, can have none ; of that I am certain. He is gone, because he was considered likely to thwart the intentions which have been mentioned to me by my mother ; do not deteriorate from your own kindness ; do not try to debase *his* excellence, by any attempt to impose upon me."

" Impose, Fanny!" said her father angrily, " this is language I must not hear. There has been nothing like imposition practised one way or the other. Suppose Mr. Welsted chose to remove himself ; I conclude it was because he felt himself uncomfortable here, where every kindness has been shown him."

" He went," said Fanny, " because he could not bear to see me sacrificed."

" Sacrificed !" again echoed Rodney, " sacrificed in a marriage with Sir Frederick Brashleigh, a man to whom the country looks up with admiration ; of whom the highest character has been given by the greatest hero of the age ; a man covered with honours and distinctions ! What are you talking of? Nothing but madness could prompt such extraordinary language." •

" What are his honours and distinctions to me ?" said Fanny. " I was humbly born ; I have been plainly bred ; I have neither knowledge of the great and gay, nor any desire to know t em. I have learned under your tuition dearest father, to despise the pomps and vanities of the world. I have trained my mind to happiness in middling life, and there alone could I be blest. To tread the same path of usefulness and content which my dear mother is now pursuing, would be the height of my ambition, and if Francis Welsted had——"

"Had what?" exclaimed Rodney. "Talk no more about him, child: the young man, were he here, would laugh at your idle nonsense. You may, perhaps, love *him*, and if it suit your ideas of delicacy and high feeling, announce your affection to the world; but that *he* loves you, is at best a matter of doubt; nay, that he does *not* love, as lovers love, is almost matter of certainty; you would indeed be acting a pretty part for a young lady who professes diffidence and principle, to hunt down your father's professional assistant, and follow a man who has quitted the house at the precise moment at which, of course, had he any serious intentions respecting you, he would have maintained his ground, and made the struggle to rescue you from the grasp of a noble and successful rival."

"Rescue, indeed," said Fanny; "I see, Sir," continued she, "by the tone and manner you assume, that I am wrong; I have spoken too freely; and yet I am not ashamed of my candour. I had a brother once, on whom I doted; he loved *me* and Francis as he loved himself: he was taken from us, and Francis was to me a brother; and had our dear William, whose place in my heart Francis supplied, been now alive, I should have been spared all this; he would have vindicated Welsted against your anger; would have restored him to your smiles; but that is over, and all I now implore, all I entreat is, that if Welsted have removed himself from our society, or have been removed by your authority and sanction, I may, at least, be allowed to remain as I am; I shall be comparatively happy, even in my single wretchedness; let me beg then that this offer of Sir Frederick Brashleigh may at least be rejected."

"Rejected!" said Rodney, "child, it is accepted; your mother gave me every reason to believe that you freely acquiesced in the brilliant proposal, and I have invited the General hither forthwith."

Fanny's countenance underwent the most singular change of expression at this announcement; a mingled look of horror, fear, indignation and grief, charac erized her features. Rodney determined to avail himself of the momentary silence to proceed.—" Therefore the affair *is settled*.—These childish attachments are soon forgotten. —Recollect," added he, more soothingly, " dearest child, the rank and station to which you will be called ; recollect the flattering preference of such a man as Sir Frederick ; above all, Fanny, recollect that the happiness of your parents depends upon it, and that your refusal would entail perpetual misery and regret upon them—recollect all *this*, and then rejoice that you have conquered whatever prejudice you might have entertained, and accepted the splendid offer which has been made you."

Fanny sat motionless, her eyes were fixed upon the ground—but word she spake not.

" And then, love," added her father, anxious to sooth as much as possible, " Welsted, whose affection for you is purely fraternal, may hereafter return amongst us, and——"

" Welsted !" exclaimed Fanny, " no, father, no ! If I could consent to marry Sir Frederick—if I am forced to marry him, I must never again see Welsted—never hear his name—either I ought to hate him, or—No," she continued, as if communing with herself, " it is right ; the ways of Heaven are inscrutable ; once more I implore, I entreat you spare me *this* marriage,—if you command— your command must be obeyed ; but why force *this* upon me ?—I repeat I am content never to see Francis again, but Si. Frederick——"

" Fanny," said Rodney—and he stood before his child the picture of despair—the pompous manner of the pedagogue changed into the downcast humility of the suppliant mendicant ; his eyes filled with tears, his voice subdued, and his cheek pale as death ; " behold your father at your feet ; your mother even does not know the extent of my misfortunes, nor can she appreciate the power which you possess to relieve them. To confess our faults to our children, to acknowledge our errors under the roof where professional duty erects us into monitors and guardians, are indeed painful trials ; but *you* must, you *shall* be told every thing. Indiscretions which it were needless now to repeat, involved me in my early days, and have deeply embarrassed my after-life; for the relief of those embarrassments, and for the purpose of maintaining an appearance in the world, I became a debtor in a considerable amount to one, to whose property Sir Frederick Brashleigh has succeeded; it was this circumstance which first brought *me* and the General acquainted; it was this circumstance which first induced him to place his grandson here; the securities I have given are of course in his possession, and although he has never remotely alluded to them, since his personal acquaintance with *you*, I cannot but feel conscious that I am in his power —in one day, Fanny, I may be lodged in prison, my dwelling stripped of every article it contains; my reputation destroyed, my character lost; think of this, my Fanny—but speak not of it. I own, my child"—and Rodney burst into tears, " *I am* asking a sacrifice—I reject all concealment, I am not blind—but—"

" Spare me, my father," said Fanny, " spare yourself: another word is useless; I would rather that my death could do you the same service, but I know my duty—I am content—and thank Heaven that I am made, even to my own destruction, the humble instrument of preservation to a parent from distress :—let me leave you now, but doubt me not—fear not—I am resolved !"

" Beloved child !" said the agitated Rodney, " what can I say—how express my feelings ?"

Fanny's head sank upon her father's shoulder, and their tears mingled as they fell ;—*hers* were tears of bitterness and anguish—*his* of joy and affection; the die, however, was cast—the right chord had been stricken, and Fanny, breaking from her trembling parent, in an agony of feeling, rushed to her room to weep and pray.

CHAPTER V.

Here is one that wishes to live longer,—
Feels not his gout or palsy,—feigns himself
Younger by scores of years —flatters his age
With confident belying ;—with hopes he may
With charms like Æson, have his youth restored.—
And with these thoughts so battens, as if Fate
Would be as easily cheated on as he.
                                        BEN JONSON.

WHEN Sir Frederick Brashleigh received Rodney's
answer to his proposal (which we too well know contained
an acceptance of it), he forthwith began to prepare for his
matrimonial expedition.   He was to sail for India in the
ensuing month : he had much public business to transact
at the Horse Guards, and at the India House ; oaths to
take in Leadenhall-street ; dinners to eat in Bishopsgate-
street, and arrangements to make in various parts of the
town and country ; considering all which, as well as his
present age, he was induced to believe that he had not
much time to lose.
    His first operation was to transmit to Miss Rodney a
splendid *cadeau*, consisting of a diamond necklace and
earrings, together with a variety of trinkets, as ill-suited
to her present condition, as necessary to the station she
was about to fill ; and with these evidences of affection he
despatched a letter to the young lady, in which he suggested that it would be extremely agreeable to his family,
if after his visit to her father, she and her mother were to
come up to London, where the necessary purchases for
her marriage and voyage must of course be made.   Mrs.
Brashleigh, his daughter-in-law, would be delighted to
see them in York-place, and, as Mr. Rodney's vacation
would very soon occur, it might altogether be made an
agreeable party previous to their departure from England.
    It would be difficult to express the placid indifference

with which the poor victim herself received all these tri-
butes of praise and affection. The calm determination
not to allow herself to reason, or indeed think, upon the
subject, and the steady adherence to her resolution not to
recur to any matter with which her adored Francis was
connected or associated in her mind, were proofs of firmness little to be expected in a girl like Fanny, full of feeling, ardour, and enthusiasm; but so it was, she suffered
her parents to direct and regulate all her actions, she
surrendered herself completely into their hands, and while
Rodney was filled with admiration at her pious resignation
to the noble sacrifice he knew that she was making at the
shrine of filial duty, her mother kept praising her for being
such a good girl, and hoping that nothing would happen
to make her miserable, which she was very much afraid
there might, &c. &c. &c.

Meanwhile Sir Frederick was occupied in divulging
his intentions to his own relations, who were overpowered
with astonishment at his choice, and accordingly resolved,
f he persisted in putting his desperate intentions into execution, to do every thing in their power to harass, annoy,
vex, and mortify the rural beauty; for they were convinced that she had by trickery and artifice insnared his
affections, and would, perhaps, by the same means eventually divert his property into a new channel; for, to all
the sanguine prognostications that *he* would have no family, a probability that there *might be* children (which it
must be confessed commonly exists in all such marriages),
opposed itself in the fertile imaginations of his expectant
and presumptive heirs.

In short nothing could be more dreadful than the prospect before poor Fanny; and if she had not, with the
piety and philosophy which I have already noticed, and
which were perfectly astonishing even to herself, wholly
excluded from her mind all consideration of the approaching event, she would have started back, even now, on the
eve of marriage, as from the edge of a precipice; while,
as if to add to her future miseries, the humbleness of her
rark, and her father's reported want of wealth, were assigned by the connexions of the gallant General, as the

true and only causes of her acceptance of his offer. Before they saw her, they had learned to speak of her with that contempt which is justly incurred by women sufficiently base and mean to prostitute themselves, legally, to age and decrepitude for the sake of money. Little did these envious flatterers of Sir Frederick's family know the real state of the case when they indulged in their sarcasms and scurrilities, their libels and lampoons.

So soon as the proposal of a removal to town after the gallant General's visit to the academy was made, Fanny referred it, as she had referred all other measures connected with the expected ceremony, to her father;—he was not a little puzzled; he saw the advantages, if not the absolute necessity of her visiting the metropolis; and saw too the impossibility of her going alone with her future husband; but he dreaded considerably the exhibition of his excellent and exemplary wife in the semi-fashionable circles of St. Mary-la-bonne, of which the gallant General (thereunto addicted by his Indian habits), was the hero. He anticipated the blunders she would inevitably make in the great world, and trembled as he thought of the homely expressions and frugal notions, which he was convinced would come into play in mixed society, with an effect the very reverse of that which it would be desirable to produce: in addition to which difficulty there arose another;—it was an essential part of such an affair to raise a sum of money, as an outfit for Fanny. Where was it to come from? It was utterly impossible to confide a detail of the delicate state of his finances to Sir Frederick, on the eve of such a ceremony, and his poetical mind was dreadfully harassed with contending hopes and fears, desires and doubts, in none of which he could make his better half a participator, inasmuch as he wished them to remain secret, which, were they once intrusted to her *safe* keeping, he was quite certain they would shortly cease to be.

At length he came to a resolution, often formed by greater and wiser men than himself in cases of nicety and difficulty, which was neither more nor less, than to " wait and see" what would turn up for the best. Of Sir ederick's visit there could be no doubt; *that* was fixed or the following Friday, and therefore he directed his daughter, in announcing her acceptance of the old gentleman's presents, to say that she had referred the question of her journey to London to her father, who had thought it best to postpone the decision until they had the pleasure of seeing Sir Frederick there; and all this Fanny said, and wrote as mechanically as a clerk in a lawyer's office, and with a callosity of feeling, as impenetrable as if she had not been in the smallest degree concerned or interested in any of the results; not a tear dimmed her eye, not a sigh heaved her bosom,—nature seemed palsied in her living frame, and she sat like an automaton, whose movements were involuntary, and the result of some extraneous power and influence.

No sooner had Mrs. Rodney been to call at Evans's about the mutton, and stepped to Miss Wilkinson's to inquire after her health, than the great mystery of Fanny's approaching nuptials became no mystery at all; even the utcher's boys knew it; and great and frequent were the sitations of the neighbours to inquire, and talk the atter over: and when it was ascertained that Sir Frederick was to pass some few days at the Academy, the Rev. Mr. Willows, the Rector, called upon Rodney, for the second time in *his* life, to hope that the family would dine at the parsonage-house on the following Saturday, for the first time in *their* lives; to state that he would himself wait upon Sir Frederick as soon as he arrived, and beg the honour of his company: and Mrs. Ewbright, the wife of a retired lawyer, who had built a small upright villa just outside the village, with a round weedy pond, looking like a basin of green pease soup in the middle of a circular lawn which much resembled a card-table in size and shape in front of it, a flight of steps leading up to the door, upon which there was a brass knocker, and a plate with the owner's name inscribed upon it; dropped in to solicit the pleasure of the Rodneys' company on the next Tuesday, and hoped that Sir Frederick would honour her by joining them; and immediately after having quitted the academy, the same exemplary lady called upon Miss Wilkinson to avow her hatred and contempt of great folks, whom, for *her* part, she could not endure; but what was to be done? there were "certain duties to be performed in certain stations of life," she had been obliged to receive Sir Frederick at dinner on Tuesday, as a mark of attention to the Rodneys, who were really very good sort of people.—" Would Miss Wilkinson come over in the evening and play a rubber?"

Miss Wilkinson, who languished for tufts, and had never been in company with any thing superior to a small cross of Maria Theresa, or an ungazetted commandery of Poyais, was afraid that her cold would prevent her going out *late* in the evening; but finding that her manœuvre failed, and that Mrs. Ewbright would *not* have her at dinner, she at length declared her intention of meeting the *great man*, about whom as much fuss was made in the little village, as if he had been Signor Rossini, or the autocrat of all the Russias.

Things went on much in the same feverish manner until Friday, and Fanny's deportment was precisely the same as it had been during the earlier part of the week. Except when alone with her father, neither sigh nor tear gave evidence of her feelings. She was still pale, cold, and still apparently senseless to every thing which was doing; and while Mrs. Rodney was praising her sweet disposition, and the perfect serenity with which she received such an accession of wealth and honour, her agitated father, whose heart in truth bled for her, and whose sorrow at her present state was augmented by the repentance of his own past conduct, saw *that* which, by the superficial spectator, passed unheeded: a forced smile would for a moment play over his child's pale cheeks, like the doubtful gleam of a winter's sun upon the drifted snow; but to Rodney's feelings the ray was cold and cheerless, and as the days passed until the Friday arrived which was to bring the bridegroom to his dwelling, he gradually regretted more and more the necessity which he saw existed for making that, which he could not blind himself sufficiently to consider any thing but a sacrifice of his daughter's happiness to his own necessities.

5

Nothing can be more grievously inconvenient than the arrival of a great man in a small establishment ; the whole day was consumed in contrivances and arrangements to make Sir Frederick comfortable ; an express had been sent off to Groves at Charing Cross for the best possible fish ; Evans was directed to select the most *elegant* meat ; and if Mrs. Tucker would be so kind as to take care that the chickens had been delicately fattened ; and if Mrs. South, who was accustomed to dress only shoulders of mutton and rounds of beef for the boys, could descend from the folio dishes of roasted and boiled, in which her culinary practice chiefly lay, to the delicate duodecimos of ragouts and fricandeaux, it would be quite charming. And, in order to set all things off to the best possible advantage, the head-waiter at the Crown, a remarkably clever person in his way, was joined in a commission with Thomas, the only civilized servant the Rodneys had,—and *he* wore hobnails in his shoes,—to attend the festive board.

To give greater facility to the proceedings, Mr. Rodney discovered that the important day in question happened to be the anniversary of some saint, whose name nobody had ever heard, but of whom he took care to relate some miraculous story to his pupils the preceding evening, in order to justify himself for doing that, which in *their* minds needed no justification ; namely giving them a holiday. The boys were relieved from discipline after two o'clock, and detached, under the command of Mr Louvel, the French master, and the younger assistant, for a walk, which Rodney intended should occupy the whole time till dinner should have been served and demolished in the parlour.

When Mrs. South, who was ancient, somewhat blind, and a little hard of hearing, understood that dinner was to be ready at six, she thought the world would shortly come to a conclusion ; even the parson dined at five, and he was the village *ultra* in points of fashion and etiquette.

But when, after incalculable anxiety, the soup, which had been safely received from London, in company with the fish, had emitted its savoury steam ; when the direful attempts at French cookery were all arranged before the fire, and half-past six chimed, and no Sir Frederick Brashleigh appeared, the agony of Mrs. South's mind was past all endurance. The lamb was shrivelled up to a cinder, the fish broken into pieces, the soup had burned on the bottom of the stew-pan, the butter had converted itself into oil, the potatoes reduced themselves to an aqueous mash, and " the green leaves all turned yellow."

At a quarter before seven, the rolling of an aristo-cratic vehicle announced the approach of his Excellency ; and his elegant travelling carriage, drawn by four posters, with a livery servant, and his own man, on the dicky, dashed up to the door. Precisely at the same moment all the schoolboys (dirty when they departed, now ac-tually covered with mud), as if by design and precon-certed arrangement, entered the gates, some carrying boughs of trees, which they had broken down on the way, others bearing gallipots full of sprightly minnows, pro-ducts of their piscatory sports ; and while Louvel was commanding silence in the loudest French, his junior assistant was endeavouring to restore order by inflicting manual punishment on the rebellious little wretches con-fided to his care.

For once Mr. Rodney ceased to be poetical, and in his heart wished the whole flock of young savages in Jericho, or any where else but where they were. The ill-manners incidental to private academies induced the young gentlemen to group themselves in the most ad-vantageous positions for seeing the debarkation of the ancient warrior from his carriage, who, affecting delight and rapture at their unsophistication and curiosity, took the hand of his intended father-in-law with an urbanity which, by doing considerable violence to his nature, he could sometimes assume.

Mrs. South, whose wooing days were past, and whose whole heart was in the pot, no sooner heard the rattle and clatter in the hall, and the ringing of the door bell, so as to be quite sure that the " company" was come than, to use her own expression, she, " upped with the

turbot and popped it into the dish," where it instantly
separated itself into sundry bits resembling the com
ponent parts of a dissected map, save and except that
the chance of ever putting it together again was utterly
hopeless. A few suitable imprecations upon the smallness
of the kettle and the hardness of the water served to
allay the fury of the culinary Proserpine, and the boiled
chickens, which were to accompany the said fish in its
progress from the fire to the dinner-parlour, were prepared for action, being, by some sinister accident, nearly
black; these, with two *vegetable dishes*, one filled with
pale limp sweetbreads fried in dripping, and the other
piled up with some half-score Maintenon cutlets, and
headed by the soup, were forwarded without any fresh
orders towards the *banqueting-room* by the hands of the
kitchenmaid, the housemaid, Mrs. Simpson the char-
woman, and little Jem the cow-boy; the whole of which
agreeable procession was encountered in the hall by His
Excellency Sir Frederick Brashleigh, K.C.B. Commander-
in-chief at Bombay, who had been delayed by the appearance of the boys in the front of the house, and by the
numerous questions he had to ask as to where his carriage
could be safely housed?—which was really the best inn?
—whether his servants could be useful? and others,
touching many important points; just long enough to
meet the establishment in its progress towards the festive
board.

"I fear I am late," said Sir Frederick; "I see the
commissariat in motion—hey? you have got mutton for
dinner, doctor—I smell it—I like the smell—good meat,
mutton, doctor, if not too fat—fine mutton, Sir, in Bengal
—little and good, hey!—but where are the ladies?"

"This way, Sir Frederick," said Rodney, ready to sink
through the red tiles of his white-washed hall on perceiving that Jem's dirty fingers had invaded more than
the *pas géométriques* of the dish he was carrying, and
that his thumb (looking like that of a rich cobbler, if we
may trust the proverb), bore evident marks of the parsley
and butter with which the dingy chickens were covered;
the fish, confided to Mrs. Simpson, who did not appear to

advantage in the hands of a lady, who, however well her dark gown and green baize apron might assimilate with the black chip bonnet which she chose to wear in the house, had not previously taken the precaution of purifying the hands which did " the burthen bear;" while the housemaid, who had rashly undertaken to convey at one trip, the sweetbreads, the cutlets, and the potatoes, having discovered that one minute's farther adherence to her imprudent design of carrying them *all* (the dish of potatoes having been placed upon the top of the dome-like cover of the cutlets), would infallibly cause the destruction of some one of her three important charges, having first raised her dexter foot with more activity than grace into one of the hall chairs to stay the descent of the slippery treasure, called out to her master, who was at the very moment gracefully ushering in His Excellency the commander-in-chief, to " please Sir—come and catch the 'taturs !"

Young Brashleigh, who had been kept at home to dine with his relation, by this time had reached the hall from the drawing-room, and even *his* approach was some relief to the agitated Rodney, who, as he told his lady when they retired for the evening, in language suited to her understanding, never was so ashamed in all his life, as ne had been of the affair now under description. Sir Frederick appeared very much pleased to see the boy, although perhaps the salutation of "grand papa," was less welcome to his ears at that particular juncture, than it would have been at any other.

When Sir Frederick entered the drawing-room, Mrs. Rodney was absent, in fact, superintending the dinner; and as Rodney presented the lover to his mistress, poo Fanny, for the first time appeared sensible of her real situation; she burst into tears and rushed from the room, —a proceeding which, while it absolutely terrified Rodney, impressed Sir Frederick with an idea that she was devotedly attached to him, and that her feelings were too much for her; and it was quite extraordinary to see with what amiable complacency he adopted that view of the case.

In less than two minutes the servant announced dinner, and Mrs. Rodney made her appearance, her dress disordered, and her face half roasted by her exertions in the kitchen, and welcomed Sir Frederick cordially as it was her nature to do.

"Come," said she, "General, the dinner is ready."

"Where is Fanny?" said Sir Frederick.

"Oh, never mind *her*," said Mrs. Rodney; "she'll find her way in time; she had some cold pork and a bit of *sassage* in the middle of the day,—don't think of waiting for *her*, General."

"Why," said Sir Frederick, "I—I—was going to make some alteration in my dress; for really I'm not fit to sit down. I did not think you dined so early; however, if you will excuse me, Mrs. Rodney——"

"Lord, to be sure, Sir," said Mrs. Rodney; "I'm quite certain at your time of life it's very dangerous to go washing and dressing yourself after travelling, like a young man; it is enough to give *you* rheumatism all over."

"My love!" said Rodney, in a fever, "where is Fanny? pray let her be called."

And a sudden thought struck him, that having rallied all her energies up to the very moment of trial, either her heart had failed her, or that suffering her distress to overcome her principle, she might at the crisis rashly dare to take that step which would decidedly secure her from all farther misery in *this* world, but which, with equal certainty would entail upon her the direct punishments of the world to come. The moment this idea flushed across his mind he rushed from the drawing-room, exclaiming, in a half-phrensied tone of gaiety, that "*he* would fetch her," and hurried to her apartment. He knocked at the door; received no answer. It was unlocked; he threw it open, his eyes travelled rapidly round the room, but Fanny was not there. Rodney, confirmed in his suspicions, hastened to her mother's room. Still was he disappointed—no Fanny met his anxious eye, until, in an agony of grief and agitation, he called to one of the servants, who was waiting in the hall, to inquire if she knew where her young mistress was?

" Yes, Sir," was the placid answer, " Miss is in the dining parlour."

No human being except a parent, no parent perhaps not circumstanced as Rodney was, can appreciate the feelings of his heart at the moment;—relieved in an instant from the most dreadful apprehensions; his child, lost to him in imagination, was restored to him in reality; he felt wild with the conflict which was going on in his mind; the mixture of serious ills with minor grievances, the conviction that every hour was hastening the destruction of his daughter's happiness, mingled with the apprehension that the vulgarity of his wife, the *gaucherie* of his servants, and the mismanagement of the establishment would disgust his intended son-in-law, and frustrate his intentions, the realization of which, he could not anticipate without sorrow for his child

When he reached the drawing-room, *that* in turn was vacant, and on repairing to the dinner parlour he perceived his lady, having without waiting for him, taken her seat at the head of the table, bestowing every sort of useable imprecation upon the cook for breaking the fish; the soup having already been dismissed as not eatable. Sir Frederick sat listening to her with great attention, while his eyes rested upon her daughter, who was placed at the opposite side of the table beside his grandson.

" Why, General," said Mrs. Rodney, " Mrs. South, our cook, is old, and can't see very well, and isn't used to this sort of fish. The last time we had a turbot, I think, must be now nearly a year and a half ago,—fifteen months I'm sure—I know it was, when we had some of the boys' fathers down here, or else we never have the prime fish, and then Mrs. Willows was so good as to lend me *her* cook."

Rodney (who devoutly wished that his wife's mouth was stopped), when he saw Fanny safe and calm, endeavouring to appear interested in a discussion upon the difficulty of turbot-boiling, thought it wisest not to recur to her temporary absence; and therefore endeavoured, if possible, to divert the conversation from its present channel, by asking Sir Frederick if there was any news in London?

" Yes, there is very important news," said Sir Frederick. " I have been told upon authority, upon which I think I can rely, that there is a probability that Ting Sang Futty How will shortly combine his forces with Dudgery Tong at Pattypatan.

" Indeed !" said Rodney, not aware that persons who have lived for five-and-twenty years in India, invariably imagine the interest of the whole British Empire exciteable by the incursions and excursions of a few troublesome natives, who are at times unreasonable enough to dislike being enslaved,—a fancy highly improved by an appointment such as that which Sir Frederick at the moment held.

" Fanny, my dear," said Mrs. Rodney, " a bit more fish ?"

" No more," said Fanny, who had tasted none.

" I'm afraid," said her mother, archly, " as I told Sir Frederick, you have been at the cold pork, or at some of them nasty, greasy, *sassages*,—you should recollect last week—you were bad enough then, I'm sure."

" Perhaps, Miss Rodney, you will let me send you wine," said Sir Frederick.

This phrase, which means nothing, but which is universally used in India, was, however, sufficiently intelligible to Fanny to induce her to accept the offer.

" What wine do you take ?" said Sir Frederick.

" Any," said Fanny. " I -——"

" She likes currant wine, don't you, Fanny?" said her mother. " And," added the lady in a whisper to Sir Frederick, " she can make it too, General, I assure you."

Rodney's agony during this scene was past description. But he feared to irritate his wife's volubility by any remark, and therefore thought it best to let things take their own course.

" General," said Mrs. Rodney, " you eat nothing; let Mr. Rodney send you some lamb ; it is a beautiful bit of meat, quite a picture. I went to Mr. Evans, our butcher, a very civil man ; we have dealt with him now seven— more than that—eight years, I think it is—and I got him to kill his daughter's pet lamb for us, that the children have been playing with all the spring."

" I am sure it is excellent," said Sir Frederick, bowing; " but I never eat lamb. Miss Fanny, shall I send you a cutlet ?"

Fanny declined.

" Fanny, take some lamb, child," said her careful mother, " it will do you good ; you are very fond of lamb, I know, and you don't get it every day, my dear. Do you know *this* is tenpence halfpenny a pound, General. Give her some, Mr. Rodney ; give her the bone, Welsted used to laugh and say she was so fond of."

This judicious allusion had nearly produced a scene ; but Rodney happening to observe, as Sir Frederick was extracting a Maintenon cutlet, that the envelopes in which they had been sent to table were neither more nor less than old Latin exercises, felt it necessary to make some remark, which might, if possible, exonerate him from any personal share in the extraordinary system of economy upon which such a contrivance had been carried into effect.

" Cordelia, my love," said Rodney, " what paper is that, in which those cutlets have been sent to table ?"

" They are old exercises, my dear," said Mrs. Rodney; " Nanny got them out of the bottom of the school-room cupboard ; they were quite clean, I assure you. I see no use in wasting nice new paper for mutton-chops," continued the lady, addressing herself to Sir Frederick, " you know nobody eats it, General."

Sir Frederick certainly did not, and when he perceived the *tempting* dish of dirty sweetbreads which was opposed to the Latin in grease, and which had precisely the appearance of some surgical preparation, his Excellency was driven to the unpleasant alternative of saying, " Well, Doctor, I *will* try some of your lamb, it looks excellent."

At this juncture a maid-servant made her appearance, and whispered something to the male attendant, whose replies to her application, of " I shan't," " ask yourself," ' to be sure," &c. were sufficiently audible to attract the

notice of her mistress, who immediately called to her from
the post of honour to know what she wanted.

" Some candles, Ma'am, for the school-room," was the
answer ; and immediate y, without the smallest disguise
or embarrassment, Mrs. Rodney began rummaging in a
pocket, apparently as large as a *sac de nuit*, and after a
considerable rattling of sundry objects hidden from mortal eye, produced a handful of its contents, consisting of
seventeen differently-sized keys, a piece of wax candle, a
thimble, three old letters, a hard-hearted pincushion, a
pair of sheathed scissors, a large toothpick-case, a dingy
red-morocco purse, containing silver and halfpence, a
small packet of white-brown paper, a pair of tweezers,
and a flattened thimble ; anging all of which before her,
on the table-cloth, she proceeded to select from amongst
them the required key of the store-closet, which she delivered to her handmaiden with a serious injunction " not
to take out sixes for tens."

Sir Frederick, during this scene, suffered more on Rodney's account than his own ; he saw the state to which
he was reduced by the homely display of his lady's domestic economy, and certainly had he known that there was
neither salad nor mint-sauce in the room, he would not
nave inquired for both those additions to the lamb,
which, having been, as I before said, burned to a cinder,
required all the aid of foreign ornament to make it palatable ; nor would he have called for a glass of soda-
water to invigorate his appetite, had he been aware that
such a liquor was as rare in Somerville House as nectar
in Pandemonium.

At any other time Fanny would have been annoyed at
the evident discomfiture of her excellent mother's schemes
and inventions to feast the General, as she persisted in
calling him, but at present it was all indifferent to her ;
one thing, however, pleased her, if she could be pleased
at all, and that was the manner in which Sir Frederick addressed her, during the repast; there was not
affectation of the young gallant, no attempt at fine acting ; he had professed his Jmiration, had confessed

her influence over him in the most serious manner, and upon the most important subject connected with her future life ; and, although, for reasons which none perhaps but gentlemen of his Excellency's age and temper can properly explain, he had laid his fortunes at her feet; he was too much a man of the world to ape the sighing lover while his grandchild sat beside his mistress. Indeed, the relief which the unexpected style of his conduct and conversation afforded Fanny was great. She felt that she could consent to be esteemed by Sir Frederick Brashleigh, she could even yield to the decrees of duty, and be the willing and obedient prop of his declining years—but Love !—It seemed as if he had read her thoughts, and knew the inmost feelings of her heart.

The miseries of the dinner were not yet concluded. In an attempt at a second course, appeared some pigeons, and, of all " the birds in the air, and fishes of the sea," a great fat roasted rabbit, intermingled wherewith were some bad tartlets, and some custards, in vessels resembling in size and shape the coffee-cups at Cloyes, (and those to whom this comparison is unintelligible, would find it quite worth while to take a journey to the principal inn of that town, in order to enlighten themselves,) and sundry other indescribable efforts of Mesdames South and Rodney, to make, " by the book," certain little confections, likely, as they thought, to please the palate of Sir Frederick.

But every thing was doomed to turn out as ill as Mrs. Rodney herself could have prophesied : and the master of the house, who lived in torments during the proceedings, was destined to receive the *coup de grace,* just at this period of the dinner.

"Allow me," said Sir Frederick, " to relieve you from the trouble of carving that rabbit. It is as difficult, I suppose, as a hare, which certainly is the most awkward dish imaginable for a lady to attempt."

" Awkward!" said Mrs. Rodney, " What !—cutting it up, General !—La ! What d'ye think of. skinning it, Sir ?"

If Rodney had not interfered with some new assault upon Sir Frederick as to taking wine, Mrs. Rodney would,

without any doubt, have proceeded to detail, in the minutest and most circumstantial manner, the process to
which she had so triumphantly alluded. Sir Frederick
gladly availed himself of his host's offer to change the
conversation; and having declined eating any of the
favoured animal, hoped to escape an observation made by
Mrs. Rodney, which in this case might have been spared,
since the party assembled were blessed with noses.

"Dear! Mr. Rodney," exclaimed the mistress of the
house, "it is quite bad, I declare. I knew it would not
keep; only you were determined it should,—for we
thought you'd like a bit of something like game, General."

"I am extremely obliged to you," said Sir Frederick,
gravely, "I seldom eat rabbits, Ma'am."

"Lord! how unlucky," said Mrs. Rodney; "I'm
afraid we have not got any thing you like; however, to-
morrow, Sir, you'll have an uncommon good dinner at
the parsonage."

"What!" said the General, somewhat alarmed and
surprised at the suddenness of the proposition, "are *we*
engaged any where to-morrow?"

"Not exactly engaged, Sir Frederick," said Rodney,
"the Rector, a most excellent person, has invited us,
and intends calling to request the honour of your company."

Sir Frederick was about to say something in the way of
acknowledgment, when Mrs. Rodney undertook to enlighten him, by observing that long as the Willows's had
been at the Rectory, they had never asked them to dinner
before; and it was only because Fanny was going to be
married to a great man, and that the great man himself
was there, that they asked them now.

The discussion into which this would evidently have
carried them, was much to be dreaded; but as luck would
have it, the boys' supper-bell resounded in the hall, and
the active matron making her excuses, in spite of all the
entreaties of her husband to allow the servants for once
to superintend the meal, hastily retired, expressing her
firm conviction that if she did not go herself, something
disagreeable would happen. To say truth, Rodney felt,

when she left the room, as an unskilful tumbler must
teel when he finds himself safe on the ground, making
his concluding bow, after a perilous exhibition on a lofty
tight-rope.   Even Fanny, she knew not why, seemed
more at her ease after her mother's departure; and the
celerity and quietness with which every thing was managed and cleared away to make room for the dessert,
when the operations of the servants were uncontrolled by
the never-sleeping watchfulness of the mistress, formed
an agreeable contrast to the perpetual mishaps, awkward
manœuvres, and uncouth noises with which the company
had been incessantly greeted during the *surveillance* of
that exemplary lady.

It would be tiresome to trace through all their minute
variations the innumerable *contre-temps* which were perpetually occurring during the stay of Sir Frederick Brashleigh at the academy; nor could much entertainment be
derived from elaborate descriptions of the dinners which
that hero was compelled to undergo, while he remained
beneath the roof of his intended father-in-law.   Lord
Springfield called upon him, and gave the party an invitation ; which of course was accepted.   But the distance
being considerable (at least *that* was the reason Rodney
gave), Mrs. Rodney did not fulfil her engagement with
his Lordship.   Poor lady, she felt herself out of her
element in good society ; and, if the truth must be told,
her constant declarations to that effect, and the many
practical proofs she gave of their sincerity, had determined
Sir Frederick, long before the expiration of the week's
probation, that to take her to London with his intended
bride, would be to excite the most dreadful insurrection
amongst his friends and relations ; indeed, so deeply was
he wounded by her excessive homeliness, and the abruptness with which she blurted out the most uncouth observations upon the most delicate topics, that he almost
began to regret the lengths to which he had carried his
negotiations with the family (little thinking what happiness his defection would bestow), and felt that if her
daughter had unluckily been destined to remain in England as his wife, the chance of an association with such a

mother, would have opposed an almost insuperable objection against making her so.

With all these varying feelings agitating their minds, how strange it appears that the match should have been persisted in! but so it was: the suitor felt that he had gone too far to retract. Honour, therefore, led *him* to complete the negotiation. Mrs. Rodney was delighted at the *éclat* of such a wedding, and her small ambition induced *her* therefore to hurry its conclusion. Rodney, as we know, was prompted to the measure by absolute necessity; and Fanny submitted through a sense of duty. And in all this composition, not one grain of love is to be discovered. The love, alas! was abstracted when poor Francis went; and how far the expectations of the other parties to the ill-omened treaty were fulfilled, we shall hereafter see.

Having, as I before said, been enabled, by his now constant association with her, perfectly to appreciate the social qualities of Mrs. Rodney, Sir Frederick determined that the safest and wisest mode of proceeding in the present affair, would be that which is generally adopted by elderly gentlemen in similar situations; namely, to marry first, and take opinions on the merits of his bride afterwards. Accordingly he submitted his plan to Rodney, who, fearing the slips, which we are told so often happen " 'twixt the cup and the lip," felt no disposition whatever to throw any impediment in the way of the marriage, which (since Fanny had expressed her perfect readiness to acquiesce in any arrangement made for her) it was now finally determined should take place forthwith; and that the newly-married couple should proceed from the Academy whither they might think proper, to spend the honeymoon; after which, Lady Brashleigh would appear in London, to make preparations for her voyage, in her proper character, and in those circles of which she was destined hereafter to be the pride and ornament.

Sir Frederick had lived too long in the world, and had seen too much of the proceedings of its inhabitants, to believe implicitly that Fanny's sweet, unruffled, imperturbable serenity was the most striking proof of devotion to him; indeed,

it afforded him some little ground for doubt, when contrasted with the strong bias of feeling with which she had
at first received him, and by which, it must be confessed,
he felt gratified and flattered : but most certainly he did
not suspect the *whole* truth, nor imagine that he had a
powerful rival in her affections —so powerful, indeed, as
to engross them all, nor think that the placid content-
ment which sat upon her brow was the result of a determination to sacrifice herself for the sake of a parent ; he
was satisfied and pleased with her conduct towards him
and not having in the first instance made up his mind
to excite rapturous love in the heart of a girl young
enough to be his grand-daughter, was pleased to find that
she treated him in a manner which gave him, and those
around him, an idea that, at all events, she esteemed and
respected him.

Under any circumstances, however, it was now too late
to doubt or hesitate ; and accordingly Sir Frederick despatched a letter, begging his solicitor to come to him
forthwith, and receive his instructions for settlements, &c.,
which mandate the man of business speedily obeyed; and
by shortening as much as possible the " law's delay," the
necessary papers were prepared in less than a week, and
a settlement made upon the future Lady Brashleigh of
seven hundred pounds per annum during the life of Sir
Frederick, and in case of his death, a jointure of fifteen
hundred pounds per annum; an arrangement considered
by Rodney and his lady extremely liberal, and highly
satisfactory.

While these matters were in progress, and after the
deeds of settlement had been signed, Rodney thought it
would be as well to ascertain whether any thing was
likely to be done about the three thousand seven hundred pounds, in which amount he was debtor to Sir Frederick, as successor to the property of Wilbraham Stevenson, Esquire, and also at what time the interest ac-
cruing half-yearly upon the said principal sum, was expected to be paid. Not liking to put any question upon
the subject to Sir Frederick himself, he took the opportunity of making his inquiries of the attorney, whose pre-

sence at the moment he considered extremely *à-propos*,
and determined to avail himself of it accordingly.

"I suppose," said Rodney to the lawyer, "if I pay you
the interest due upon the money to Sir Frederick, during
his absence in India, it will be the correct mode of proceeding?"

"Do you mean the bond debt?" asked the lawyer.

"Yes," said Rodney, "granted by me to the late
Wilbraham Stevenson for three thousand seven hundred
pounds."

"Oh, Sir," said the lawyer, "Sir Frederick Brashleigh
has nothing in the world to do with *that*; he succeeded to
certain estate of the late Mr. Stevenson in right of his
maternal uncle; but all bonds and securities for debts due
to that gentleman's estates are in the possession of his
immediate heir, and Sir Frederick has neither interest
nor control over them; indeed, the coolness which exists
between Sir Frederick and young Stevenson entirely
prevents his interfering one way or the other about them."

Rodney was astounded; indeed, it was with difficulty
he could conceal his feelings. He had compelled his
child to sacrifice herself for life, he had exiled from his
house the exemplary Welsted, he had toiled and laboured,
and contrived and planned—for what? To be deprived at
once of the being who absolutely supported his credit as a
schoolmaster: to be robbed of the society of an only
daughter, and yet to be left as much exposed as before to
the perils of a debt, to cancel which had been the great
object of all his schemes and toils. And not only was
this the case, but from the declared hostility which existed
between young Stevenson and Sir Frederick, the very
fact of Miss Rodney's marriage with the General, would,
it was pretty clear (if it had *any* effect upon the young
gentleman's conduct touching the fatal security), induce
him to act with harshness rather than lenity towards her
father.

Rodney felt at that moment the meanness, the needless,
fruitless meanness, of which he had been guilty: that the
match *was* advantageous to his daughter, in a worldly
point of view, nobody could deny, but its advantages

were most assuredly not sufficiently great to have induced him to excite the animosity of his principal creditor, in whose hands his fate literally rested.

In this, as in all other trying situations, the unhappy poet was more to be pitied than his fellows ; he was not a man of the world himself, and moreover had not to look for the solace of compassion, nor the relief derivable from a communication of his sorrow to another : he was afraid, nay certain, that if Mrs. Rodney were put into possession of any of the facts which agitated him at this moment, they would infallibly burst out in the course of the succeeding day in the shape of little jocularities or direful presages ; and, therefore, stifling his remorse for what was past, and his apprehensions of what was to come, the unhappy father proceeded with the arrangements for the nuptial ceremony which was so shortly to take place.

CHAPTER VI.

All the world's a stage.—SHAKSPEARE.

WE left poor Francis Welsted, as perhaps the reader may remember, on the outer side of a stage-coach, journeying towards the metropolis, and perhaps, considering all that has been doing since his forced march from the academy, the reader may also wish to know how the unhappy exile has been employing his time since we have been compelled to lose sight of him.

Francis had never been in London, and felt an almost indescribable awe of his first visit ; as the coach proceeded at its wonted pace, the desire to reach the end of a journey, rendered pleasant neither by the weather nor his companions, was mingled with an apprehension of entering the mighty maze of which he had heard so much, but which he had not yet beheld ; and as the day closed in, and the sun retired into a black mist, such as the young adventurer had never before seen, and left in deep purple

6

shadows the clustering spires of the great city and the
stupendous dome of its towering cathedral, he felt something like a dread of the scene before him, which he was
so rapidly approaching, and which, in all probability, was
destined to be his future sphere of action.

Having made sundry inquiries of his fellow-travellers,
and, for a miracle—not having been misled by them, he
ascertained that the stage-coach "*inned* at the sign of the
Bell and Crown, Holborn." The sound was any thing
but romantic—any thing but inviting; yet Francis determined at all events to take up his abode there in the first
instance, considering that the coach and his luggage
would satisfy the inmates of the house that he was *bonâ
fide* a traveller, and a stranger fresh from the country;
whereas, had he proceeded to some more agreeable domicile in the first instance, his self-introduction might perhaps have been more equivocal.

As the vehicle entered London, and commenced its rapid progress over the wretched metropolitan pavement,
threading, as it were, the apparently impervious mass of
coaches, carts, and other conveyances, in the midst of
cries and yells, and most discordant noises, Francis felt
himself bewildered, and congratulated himself that from
his situation he was exalted above the necessity of making
his own way amongst the crowd and confusion by which
he was surrounded.

At length the broad street of Holborn presented itself,
and the stage dashed rapidly beneath the gateway of the
Bell and Crown, at the door of which, assiduous waiters
and active chambermaids made their appearance, offering
all sorts of aid and attentions, while the landlady (much
too important to take a personal share in their toils) enlivened the scene by keeping up a continual ringing with a
huge bell in the bar, which might have served for the sign
itself: a group of well ringletted daughters peeping over
the blinds to witness, if not welcome, the arrival of the
passengers, gave an air of doubtful gaiety to the dingy
apartment in which they were immured; and tired as he
was with his journey, Francis felt relieved and comparatively comfortable, when he found himself ushered into a

neat sanded slip of a coffee-room, the windows of which opened to the street. He inquired if he could have a bed; was answered in the affirmative; and taking it for granted that the kind hostess, whose assiduities in noise-making had attracted his early attention, would select a comfortable apartment for his use, left it entirely to her good nature to provide one, and did not take the precaution of reconnoitring his room until bed-time, when he was deposited in a cell, high up in the house, and far down the yard,—in which the bed was of the smallest size, the glass of the worst quality, the sheets not clean, the washing-stand soapless, the ewer and water-bottle empty, the door without a lock, and the bell without a string; in short, he was " stowed away" in a manner perfectly suitable, as the chambermaid thought, to the condition of an outside passenger on a heavy-coach, who took tea instead of dinner, and carried his own portmanteau up stairs.

Francis, as it may be imagined, was wretched during the evening; he attempted to abstract his mind from the objects which engrossed it, by reading all the newspapers, spelling the red-book and the directory, and subsequently all the framed and glazed bills of steam-packets, and patent soda-water manufactories, with which he found the coffee-room plentifully adorned. He feared stirring out; the crowd and darkness combined with the total absence of pursuit and want of knowledge of the streets to keep him prisoner; he ventured, it is true, as far as the side-door of the house, which opens into the inn-yard, and saw the Poole mail take its departure; but he returned to his old seat in the window, where he remained until the sound of ten o'clock striking, justified, he thought, his proceeding to bed; and accordingly, marshalled by the chambermaid, bearing in her hand a flaring tallow-candle, in a japanned candlestick, he quitted the coffee-room, and ascended a dreary staircase, passed through a dismal narrow passage, and found himself abandoned to his fate in a garret, the merits and conveniences of which I have already attempted to describe.

The reflections which Welsted's situation gave rise to in his mind, were, at the moment he lay down, any thing but consolatory. In novels and romances, love, when it once gains the ascendancy, is represented as banishing, in the most arbitrary and tyrannical manner, every other feeling, every other wish, every thought, indeed, unconnected with the one object of its tender solicitude ; but in real life the case is somewhat, though not greatly, different, and although Welsted's heart was sore when he thought of his beloved, and although her ill-executed portrait slumbered that very night beneath his pillow, he could not, in considering dispassionately the line of conduct which he had adopted, fail to recollect that his prospects, at the moment, were any thing but flattering.

The state of the case was this—(for as the historian of Francis Welsted, I must develop *that*, which his pride assiduously concealed), the young man had arrived in the metropolis, friendless, unknown, and unpatronized ; and although with *his* talents and application, and the highly satisfactory testimonials which Rodney would doubtlessly be ready on any proper occasion to afford of his exemplary conduct and character, he had a fair chance of employment, still things do not so speedily fall out as sanguine persons often wish ; and though he might in time procure the situation most desired by him, that of assistant in an academy removed from the scene of all his past happiness and present sorrow, still, it was highly improbable that such a vacancy should present itself until the termination of the current half-year,—a period when changes are made, and new plans arranged in such establishments. Seeing therefore that his stock of worldly wealth amounted but to eighteen pounds and some few shillings, the vista which opened before him was, it must be admitted, neither very gay nor very cheering ; and little as *he* knew of the world, he knew enough to be convinced that such a pittance would last but a few days in the metropolis, live as frugally and abstemiously as he might.

The journey, the rapid progress through the air, the strong present excitement of his feelings, nay, the very fatigue of sorrow itself, and those who have felt it will perfectly understand what I mean, " weighed his eyelids

down, and steeped his senses in forgetfulness." And in
spite of the vigorous attacks of a large army of small animals, whose *persons* are unknown in the country, and
whose names are never mentioned in London, he slept
soundly until nine o'clock the following morning : perhaps he would have reposed longer, but the chambermaid,
having first opened the door of his room, in order to ascertain whether he had absconded in the night with the
sheets and counterpane, finding he still slumbered, and
considering that all her other beds being made "she
should be thrown back in her work," if he did not get up,
and allow her to make *his*, began to bang the pails about
the passage, shut the doors which opened into it violently,
rattle down the Venetian blinds, and sweep out the sharp
angles of the narrow staircase, carefully and assiduously
bestowing sonorous tnumps upon each step in her progress
downwards, so as effectually to mar the repose of her solitary *patient*, and give him a distaste for late hours in future.

The well-schooled handmaid perfectly succeeded in all
her undertakings ; and lest he should by any chance relapse into a doze, the moment the creaking of his rickety
bedstead announced a movement, she was at his door inquiring if " *he* called ; " to which, imagining it quite time
to rise, he answered in the affirmative ; and having procured some hot water, proceeded to dress. It might appear like trifling to detail all the minor miseries which he
underwent during the operation, or the laborious efforts
he was compelled to use to make himself heard, when the
chambermaid had once taken her departure from his vicinity. After protracted delays, however, his clothes were
returned brushed ; and once more arrayed in his morning
costume, he proceeded to breakfast in the coffee-room.

As he surveyed the tenants of the different boxes,
Welsted felt an entirely new sensation ; he had in fact
never, until the preceding night, when the coffee-house
visiters were few, been in any thing more like a public
room, than that in which the oyster club was held in the
little village which he had left ; and when he saw the variety of strange faces, and the variety of expressions which

characterized those faces. he started back like a novice
on his first appearance at a masquerade.

Some of the parties were farmers and graziers, making
calculations upon the price of live and dead stock ; others
(and mostly those) were small attorneys, discussing points
with country worthies, whose huge great-coats, piled upon
the seats beside them, announced them to be fresh import-
ations ; while heaps of dirty letters, tied with red tape
which occupied the major part of the breakfast-tables
gave proof of ample employment for the ill-dressed, well-
powdered persons, who were listening with greedy ear to
catch the " state of the case " from the rubicund rurals
whom they had secured as clients.

Contrasted with these hale and healthy specimens of
English yeomanry, stood the smoke-dried waiters, whose
pale and yellow cheeks gave horrible evidence of the con-
finement which they suffered in the atmosphere they were
doomed to breathe ; for, in addition to the ordinary smells
of London, a stable-yard, a coach-office, the country farmers and the London lawyers, coffee, rum, hollands and
water, tea, toast, brandy, and tobacco, all conspired at
one and the same moment, with the never-failing odour
of gas (when used in the interior of houses), to give fra-
grance to the residence of poor Francis Welsted.

A pale object, which looked like the ghost of a departed
attendant, moved towards Frank, and asked him if he
chose breakfast, to which Frank naturally answered in the
affirmative. And accordingly the waiter (for it *was* a
waiter) spread over the table (rendered clammy by sundry
circular deposits of ale and porter, the accidental spill-
ings of last night's carouse) a cloth, not larger than an
ordinarily sized napkin, darned in sundry places, and
bearing strong evidence upon its face that eggs and mus-
tard had been eaten upon it for several previous mornings.
He then proceeded to exhibit a pewter tea-pot, with a
Davenanted spout, a small jug, containing three or four
table-spoonfuls of a light-blue liquid professing to be milk,
which, with some half-dozen lumps of dingy sugar, recum-
bent in a basin, and attended thereon by a pair of brown
japanned tongs, shared the board with a bit of salt but-

ter, and a French roll, three inches long by two inches in circumference.

Poor Welsted, who had been accustomed to the substantial breakfasts of his kind patron, where magnificent rounds of beef and roseate hams, and other viands of solid contents, garnished out the board, and where rich cream, and loaves and rolls, and marmalade and honey, and butter at discretion, formed a strong and painful contrast to the retail exhibition now before him, looked, lover as he was, wistfully after the waiter when he departed, leaving in a tea-cup not larger than a thimble, a small amount of dried sloe-leaves, mixed with small bits of birch-brooms and raisin-stalks, known in the London trade as bohea tea ; and when the man, being told by Francis to " make the breakfast," cast the dark mixture into the metal pot, and scuffling slipshod along the sanded floor to a huge black kettle, which swung over the fireplace, deluged the miserable pittance with a flood of thick Thames water, our hero, with a more worldly feeling than either novel-writers or novel-readers would in general allow a desponding swain to cherish, abstracted all his thoughts for the moment from other subjects, and really felt uncomfortable in the anticipation of a London life, passed as he fancied his was doomed to be ; considering as he did, that even the *style* in which he was then temporarily indulging was much too *gay* and expensive (his slender means considered), to be adopted for a constancy.

Having, however, despatched the meal, which was, it must be owned, not " long a doing," Welsted felt anxious to try a flight in the streets, which, now that daylight and a bright sun had changed their appearance, held out something like temptation for a stroll. To ask his way as he left the inn, would be, he thought, to confess an ignorance which he did not choose to avow, because he imagined such an admission likely to lay him open to the designs and depredations of London sharpers, and if overheard would offer a luring bait to the adventurers by whom he fancied himself surrounded, even in the coffee-room itself; accordingly, he sallied forth from the inn, and instinctively proceeded towards the west end of the town, where, bewildered with the noise and bustle, the gaiety and activity of every thing around him, he continued strolling, until his wearied limbs and the darkened state of the atmosphere warned him that his excursion had been sufficiently prolonged; he retraced with very little assistance his road to the hotel, and the day closed without one step having been taken to forward his views or better his condition. A bad dinner swallowed without appetite, and succeeded by a pint of that dark-red mixture which is generally retailed in London as port wine, terminated the proceedings of the first twenty-four hours.

The state of his mind at this period was pitiable; the one subject—his beloved Fanny. wholly and entirely engrossed it; and although the varying objects by which he had been surrounded or pleased, amused or excited, for a moment, during his brief residence in town, occupied him temporarily, yet to the one fatal point he again invariably recurred; and the chilling feeling of utter hopelessness and despair was on him, as, for the second time, he wound his weary way to the dark and dismal apartment, in which he was doomed again to pass the night.

When he rose the next morning, he felt more refreshed than on the preceding one: and, while mechanically swallowing his melancholy breakfast, resolved not to let that day pass without making some effort to secure himself, if possible, from the distress which must inevitably overtake him, unless his faculties were employed to some useful purpose: he read the advertisements in the newspapers, saw several inquiries for assistants at schools, for tutors to young gentlemen, for steady clerks, and other officers; in which industry and integrity were mentioned as indispensable, and excellent characters from their last places absolutely necessary. Of several of these he made memoranda, and so soon as he had finished his repast, proceeded, by the help of a map, which he had purchased the preceding day, to go in search of the employments promised by the several advertisements.

The first reference was to a boy's school in Gray's Inn lane; he approached the house with a certain degree of respect, associating in his mind with the very appearance of an academy, the amiable Rodney and his delightful daughter; but the bright vision did not last long; the terms of the assistantship were twenty pounds per annum, for which stipend, besides the scholastic duties necessarily attached to the situation, it was expected that the young man should look after a horse and chaise.

In the next instance Welsted was received by the lady of the house, who really seemed somewhat pleased at his appearance, but the flattering amenity of her first approaches was suddenly changed into absolute coldness, upon discovering that Francis could not dance quadrilles, which Mr. Dobson's young men were always expected to do, to keep the young ladies in practice.

In his applications for the situation of clerk, he was as unsuccessful as in those for assistant. Was he acquainted with the silk market? How did he keep his accounts? Who would be his sureties? Was he the son of a freeman? and many questions of similar import were asked; to which he gave either answers that were unsatisfactory, or no answers at all; and he departed from the counting-house of Mr. Bunyon, wretched and depressed.

At length, he found it necessary to conclude his morning's toil, and again returned to his inn, where, although occasionally spoken to by various visiters (chiefly passengers by stage-coaches), he met with none of those surprising adventures which ordinarily befal the " wandering children of adversity;" and when he again reposed himself, it was not in the same cell to which he had at first been consigned. His protracted residence, his punctual payments, and his regular mode of living, had induced a change of dormitory, and he was shifted to a more commodious apartment, which, though far from being the best, was extremely fair for a " pint of wine" man, and by comparison with the dungeon which he at first tenanted, absolutely delightful.

It would be quite useless here to expatiate upon the qualities attributable to the number Three, or quote the Graces, the Fates, or the thousand trite combinations adducible in support of its mysterious merits; certain it is (and that is quite sufficient for me), that on the third

morning of Welsted's residence in London, something *did*
occur to distinguish it most strikingly, not only from the
two mornings which preceded it, but in its consequences
from every previous morning of our young wanderer's
existence.

After a long and fruitless march in search of something,
—what, poor fellow, he hardly knew,—he was proceeding
on the third morning, along the busy part of Piccadilly,
confused by the noises around him, with his mind (all the
energies of which would have been requisite for the safe
guidance of his body through the bustle) wholly abstracted, when he attempted to cross the street, just as a
black cabriolet, driven by a young man of elegant and pre-
possessing appearance, and drawn by a horse showing as
much blood as his master, dashed by him so closely, as
nearly to strike him down; failing in which, its wheel
suddenly rolling into one of those deep holes with which
the pavement of Piccadilly so plenteously abounds (and
which was more than half full of dirty water), produced
an effect upon his body not unlike that of a Shrapnell
shell upon a solid square of infantry; in short, such were
the shock, the dash and the splash, that he was nearly
covered with mud.   Considering this to be one of the

—————— ——— ——— " Spurns
That patient merit of the unworthy takes,"

poor Francis merely cast a compassionating eye over his
own figure, and hastily concluded the perilous operation
of crossing the street, thinking no more about himself, or
the great man who had bespattered him; when his surprise was excited by finding the same black cab, and the
same blood-horse again at his side, splashing him in a
minor degree, but with greater constancy and regularity;
he turned his head in order to ascertain whether the as-
persions with which he was thus favoured were inten-
tionally bestowed, when the gay driver checking his fiery
horse, and bringing him nearly on his haunches. by his
animated manner of pulling him up, astonished the rural
usher by exclaiming, " Welsted, my dear good Frank
Welsted! I thought it must be *you.*—Mercy on us! how
my infernal horse has splashed you!—What *are* you doing

in town? where are you staying? when do you go? how's old Rodney? how's Fanny?—gad, how ill you look, eh?"

This speech, delivered in the midst of the noise of Piccadilly, the bright bay horse alternately rearing and pawing the ground, as the heavy laden carts grazed the wheels of the cabriolet in passing, and while the speaker's companion in the carriage (who clearly saw that Welsted was nobody) kept warning him of the near approaches of more heavy vehicles, was perfectly unintelligible to the wondering young man; he endeavoured to explain that he really did not recollect his " dear friend," whose appearance was so highly aristocratic, as during the short colloquy to attract the eyes of wondering shopkeepers and wandering milliners—but all in vain; the noise, the restlessness of the horse, the crowd, the exclamations of the coachmen in the rear, desiring the cab-driver (invisible to them), to " pull on a bit," and the embarrassment under which Welsted himself laboured, prevented the accomplishment of the desired end.

" The deuce take the horse!" said the driver, " there is no use in trying to make oneself heard here ;— give me your card my dear Welsted, and I'll call on you to-morrow without fail, for I have ten thousand things to ask and as many to tell you."

Still in " amazement lost," hardly knowing what he did, Welsted, who had prepared two or three cards as reference, in case of discovering any promising situation, handed one of them to his unknown friend, who, receiving it in the most grateful manner from the wondering rustic (who to the astonishment of the groomlet behind the cab, and the discomfiture of the dandy within it), safely deposited it in a small pocket of the carriage, and giving the steed his head, dashed away along the heavy sea of the Piccadilly pavement, and was out of sight in a few seconds.

Welsted watched the progress of the cabriolet, wondering what it all meant, and who the elegant, graceful personage could be, who was so very intimate with *him*, and with Rodney, and Fanny, and who apparently took so much interest in his present proceedings ; he thought too, that he could trace something like a resemblance in the stranger to some boy who had formerly been at school at Rodney's, but could fix upon no name wherewith to iden- tify him ; and the volatile personage taking it for granted that Welsted remembered *him* as well as *he* remembered Weisted, had given him no clue whereby to discover him ; so, as Francis walked homewards, he repeated all the bills of the school that he could remember, in hopes, by some indescribable association of ideas, to ascertain who his new and elegant friend could possibly be.

On his return to his inn, however, he was still in a state of perfect ignorance on the subject, and felt a degree of uneasiness as to his worldly affairs, to which he had hitherto been a stranger ; the days were gliding away, and no prospect of employment or advancement opened, and the poor stranger in London again swallowed his din- ner as a mere matter of course, with his mind divided between the bitter recollections of his beloved Fanny, and the dark anticipations of his own ill success. He sought his bed earlier than usual, not without exciting in the minds of the landlady and her daughters a strong appre- hension that he harboured some intention of committing suicide :—so strikingly changed indeed was his demean- our, and so probable did such an event appear to the kind females, that immediately after his departure from the coffee-room, for bed, the mistress of the house rang her bell for the head waiter, and inquired if Mr. Welsted had paid the day's bill ? A reply in the affirmative considera- bly appeased her personal apprehensions for his safety, and she slept soundly during the night ; she was however not the less pleased to see her young guest again in the morning, alive, and if not merry, at least eating his breakfast at his wonted table in the coffee-room.

While going through this indispensable operation, Francis, as was his custom, carefully perused all the ad- vertisements of the various journals, and at length saw in one the promise of something favourable to his wishes for employment. The reference was to a school at Hackney, and having consulted his map, he resolved that the busi-

ness of the morning should be a visit to that place, which
he ascertained might be reached on foot, without much
fatigue. Thither he determined, therefore, forthwith to
proceed. There had been an unusual degree of gloom on
his mind in the early part of this morning, and he felt
relieved and invigorated by the appearance (fallacious as
it might eventually turn out) of better times ; and cheered
by his hopes, started upon his expedition with a firm step
and a heart full of expectation, and, after losing his way
two or three times, found himself at length at the termination of his journey.

The house to which the advertisement directed him was
conveniently situate, and highly respectable in its appearance; its broad red brick front was set off to advantage by a close-shorn lawn, separated from the high road
by a low wall, iron railings, and a pair of well-wrought
gates ; over-arching which, appeared a board, whereon the
word " Academy," in highly burnished letters, upon an
azure ground, glittered in the sun ; he approached the
grand entrance, and pulling a pendant bar with all his
might, produced a sound at once powerful and majestic.
The silence which followed the peal of the great gate-bell
seemed doubly awful, and when from a side and smaller
door a female enquired " whom he pleased to want," the
sensitive applicant perceived that he had taken an unusual
liberty, in making his appeal at a portal evidently designed
for the admission of much greater personages than himself.

Having mentioned to the housemaid his desire to see
her master, she ushered him through a passage across the
hall into a drawing-room, in which every thing gave evidence of the most scrupulous exactitude and formal precision.

The prints from the Scriptures and Shakespeare were
in frames, covered with paper nettings, and a large picture
over the chimney, probably that of Mr. Tickle himself,
was entirely eclipsed by an extensive cotton cover ; the
chimney ornaments preserved indeed their forms, but they
too were all closely cased in paper, and a lamp pendant
from the ceiling was equally well secured in an elongated

canvas bag. The curtains and chairs wore domestic suits of calico, and the well-polished grate, filled with fantastic shavings, gave similar indications of the care and attention of the superintendants of the establishment to their household goods.

To describe the delay, the anticipation, the interview with Mr. Tickle, the master of the said academy, the conversation which he held with Francis, or the various anecdotes of himself which he related, would be useless;—the point, I presume, to be all that the reader desires, and that he shall have as briefly and as speedily as possible.

Mr. Tickle wanted an assistant to come to him in ten days:—he described the qualifications requisite, and Francis displayed his abilities; gave satisfactory proofs of his competency, and referred Mr. Tickle to his late employer, Mr. Rodney, for testimonials of character. Mr Tickle was pleased with what he saw, congratulated himself upon the acquisition he was about to make, and promised to address himself forthwith to Mr. Rodney.

The terms were moderate—forty pounds per annum;—but then the assistants lived with the family. Mrs. Tickle was an amiable woman, and her two daughters sensible, charming girls; indeed the warm commendations which the head of the family bestowed upon all its members gave Francis a desire to behold the perfections of those with whom he was destined to pass, perhaps, the remainder of his life.

He was, as indeed he had almost expected, invited to partake of an early dinner; and having been duly introduced to the ladies, was cautioned by Mr. Tickle not to make any allusion to the real object of his visit, as one of the assistants, to whose place he was to succeed, would be at table, of whom Mr. Tickle chose (perhaps with a view of slily cautioning the stranger in his future conduct), to relate several anecdotes, tending to explain that the principal reason which he had for removing him, arose from perceiving a disposition on his part to be upon too friendly terms with one of the Misses Tickle;—he played the flute, and copied out music for the young ladies, and drew landscapes, and sang love songs, and did an infinity of those sorts of things which were not professionally required of him, but which it appeared had made him, by Mr. Tickle's showing, somewhat more of a favourite with the young ladies than their father desired.

The moment Mr. Tickle had hinted at the cause of the young man's removal, Welsted felt interested for him; and when he sat down at dinner, not five minutes had elapsed before he was convinced that Mr. Tickle had begun his preventive system a little too late: in five minutes he perceived that there was a well organized communication established between the eyes of Miss Elizabeth Tickle and Mr. Frederick Stevens; and moreover, that both those personages were as perfectly aware of the object of his visit, and of Tickle's display of civility and hospitality towards him as if " New Usher " had been painted on his forehead in large black letters.

It is impossible to be in a mixed society, even for the first time, without detecting before the expiration of a quarter of an hour, the pair (or pairs, if there be more than one) between whom this sort of good understanding exists ;—they fancy themselves secure, and think their proceedings are hidden from mortal eye, because those who ought to know most about them are generally the last to notice them ; but the stranger, who comes into their company, like the sober man into a party of drunkards, if he have but an ordinary share of common sense and common observation, can never fail to see and understand the whole of the performance, in less than the period which I have liberally allowed for the discovery. Elizabeth and the usher were carefully placed opposite to each other ;—(judicious precaution)—and the remotest allusion to change of circumstances, or the most obscure remark upon Welsted's visit, was followed instantaneously by an interchange of looks, which, although as clear in their meaning to the new-comer, as his coming was to those who gave them, appeared to excite neither discontent nor observation in the watchful parents of the favourite daughter.

Sympathy for poor Stevens had so worked upon Welsted's heart during the latter part of the day, and the look the fond girl gave him as he was retiring after tea to grind Greek with the juniors, reminded him so forcibly of those which his fairer and fonder Fanny had been used to cast on him, when he departed for some similar purpose, that he almost repented having accepted the situation in which he was to supersede the lover. As it turned out, he was perfectly right, when he supposed the young couple perfectly aware of the nature and object of his visit, for it seems that Tickle had disclosed the secret to his wife, as an excuse for inviting a stranger to dinner without her special permission. That being the case, Mrs. Tickle, as communicative as Mrs. Rodney herself, imparted the fact to her daughters; to whose desire to know whether, as there was company, they should dress, she gave the chilling answer that there was no occasion, "as it was only the young man come after Stevens's *place*."

After having participated in the perilous luxury of hot weak tea, and having formed his opinion of the society in which much of his future time was to be passed, Frank quitted the academy, having been warmly shaken by the hand by Mr. Tickle, whose pleasure at securing a young man evidently of great ability, and extensive attainments, was not at all decreased by hearing from his wife in a brief *tête-à-tête* between dinner and tea, that the girls thought his young friend, Mr. Welsted, a great quiz, and had been roasting his shyness prodigiously.

Tickle knew as little of the world as our friend Rodney. Elizabeth and Harriet in their spleen at losing Stevens, saw with jaundiced eyes the modest, unassuming manners of his intended successor, and ridiculed his diffidence and delicacy of manner; but this spirit was conquerable by time; and the young lady whose heart was disengaged, might perhaps have lived long enough to change her opinion.

As poor Welsted returned towards town, he felt, amidst his gratitude to Providence, for having thus placed him in an honourable situation, where he might earn his livelihood, and at the same time do justice to those with

whose education he might be charged, a regret that he
must necessarily be mixed up in the family politics, and
enter a circle of which two members would be naturally
prejudiced against him. Harriet was evidently her sister's confidante, and Elizabeth would doubtless hate the
successor of her beloved ; and Welsted felt besides, that
the circumstances of the case were too nearly resembling
his own, to be regarded by him with perfect indifference,
and should his duty to his employer be put in competition
with his feelings towards the divided pair, upon any occasion which might present itself, he feared that he might
be induced to lean more towards the side of unprosperous
love than strict impartiality would dictate.

Still, poor fellow, he *was* settled, and he determined to
lose no time in writing to Rodney to apprize him of his
success, and of the application which would be made to
him for testimonials ; and so entirely was he absorbed in
his thoughts and considerations of the subject, that he
reached his inn, with very few variations from the direct
course, before he thought himself half-way towards his
journey's end.

When he entered the coffee-room—indeed the moment
his face was seen through the glazed door of the bar, the
large bell rang, and the landlady screamed with all her
"might and main" for John, Thomas, Betty, chambermaid, who, thus urged to speedy measures by the noises
of their mistress, were all shortly in attendance. The
waiter in an instant was seen lighting two candles ;—he
approached Welsted, bending as it were under his humility, and requested to know whether he would not prefer
a private apartment to the coffee-room, as there was a
very convenient one disengaged at present up stairs.

" No!" said Welsted, staring at the extraordinary difference and deference in the waiter's conduct, " this will
do."

Here the officer of the household, known as Boots, appeared with a boot-jack, and an entirely new pair of blue
morocco slippers.

" Have your boots off, Sir !" said the man ; to which
hardly had Welsted replied, ere the landlady's eldest

7

daughter, with Medusa-like head bore testimony to the opinion she entertained of the beauty of her hair, as well as of her own skill and industry in its decoration, stepped " Hebely" along the sanded floor, and presented him with a note and card, which she said had been left for him during his absence. The look which accompanied the delivery of these important documents startled the young rustic, who had often before seen the young lady's eyes, but never so lighted up, so animated as now.

Welsted looked on the ticket, and saw the words " Earl of Farnborough" engraven upon it in good Roman capitals, beneath which, in pencil, was written " Viscount Feversham," the address below, " Grosvenor Square."*

The accompanying note, which had been written at the inn, and left unsealed, ran thus—

" DEAR WELSTED,

" My Father insisted upon accompanying me in my visit to you this morning, in hopes of prevailing upon you to dine with him to-day.   Your being from home, and the uncertainty of your return will, it seems, prevent our making this out; but the Earl will be delighted if you will join our family party at seven to-morrow, as he wishes very much to make your acquaintance ; and I wish very much that he should do so.   Pray do not fail.   Your old and affectionate friend,

" FEVERSHAM."

Welsted read the note, and then the card, several times alternately; and had not recovered from the amazement into which he had been thrown by the perusal, when he observed the very best chambermaid in her very best attire, waiting to usher him to bed, bearing in her hand a plated candlestick, containing a wax-light ; he looked at her with

* Since this book was written the title of Farnborough has been conferred upon the amiable and accomplished Sir Charles Long, G.C.B.; but as the dates speak for themselves, it has not been thought necessary to change the " peerage" of the fictitious Earl.—1836.

a vacant stare, which she mistook for a signal that he was ready, and he followed her, so completely overcome by the call and invitation of a Peer, whose title he had never heard, and the affectionate regards of a young nobleman with whom he never had been acquainted, that he did not perceive until she had put down the candle and departed, that he had been conducted into a spacious, well-furnished room, stored with conveniences and luxuries of every kind, and as different from the cell in which he had first been deposited, as light from darkness. "The Earl of Farnborough!" murmured Welsted. "Now, who *can* the Earl of Farnborough be;—who the Viscount Feversham?" A book of the peerage, which would have given him his Lordship's name, might have unravelled the mystery in which the important visit appeared to be enveloped : this, however, did not occur at the moment, nor at the moment, perhaps, would it have been attainable. Frank went to bed, disturbed by his thoughts, which (unlike what they had been heretofore) were not exclusively devoted to Fanny Rodney. He could not conceive, how, when, or where, he could have become acquainted with the noblemen in question ; and in the consideration of the important subject, all his cares and interest about Elizabeth Tickle were lost. A new field appeared to open to his view ; he felt that there could be no mistake in his name, and concluded all his cogitations with a resolution, that whoever Lord Feversham might turn out eventually to be, he was doubtlessly the driver of the cabriolet to whom, on the preceding morning, he had so bashfully presented his ticket.

Scarcely had the London morning dawned, ere Francis heard the door of his bed-room gently opened, and the head waiter himself steal softly and shoeless into the apartment, and remove his clothes and hat, in order that they might be properly and carefully brushed and cleaned ; and just before his usual time of rising. a gentle tap announced the modest chambermaid, who bore in her hand a silver mug, teeming with the hotest water ; while in his hand, the obsequious porter, unasked, paraded his boots shining in all the refulgence of Day—and Martin

When he descended to the coffce-room, he found his
breakfast laid on a large table in the largest box; the
private platc of mine hostess was furnished out to do him
honour; an ewer, of antique form, held his cream; his
sugar reposed in a basin of similar pretensious; a teapot,
of the same material, superseded the pewter one of former
days, and the "haymakers" of ordinary guests gave way
silver forks fit for a human being to eat with.

The manners of the attendants were not less changed
from what they had been, than the articles for his use;—
common civility gave place to uncommon servility, and
the whole establishment seemed to vie with each other in
offering attentions and respect to the gentlcman upon
whom an earl and a viscount had called at the sign of the
Bell and Crown in Holborn.

Welsted was not long before he had recourse to the
Red-book, wherein he discovered that the Earl of Farnborough's family name was Rutherford, and that his eldest
son's Christian name was Thomas: at once the truth
flashed upon him; Lord Feversham was neither more nor
less than little Tom Rutherford who was at Rodney's for
two or three years before he went to Eton; and the moment this fact was ascertained, the recollection of the boy
brought to Frank's mind a striking resemblance to the
cabriolet driver, whom he had before identified with the
Viscount.

There was one part of this discovery satisfactory to Welsted; it was clear that the invitation did not proceed from
mistake, and he felt pleased and gratified that one of his
earliest pupils should thus kindly remember him, and that
the Earl (recently ennobled by the death of his brother)
should unite with his son, in bestowing upon him so singular a mark of personal approbation.

Scarcely had Frank ascertained the fact that he was
really known and really invited by the noblemen, before
the waiter, marching pompously up the centre of the
coffee-room, delivered him a small triangular note, saying
in an audible voice, " His Lordship's servant is waiting
for an answer, Sir:"—the eyes and ears of the hay-sales-
men and pettifoggers were forthwith turned on Welsted.

The note was from Lord Feversham, stating, that they were anxious to know if he could dine with the Earl. Welsted forthwith wrote his reply, accepting the invitation, and having despatched the note, proceeded to breakfast with what appetite he might.

His first business for the morning, as he had previously arranged it, was writing a letter to Rodney, but there appeared something so singular in the event which had just occurred—something like a *probability* that his talents might be required in some other sphere—that he resolved to defer his letter to his old master till the following day, since the delay of one post could do no mischief, and might possibly produce some new adventure.

The morning passed feverishly with Frank, for he was unused to society, and had, moreover, since truth must be told, a kind of contempt for nobility. Whence this feeling originated I know not, unless in the perusal of works and public papers, whose writers have the worst of objects in endeavouring to ridicule and vilify the best of people; and who, without ever having had an opportunity of judging personally of good society, consider it part of their daily duty, as tending to the great end they have in view, to make it appear that every individual superior to themselves is either a fool or a knave: that it is only necessary to place a coronet on a man's head to weaken his intellect: and that vice and dissipation (which in truth flourish more in the lower and middling classes, than any where else), are the exclusive characteristics of the best-born and best-bred part of the British population.

To analyze a feeling so absurd, and so unworthy of a man possessing an average share of common sense, is needless. It is sufficient to state, that under the misleading influence of these underlings of literature, poor Frank had established in his mind as a fact, that all lords lolled and lounged about, and looked through " quizzing glasses" and said, " 'pon my honour," and " gad, how charming," and had no feelings, and were proud, and senseless, and rude to their inferiors; and that ladies of family invariably lisped out nothingnesses, and talked the same silly stuff as their fathers and brothers, and husbands;

in short, he knew no more of such people, than he had
learned from those who knew as little as himself, and
fretted himself into half a fever with considering how *this*
was to be done, and how *that* was to be managed in his
visit to the Earl, doubting even until the tavern-clock had
stricken seven, whether he should not send an apology,
and eat his mutton chop in the coffee-room as heretofore.

Rallying however, all his energies, he resolved, full of
disagreeable anticipations, to undertake the expedition ;
and as the clock of Saint Andrew's proclaimed the first
quarter after the seventh hour, Frank Welsted mounted
the iron ladder of a hackney coach, and depositing his
legs amongst the dirty straw beneath, directed the d.iver
to Lord Farnborough's house, in Grosvenor-square.

CHAPTER VII.

Oh ! call not to my mind what you have done;
It sets a d bt of that account before me,
Which shows me poor and bankrupt.
                                        CONGREVE

THE pre-disposition against nobility with which, as I
just observed, Welsted was so unaccountably gifted,
preyed upon his mind during his rattling drive towards
Grosvenor-square, and, as the coach turned into that
splendid street, which, while it does honour to the monarch
under whose auspices it was designed, will confer immortal fame upon the highly-gifted architect by whose taste
and industry it has been so splendidly and rapidly exe-
cuted, the heart of our hero sank within him ; and even
thus far advanced in his progress, he was half determined
to abandon the enterprise : as it happened, however, the
coachman having nothing to think of but getting to the
end of his distance and receiving his fare, proceeded at a
more regular pace than the thoughts and resolutions of his
inside passenger, and before the young gentleman could
perfectly decide upon the measure, the vehicle stopped at

Lord Farnborough's door, which trembled with the loud but bungling assaults of the hackney driver's knocking.

Welsted stepped from the coach, defrayed the travelling expenses, was ushered up stairs, and, having been duly announced, made his *entré* into his Lordship's drawing-room ; and if the civility of the waiters and landlady at the inn in Holborn, on his return from Mr. Tickle's, had astonished him the night before, the warmth and cordiality with which he was received into Lord Farnborough's family circle, were, if possible, still more surprising.

When Welsted's name was announced, his Lordship was standing in one of the windows in earnest conversation with another nobleman, and the Viscount Feversham was reading a letter which the Countess his mother had desired him to give an opinion upon ; but the moment Welsted made his appearance, away went the letter from the Viscount's hand, away came the Earl from his noble friend, and up rose the noble lady from the sofa, all apparently eager to do the young stranger honour, all equally anxious to bid him welcome.

" This, my Lord," said Feversham to the Earl, " is my friend Welsted."

" Mr. Welsted," said Lord Farnborough, " I am truly happy to see you, truly happy to make your acquaintance, and the Countess, to whom allow me to present you, is equally gratified with myself in having the opportunity of acknowledging personally, *that*, which we can never cease to remember gratefully."

" I am sure," said the Countess, with one of her kindest smiles, " Mr. Welsted will do me the justice to believe how truly happy I am to see him here."

" And *I*," rejoined the Viscount, with perfect enthusiasm, " need say nothing, I think, to convince him of the pleasure his visit gives *me*."

Welsted kept bowing and muttering something in the way of acknowledgment for treatment which was to *him* utterly unaccountable : nor were his wonder and surprise at all decreased, when, after whispering a few words to his noble friend in the window, Lord Farnborough ap-

proached Welsted and presented him to the Earl of Headington, who expressed the greatest satisfaction in being
known to a person who must be so interesting to his friend
Farnborough's family.

Again Welsted bowed, and again felt embarrassed, but
not as he had expected to be ; he was embarrassed, because continual references were made to something relative
to himself, which he did not in the least understand, but
of which it was evident he ought to be fully aware; and
the awkwardness arising from this want of comprehension
would, of course, have occurred, had he been suddenly
domesticated and similarly situated with the family of a
tradesman or mechanic; but in the house and circle of
Lord Farnborough, he saw none of the mingled pride and
folly which he had so weakly anticipated, while labouring
under the erroneous impressions made upon his mind by
designing knavery or pretending ignorance, kindness and
unaffected good-nature, sweetness of manner, and gentleness, characterized the conduct and conversation of the
group; and although he felt a difficulty in receiving such
incomprehensible praises and acknowledgments; on all
other points he was perfectly at his ease, and found himself, in ten minutes, enjoying the histories of the olden
time with the Viscount Feversham, with as little embarrassment or shyness, as if his Lordship had been the young
curly-headed Tom Rutherford, with whom he had parted
some eight or nine years before.

But Welsted had not yet seen all that was to be seen
in Lord Farnborough's family ; nor did he know, when
first introduced, that his Lordship had other children than
the Viscount—he was doomed to be better informed.

" I cannot imagine where your sisters are," said the
Countess to her son.

" It is opera night," said Feversham ; " your Ladyship
will please to recollect that there are hearts to be caught,
and therefore more time must be allowed the young ladies
for their toilettes ; however, I shall say nothing, for here
are the culprits to speakt for themselves."

These words directed Welsted's eyes towards the door
of the drawing-room; but little was he prepared to behold

such fascinating creatures as the " culprits," who at the moment made their appearance.

The Lady Anne and the Lady Maria Rutherford were beings of a different sphere from that in which the rusticated usher of Somerville House Academy had been accustomed to move; strikingly beautiful, and very much alike in their persons, the fascinating young creatures burst upon his astonished senses, like bright visions from another world. Lady Anne was, if any thing, fairer than her sster; but there was a clearness in their beauty, a pure and sparkling brilliancy in their eyes, a sylph-like gracefulness in their figures and actions, which cast into the shades of utter darkness all that the unworldly Welsted had before thought lovely.

Feversham saw the effect produced upon his rural friend by the appearance of his sisters; and taking the Lady Anne, who was the elder of the two, by the hand (after she had spoken to the noble Lord in the distant window), led her up to Welsted, who, as the delicate creature advanced, and underwent the friendly ceremony of introduction, felt his cheek glow and his heart flutter, and ten thousand other disagreeable symptoms of perturbation, which had by no means subsided, when the witching eyes of the Lady Maria, who, in her turn, underwent a similar formality, for a moment met his; the sweet smile, the urbanity and easy grace of manner with which the unaffected young noblewoman received him, and the artless language in which her Ladyship expressed her delight at seeing the friend of her brother, to whom they owed so much, completely overcame him—he stammered a few words which were as unintelligible as unmeaning, and resumed his chair, being, as it did not occur to him at the moment, the only person at the time seated in the room.

The truth must be told; the instant he was able to collect his scattered thoughts, they as usual reverted to Fanny, but the spirit which animated him was wholly different from that by which he expected to be actuated, while making comparisons between his unsophisticated rural beauty, and young ladies of high birth and station; he had been told by all the little, low, and levelling writers of the day, that fol'y was inseparable from fashion, and pride the constant companion of noble blood ; he anticipated, therefore, as I have said before, nothing but nonsense in the conversation of his aristocratic acquaintance, nothing but heartless folly in their conduct; and when he found himself in the midst of kind parents, and amiable children, intelligent and accomplished companions, and agreeable associates; when he saw resplendent beauty unalloyed by pertness or affectation, exalted station and high rank adorned with every social virtue, and appropriately supported by high feeling, he wondered at the delusion under which he had so long been labouring, and felt heartily ashamed of the prejudices which he had suffered to gain an ascendancy in his mind.

The dinner was announced, and proceeded in the common order of dinners, and the only thing worthy of remark during its progress, was the silent admiration, mixed with wonder, with which Welsted regarded the lovely daughters of his noble host: but, as the day advanced, and the allusions to the obligation under which the whole family acknowledged themselves to Frank, became more frequent, his embarrassment, it must be confessed, gradually increased. He resolved, however, to do that, which many a greater man had done before him, namely, to bow and say nothing, satisfied that whenever he had an opportunity of speaking to Lord Feversham alone, he should be able to extract the truth from *him*, and ascertain what the deed really was, which " gilded his humble name" in the minds and memories of the noble house of Rutherford.

After dinner, when the ladies left them, the Countess stopped a moment *en passant*, and whispered something in the ear of her son, who seemed highly pleased with her proposition, and when the door had closed upon the departing *procession*, he turned to Frank to communicate her Ladyship's message, which conveyed a kind invitation to her box at the opera, for which she told her son she would leave a ticket in addition to that which belonged specially to his Lordship. This latter part of the message Feversham (not recollecting the rusticity of his friend, or his ignorance of " things in general"), did not think worth mentioning; and therefore, when the usher from Somerville House heard the proposal, he was most disagreeably puzzled. To be admitted into a theatre, he naturally concluded it was necessary to pay; what the amount might be required for entrance to the opera might be, he did not of course know, farther than the gallery price being five shillings, and the pit half-a-guinea (which he *did* know), he was led to fix in his mind a much larger sum as necessary for a passport to the boxes: he felt how greatly he should enjoy going to a place where, under the most auspicious circumstances, he should see the gay world congregated together, but this natural desire was checked by the consciousness that he had only a few shillings in his pocket, and his honest pride bade him reject the gratification he so much desired, rather than submit himself to a pecuniary obligation in order to enjoy it.

His noble friend, who could not exactly make out what reason the young rustic could possibly have for his firm refusal of the ticket, rallied him on some lady to " whom all other things give place," and offered, if he persisted in declining to accompany him, to drive him to his place of destination, in his way to the Opera-house. In vain poor Francis protested that he had no such engagement, in vain urged various objections to the Opera; but such was the force of Rutherford's raillery, that he had nearly consented to abandon himself to his guidance, when the noble father of his noble friend luckily happened to enquire if Lady Farnborough had left a ticket for Mr. Welsted, (it having evidently been arranged between them, that one should be reserved for him;) and during the discussion the other noble lord, in making some general observations on the subject, let fall a remark, that he hated opera tickets to be lost. " I like to save young fellows from Eton or Harrow, their half guineas, and when my family are out of town," said his Lordship, " you would mistake me for a poor player pushing his interest amongst his friends, if you saw me distributing Lady Headington's five spare tickets on Tuesdays and Saturdays."

From this observation, our poor, yet proud Francis discovered that there would be no call upon his pocket, no

compulsion to request assistance, and therefore, during
the next quarter of an hour, when coffee was ordered, he
allowed himself to be persuaded to do that, which in truth
it had been all along his most anxious desire to do; and
accordingly having *chasséed* the refreshing beverage with
some Maraschino, the gay young nobleman stepping into
his cabriolet, gave the spare seat to Frank, and the unconscious steed dashed forward towards the Haymarket,
bearing on his willing shoulders, the very individual whose
garments he had, but two days before, bespattered with
his prancings and curvettings in Piccadilly.

The *trajet* from Grosvenor-square to the Opera, as cabs
go, occupied but little time, and with due instruction from
his noble friend (having reached the doors of the theatre),
Francis, after considerable squeezing and pushing, and
knocking his hat off twice in the struggle, contrived to get
out of the watch-box on wheels, in which he had been wafted
to the scene of gaiety, and having passed over the pavement, through the ordeal of link-boys' odorous torches, and
the motley crowd collected to see the company, his senses
were a little disordered; nor had he completely rallied his
energies, when Feversham, presenting the tickets at the
door, led him forward towards the pit. "The Countess
of Farnborough, too," sounded in his ears, for his eyes
were dazzled, and he mechanically ascended the steps
which lead to the area of the emporium of fashion. At
the same moment in which the vast and splendid theatre
opened to his view, the rich voice of that queen of singers,
Catalani, burst upon his ear; she was delighting the brilliant audience with one of Mozart's most splendid pieces
of vocal music; and not a sound, save her own unrivalled
tones, and the soft accompaniments of the orchestra, were
to be heard.

The effect produced upon the well-informed elegant
mind of a being like Welsted, sensitively alive to all the
charms and attractions which simultaneously assailed him,
but who had never before seen the interior of *any* theatre,
must be imagined;—an attempt to describe it would be
vain: his breath stopped, and an exclamation which
modern Saints would pronounce impious, escaped him;

but he was serious in the appeal ; he was completely overcome from the sudden transition from the dark streets, the rapid, and as he thought perilous, whirling of the great-headed vehicle in which they had travelled, and all the noises, cries, whistlings, singings, screamings, bag-pipings, fiddlings, trumpettings, and news-hornings of the public streets, to the placid stillness of the vast sa-loon, broken only by the warbling of the unequalled singer.

Lord Feversham, who was a straight-forward fellow, and never stopped to consider the sensations of his friend, and never recollected (perhaps did not know) that this was literally his " first appearance at that theatre," pushed on, amidst the yielding crowd ; and as he spoke to one, and nodded to another, although the noise was scarcely audible, poor Welsted felt agonized that even a breath should disturb the harmony with which his ears were filled ; but, when led onward by his youthful Mentor, he gained the " 'vantage ground" of the centre alley, and beheld the sea of heads about him, the splendid stage and all its gay accompaniments, and saw the lovely being, whose voice had before enchanted him, looking as divinely as she sang, he felt a relapse of his disorder, and actually sank on one of the benches, completely overpowered by his feelings.

There are moments of our lives when the mind is pecu-liarly disposed to receive the strongest impressions from the slightest causes. The present one was such to Wel-sted. The sudden burst of splendour, and the magic swell of sound, acting upon feelings, which, during the last few hours, had been kept in a high state of excite-ment, were too much for him.—But whither and towards what centre did his scattered thoughts converge ?—what was the first wish he felt, when recovering himself, he threw his eye around the glittering crowd, and could endure more tranquillity to gaze upon it ?—*Fanny*,—his own dear Fanny was the object of those thoughts ;—that she were with him, the first wish of his heart ;—how *she* would have felt had she been there, was his only specu-lation ; and so lost was he in the pleasing delusion, that

at the instant he forgot that he and Fanny were parted—
never more to meet;—that she was left to the assiduity
of an avowed, an accepted lover, and that her first visit
to this very theatre, if ever made, would of course be made
with *him*, whose wife she was to be.

However the combination of his feelings might have
affected him, certain it is, that Feversham was obliged to
rouse him from a kind of stupor, into which he appeared
to have fallen, to announce his intention of conveying him
to the Countess's box ;—a proceeding which Welsted anticipated with some degree of horror, inasmuch as he felt
his inadequacy to maintain the sort of conversation adapted
to the present scene and circumstances ; of course he
" followed his leader," and having ascended to the first
tier, was ushered into what appeared to the ignorant young
man, an ordinary-sized four-post bedstead, his entrance
to which was impeded by the curtains ; having, however,
been thrust forward into the little den, he found it occupied by the Countess, her two daughters, and two tall
aristocratic-looking men, one wearing martial mustachios,
the other more civilly attired, but both appearing to him
as of a new order of human beings.   The addition to the
party of Feversham and Frank completely filled the box,
and the novice had to maintain whatever conversation was
to occur with the Countess, from the distant corner (if
any corner of it could be distant), of the little apartment.

The perfect unconcern with which the party continued
talking in the ordinary pitch of their voices, while a poor
thin lady in sky-blue satin, and a tall man with a black
beard and a tin helmet, were on the stage, doling out the
unimportant griefs of an under-plot in recitativo, annoyed
and suprised poor Welsted, who was ignorant enough to
suppose that people frequented the king's theatre in the
Haymarket, to hear and see, instead of being heard and
seen, which, as every well-regulated person knows, are the
real objects of their visits there, and the actual *quid pro
quo* of the subscription.

And what is there in civilized society more agreeable
than the exclusive enjoyments of one of those dark
dusty, well-curtained, fustian-lined pigeon-holes, called

opera-boxes, in the heat of a fashionable winter ? So snug, so small, and so obscure ;—where else can one so well carry on those sweet and innocent flirtations, which speak in " whispers," if not of conscience, at least of something quite as agreeable ?

The proverb says, " Marriages are made in heaven." The lady patronesses say, " they are made at Almack's.' But I believe more has been done in the way of matrimonial speculation in the compact recesses of the opera circle, than any where else in London ; and more so now than ever, when the time which was devoted to flirting when English contre-dances were allowed, is bestowed upon the *figurante*-like display of grace and agility in more elaborate exhibitions. To these should be added the waltz, where practice supersedes persuasion, and prudence gives way to feeling ; and certain it is, that it has been ascertained by a committee of experienced dowagers, that fashionable marriages have considerably decreased in number, during the period in which that fanciful performance has obtained. Indeed, to whatever else such an audacious exhibition may tend, matrimony appears by no means its most probable result.

As for the opera pit, it is the Royal Exchange of good society, and divided into *walks*, as regularly as the Exchange in the city. Some persons indeed shine in the one arena, who would not be admitted into the other : in the one the smallest difference in the rate of exchange is calculated to a fraction ; in the other loans are effected without interest, and transfers made without the intervention of a broker. The *policy* of *assurance*, however, seems to be understood in both ; and in both, the transactions of the Alley are somewhat mysterious ; although in the earlier part of the season, those of the Haymarket certainly present a bearish account. In the Haymarket the state of fashionable parties forms the current business of the night, as the state of foreign funds engrosses the attention of Cornhill during the day. Invitations to a noble gourmand's dinner stand relatively in the one, to the four per cents. in the other. *Blue* coteries rank with Prussian stock, and a rich widow's assemblies, with Spa-

nisn securities; small dances without supper run parallel
to Poyais bonds, and water parties in the spring to Chili
scrip.   In short, the dandy and the dealer might shut up
shop, were they not in their different vocations regularly
to visit one or other of these great national marts, during
the hours of business.

Overhanging the motley group, which filled the varied
space below, Welsted remained for some time, luckily for
himself, somewhat in the back ground; the retirement of
the graceful occupants of the front part of the box, however, at length brought him forward, and he was placed
next to the Countess, on the side opposite to the young
ladies.   Here he existed for some time in a dreadful state
of embarrassment; for her Ladyship, being extremely
mild and gentle in her conduct and conversation, spoke
very softly, while the overture to the Ballet was played as
loudly as possible, and the urbanity with which she entered into what were evidently minute details of some
interesting subject, with her son's dear friend, was to that
friend (who could not comprehend more than one syllable
out of every twenty which glided over her Ladyship's
lips) the most painful kindness ever conferred upon mortal man.

A relief of dandies fortunately arrived to flirt with the
young ladies, but their easy familiarity of manner startled
the novice, and kept him in a perpetual state of amazement; yet even his astonishment at their observations and
anecdotes sank into insignificance before the wonder he
experienced when the Ballet commenced, and he saw the
unblushing indecency with which the half-dressed women
on the stage exposed their figures to the wanton gaze of
the multitude.   He looked first at the scene, and then at
his companions;—their glasses were at their eyes, but he
watched the expression of their countenances, and turned
with an inquiring and unnoticed gaze towards the men;
but as the exhibition went on, he remarked that the more
indelicate the display on the stage, the greater was the
applause on the part of the audience.   The sensation he
felt was one of constant apprehension, and his breath actually failed him as he beheld the tenfold pirouette of a

lovely girl, which presented to the public eye the whole
of her form and figure ; but his feelings were changed
from alarm and apprehension lest the sensibility of his
female companions should be shocked by what he considered such a flagrant violation of decorum, when he heard
the exemplary Countess herself exclaim with greater
energy than she had hitherto evinced, " Brava, brava,"
and beheld the lovely Lady Maria turn round to one of
her male associates, to praise the dexterity and ease with
which the unfortunate and degraded creature had performed the ungraceful evolution, the only merit of which
is the gross exposition of person, at which modesty shud-
ders, and from which common decency revolts.

This was the first symptom of aristocratic depravity
which struck Welsted, and he began to fear that he had
somewhat too hastily formed a favourable opinion of his
new associates ; but he had not reached the *acmé* of suspicion ;—he heard, to his infinite amazement, a conversation
amongst the party relative to the kept mistresses of married men who shared with their " protectors" the fronts of
the best boxes in the theatre, while the wives and daughters of the hoary rakes sat opposite, and witnessed the
debasing exhibition. He saw too, with wonder, men con-
versing with females in the pit, whose character and profession, even to the unpractised eye of Welsted, were unequivocal, and then, without the semblance of concealment, or a change of place, turning to their wives or
sisters (or, at all events, the wives and sisters of their
friends), and addressing them in precisely the same manner (perhaps on the same subjects) as that which they had
adopted towards their unfortunate associates of the preceding minute.

Our young friend however was wrong—that there are
in all classes exceptions to general rules, unfavourable as
well as favourable, every body knows ; but when the number of the aristocracy of this country is calculated, and
the constant watch kept upon all its actions duly considered, I am apt to believe that the vices of the higher
grades, however much more exposed to view, will be
found infinitely fewer in proportion to their numbers, than

those of middling society; in the classes below mediocrity it will not be thought too severe (since the statement
is founded upon observation) to say, that those virtues for
the absence of which, the great are most satirized, are
beyond all measure rare.   Police reports, the daily press,
common remark itself, will prove the truth of this assertion.   At all events, taking a view of society in other
countries relatively to that of our own, whatever may be
the equivocal merits of the community at large, we believe
it will not be denied, that the British nobility, taken as a
body, is the most moral nobility in Europe.

Francis literally felt happy when the curtain fell, and
he saw preparations making for their departure; the
Countess, who considered Welsted as a " safe person,"
consigned the lovely Lady Maria to *his* care, and securing to herself the beau she thought least eligible for either
of her daughters, and entrusting the Lady Anne to old
Colonel Sassafrax, of whom she had not the slightest
apprehension; the party, led by her Ladyship, proceeded
to the room, where a new scene presented itself to the
astonished eyes of Francis, whose horror was complete,
when, her Ladyship not being quite satisfied with his appearance in the saloon as her daughter's *cavalière ser-
vente*, gathered the Lady Maria under her wing, and
begged him " just to get up her carriage."

He evinced practically all the readiness which he professed, to perform the required service, and gave the lovely
daughter safe into her noble mother's charge; but having
done so, the thought of what it was he had to do next,
and how it was to be done, came into his mind—to get
her carriage up?—up where? and where was " down," if
that were " up?"   At length his good sense told him,
that even in such scenes of luxury as these, carriages were
not literally expected to be got *up*, and therefore that he
must find his way down to the door of the theatre. What
he was then to do he did not clearly perceive, but, trusting
to fortune and a certain degree of animal strength, he
pushed his way through the titled mob, and catching a
glimpse of a staircase, made his way manfully towards it,
and at length succeeded in gaining his object, to the infi-

nite embarrassment and utter derangement of certain
knots and parties who appeared to him, especially to have
chosen that vicinity for their conversations. The staircase was empty; he descended rapidly, and opening a
door, found himself in the Royal Arcade, where no vestige of a carriage appeared. The yawning porters of one
solitary chair, together with the sentinel, were all the
living creatures he beheld; but, perceiving a host of
coaches at the end of the avenue, he proceeded hastily
into Charles-street, where, indeed, the phalanx of fashionable vehicles was to him imposing and surprising. How
to discover out of the five hundred which he saw, the one
which actually belonged to Lady Farnborough, he did not
exactly know; and even the object of ascertaining that
fact, when it seemed to him that neither fate nor steam
could so ordain that any of the carriages he saw should
move, did not appear quite clear: however, having a
knowledge neither of police-officers, nor link-boys, nor of
their respective uses, he proceeded to inquire of the servants in detail, for the Countess of Farnborough's carriage. To his questions he got from some civil answers,
from others vollies of abuse; he persisted, however, most
philosophically, until he at length reached the corner.
As ill-luck would have it, a large dinner had been given
at the United Service Club, the carriages in attendance
upon the guests at which had mingled with those of the
Opera crowd, so that when he began questioning the military and naval coachmen about the Countess's equipage,
ne received such replies as to a quiet, modest, young
man from the country, were any thing but agreeable or
satisfactory.

In this pursuit, hunting Lady Farnborough's carriage,
Welsted traversed Regent-street, returned through Water-
loo-place up the Arcade again, and at length into the
theatre, through the door by which he had left it. In the
hall he found few people,—on the stairs none; he reached
the room whence he had just descended; some four or
five persons alone remained, who at the sound of " Lady
Winterbottom's carriage stops the way," fled before his
approach like frightened birds. Finding nobody in *this*

place, he followed those who were leaving it, and found the hall, towards which he then discovered he should first have directed his steps, equally deserted : men were extinguishing lamps, the doorkeepers were mounting their great coats, and the guard falling in, to march off. At this moment the mystery of his failure was discovered, by the application of a link-boy to know " whose carriage he wanted."

The conviction that he had made himself absurd, and perhaps offended the family, who had shown him such civility, now was his torment; and resolved in his own mind that after all, he was not " fit company for such high-flying people," he inquired and found his way home to the Bell and Crown, and went to bed, determined to write in the morning a note of explanation to his friend Feversham, in the first instance, and a letter to Rodney in the second ; and thus secure, as he hoped, an honourable though humble subsistence, in a sphere of life more suited to his views and principles than the gay world of fashion.

CHAPTER VIII.

The boy thus when his sparrow's flown
  The bird in silence eyes;
But soon as out of sight 'tis gone,
  Whines, whimpers, sobs, and cries.

GAY.

WHEN Welsted awoke in the morning, he felt a strange and uncomfortable assurance upon his mind, that he had, by his mismanagement and want of fashionable knowledge on the preceding evening, at least incurred the ridicule, if not provoked the anger of his noble friends; and this puzzled and distressed him the more, because, not exactly knowing what he *really* ought to do, he feared that calling in Grosvenor-square, in the course of the day, to explain and apologize for his conduct, would look like pushing himself, and a desire to be again invited to his Lordship's table. From this his high spirit revolted ; and he arose, his head aching violently, his eyes filled with bright visions of half-dressed opera-girls, and his ears still ringing with the silvery sounds of the syren's voice which had enchanted him the evening before.

His difficulties and embarrassments were, however, not of long continuance : a note of inquiry, half serious, half waggish from his affectionate friend Feversham, reached him just as he had breakfasted; containing, besides the expression of his Lordship's solicitude, and that of the Countess for their young rustic's safety, an invitation from the Viscount to meet him in Grosvenor-square, and accompany him in a drive through London ; that is to say, up and down those two or three streets which alone are known, acknowledged, and visited by persons of intelligence and consideration.

To refuse the invitation would have been needlessly rude ; and although all the time Welsted could spare from thinking of Fanny was devoted to his endeavours to discover the cause of that particular and marked kindness which every branch of the Rutherford family appeared to vie with each other in displaying towards him, he thought it right to announce, without farther question on that part of the subject, his intention of complying with the request, or rather of obeying the challenge of Lord Feversham ; and having despatched his answer to the note, proceeded (since the decreasing weight of his purse warned him of the absolute necessity of doing something in earnest) to address Rodney, and request the testimonials requisite to secure the situation at Tickle's academy. In the letter he endeavoured as much as " in him lay," to abstain from alluding to Fanny, and intended, when he sat down, to confide its purport strictly to the business in hand : he begged to be remembered kindly, and when he concluded, fancied he had said nothing whence could be extracted a confession of his present feelings. Whether he had been as successful in restraining those feelings, as he thought he had, we shall hereafter see ; at all events, when he had sealed the letter, and delivered it to the waiter for the general post, he lost the command which he previously fancied he held over himself, and his eyes were dimmed with a tear as he reflected whither the senseless paper was so soon to be conveyed, and how irrevocably closed against *him*, were the doors which would be readily opened to receive it.

Still he was borne up and supported by the consciousness that he was acting properly, and by the reflection that in after days he should be able to look back on his present trials and troubles, with feelings far different from those which result from the inconsiderate indulgence of passions, which, involuntary as far as regards ourselves, or blameless as relates to others, are in principle, opposed to the duty which we owe our fellow men.

His present circumstances were by no means pleasant: his small *modicum* of worldly wealth, as I have before said, was rapidly dissipating, and during the six days which had elapsed since his departure from *home*, as he called it, had been reduced to less than one half of its original amount ; still in a few days more he should be officially installed at Hackney, and his industry again would enable him to meet the very trifling demands of his limited desires. Having thus reconciled to himself the present inconveniences of a small capital in a large one, he made his arrangements, and proceeded to Grosvenor-square.

In his way thither, the principal object of his speculations still, was the motive which could have induced this noble family so warmly to patronize him at first sight; it must, he thought, be something more than the mere relative position in which he stood to the young Viscount, and he again resolved, if it were possible, to ascertain from that noble personage himself the real cause of such unusual kindness as that which he had experienced from every member of his family.

On his arrival in Grosvenor-square, he found his noble friends, with the exception of the Earl himself, who had quitted town unexpectedly for a few days, seated at luncheon. Here the novice from the country beheld the younger branches of a family of that class which he had been taught at once to deride and despise, even more happily congregated than they had been the day before.

The kind and really interested manner in which the Countess inquired the cause of his protracted absence on the previous night, and the genuine way in which she apologized for having thoughtlessly sent him on a service for which he was not well qualified by experience, perfectly delighted him; and in listening to the lively sallies of his former pupil and the playful yet elegant conversation of his Lordship's sisters, he nearly forgot for the moment the rural bower which he had so recently quitted, and I am almost afraid to add, its bewitching mistress.

Rain, which interferes more or less with every day's proceedings in this country, began to fall, shortly after luncheon; Feversham proposed billiards to Welsted, until the weather should mend; and Welsted, who could play no billiards, acceded to the arrangement, because he felt (strangely perhaps), that he was listening with too much interest and too much pleasure to the opinions and observations of the female part of the circle, and that it would be right and better to quit it immediately.

I believe I have somewhere before observed that it appears as if every thing pleasant were wrong—I by no means intend to say, that the converse of the proposition is equally evident :—certain it is, that no physic is palatable, nor indeed do any of the habits which are considered most likely to benefit our bodily health, come under the definition of agreeable. Welsted felt as *I* do upon this point; and whenever he found himself extremely comfortable, and enjoying himself more than usual, immediately apprehended that he was doing something extremely incorrect. If a momentary forgetfulness of *her* who was dearest to his heart may be called *wrong*, he certainly was sinning even now; for, during the morning in question, he had ceased to compare the Lady Anne and the Lady Maria with his lost Fanny, as heretofore, to *their* disadvantage, and had gone on listening and looking, and looking and listening, with an absorbing admiration, until the only comparison he felt disposed to make, was one between the relative attractions of the two noble and highly-gifted sisters.

He did the gentle violence to his feelings which he thought correct, and accompanied the Viscount to the billiard-room, not displeased, since constrained at all events to leave the presence of the fascinating fair ones, that he should perhaps have an opportunity of discovering, during the present association, the desired secret, relative to the friendship which every hour, and in every incident that occurred was so evidently displayed towards himself by the Rutherfords.

The balls placed, the cues filed, scraped and chalked, he rival players took their places, when ere a blow was given, the Lady Maria made her appearance in the room, and volunteered to score the game. Had Welsted played as well as Bedford, this would have destroyed him; his hand trembled, and his eye wandered from the table to the fair marker, who with the open-hearted, unaffected feeling of kindness generated by the eminent service he had done her family, expressed in her arch and intelligent countenance to Welsted, the certainty that her brother would be beaten; little thinking that the novice, whose efforts she was thus encouraging, had hardly ever before attempted the game.

While this scene was acting in the billiard-room, on a sudden the sweet tones of a harp, whose strings were swept with a master's hand, sounded through the adjoining saloon, and a rich and melodious female voice burst upon Welsted's ear. The air was familiar to him, for he had heard his Fanny sing it; but the style, the grace, the manner, with which it was given, were so different from her simple performance, that delighted as he was by the reminiscences which the well-known notes awakened in his mind, he stood motionless to listen.

"Come, Welsted," said Feversham, to whom the sound of his sister's voice was neither novelty nor treat—" play on."—

"How beautiful that music is!" said Welsted.

"'Tis Anne, practising," said Feversham.

"Practising?" said Francis.

"Yes," answered the Viscount. " By the way, do you like music, Frank? This young lady is reckoned a great hand ; if you prefer it, I dare say her Ladyship and her sister will favour you with a morning rehearsal—won't you, Maria ?"

Welsted was abashed and mortified that he had thus subjected himself to a refusal, or at least to that sort of yea and nay exhibition, in which he had seen Miss Amelrosa Ewebright and Miss Margaret Hodges, and persons of their standing in the select circle of his country acquaintance, indulge themselves ; and anticipated a scene of affected shyness and coy willingness, with at least a concluding speech about having a cold, or the instrument being out of tune. But no—the Lady Maria Rutherford knew that she was mistress of the art, and that her sister was equally skilled with herself. She was assured by his manner, that her brother's friend really desired to hear them ; and she felt conscious that their performance would be worth his listening to. Without the slightest hesitation, and with a smile of the sweetest good humour beaming in her beautiful countenance, she sprang forward to apprize her sister of Feversham's request, and in a few moments the cues and balls lay dormant on the verdant board, and Francis Welsted was sitting, lost in wonder and delight, at the splendid execution and exquisite judgment with which the accomplished creatures performed the difficult task they had so kindly undertaken.

Feversham, who "had no music in his soul," had quitted the drawing-room ; and when the young sirens had concluded the first duet, and Welsted had expressed in all the varied language of which he was master, his unbounded admiration, there came a pause—a silence—which he broke by requesting, if he *might* ask such another favour. With equal good-nature they performed a second duet, by a different master, in a different style, with equal success. Seeing, when *this* was concluded, that Welsted was too diffident to " go on asking," the Lady Anne inquired whether they should go on singing, or whether they tired him, in a manner which convinced him that the question was genuine, and that she wished him to answer her candidly. He however expressed his desire with diffidence, and said he hardly knew how he could venture to make such a request.

" Mr. Welsted," said the Lady Anne, " I dare say you think Maria and me strange creatures ; but, somehow, we fancy you quite one of ourselves ; and I am sure we are bound to do every thing we possibly can to amuse or please you."

Welsted bowed, and muttered something perfectly unintelligible, as was his custom whenever the conversation took this turn.

" We should be extremely ungrateful, if we did *not*," said the Lady Maria.

Welsted would have given the world at this moment to have made his inquiry, but it was impossible.

" As for mamma," said Lady Anne, " I am sure she would have died if it had happened ; and even now she never thinks of it without crying. We were even afraid her seeing you at first would have been too much for her."

" And papa," continued Lady Maria, " has every season wondered that you never came to call upon us. We have been abroad to be sure, for five years ; but both the Earl and mamma have been always extremely anxious to prove to you how deeply they feel their obligation ; and, as we are good, dutiful daughters, it is but right and proper that we should add our efforts to convince you of our estimation of your services."

Still Welsted bowed and muttered, and still wondered the more, when the Countess, entering the room, and seeing her daughters at the piano-forte, and Welsted occupying the place of a listener, desired him to lay his commands on them for as much music as he liked. " I am quite sure," said her Ladyship, " for *you*, Mr. Welsted, they will exert themselves in earnest."

All these various hints and observations added to the mystification under which the young man was labouring. Feversham returned to the room, but the rain still continued, and the billiards were resumed. The day drew to its close, Welsted prepared for a departure, when a snort whispering conversation took place between the Viscount and his noble mother, which ended in his Lordship's asking Frank if he were engaged anywhere at dinner; a question to which one answer only could have been expected, had his Lordship known the state of his friend's connexions and circumstances.

The reply was genuine and true : he was *not* engaged. The Countess pressed him to give them his company, in which invitation the Lady Maria, with an archness and *naïveté* peculiarly her own, earnestly joined ; and upon a hesitating look which Francis gave towards the window, expressive of the perilous state of the weather, Feversham undertook to make his excuses to the ladies for dining in boots, if he would remain where he was, and resume their billiards until dinner-time. In short, the whole tenor of their conduct towards him was marked by kindness and attention, and an apparent desire to make him perfectly an *enfant de famille.*

To such an invitation, so warmly given, what could Francis object?—he would be but too happy ;—and when he said so, he spoke the truth. There was something so new, so charming, so exciting in the society into which he had thus so miraculously fallen, that he looked back upon his past life as so much time lost, and forward to the portion of which was to come, with apprehension and dismay. If the delightful Lady Anne, and the fascinating Lady Maria, could keep his thoughts from Fanny for an hour together, how would he feel when compelled to relinquish such companions for the dowdy daughters of his new patron, Mr. Tickle? how pass his evenings with those young ladies and their *ma* with common patience, after the taste of happiness which he was now enjoying? To " take the goods the gods provide," is no unwise determination ; it is not because we may be wretched to-morrow, that we are necessarily to make ourselves miserable to-day. Debarring himself from the delights of good society now, would not render bad company more agreeable to Francis hereafter ; nor would the most philosophical abstinence from the alluring pleasures of Grosvenor-square, make the dingy delights of a Hackney parlour one pang the less unpleasant in future. It was upon this principle that he gladly accepted, what could not but be considered a most flattering bidding ; and, being told that the ladies, who were engaged to two assemblies and a ball in the evening, would relieve his blushes about his boots, by dining *en deshabille*, he felt as much at his ease in the " great lord's mansion," as he would have been in the sanctum of the village schoolmaster whom he had quitted. Indeed, I doubt whether, from the force of habit, he ever breathed so freely in the presence of the pedagogue, as he did now in that of the peeress.

The Earl, as the reader may recollect, was in the country; Feversham and Frank were the only *beaux* at the dinner-table. The ladies looked at the dishes, but ate nothing ; and Frank would either have pronounced them indisposed, or have compared, much to poor Fanny's disadvantage, the rural appetite of that young gentlewoman with those of the belles of quality before him, had he not, unluckily for their display of abstemiousness, been present at luncheon.

Well may such " delicate creatures " who (unlike those spoken of by the immortal bard), have " no appetites," sit and play with a morsel of fricandeau, or satisfy themselves with a trembling spoonful of jelly, while others feast; when it is notorious that they have effectually guarded against the ill effects of squeamishness, by eating a good, substantial, hot luncheon—in fact, a dinner—at three o'clock. It was having witnessed this unceremonious performance at that early hour, which made Welsted perfectly easy, when he saw his lovely associates absolutely fasting at a later period of the day.

When the " solemn mockery " of dinner was over, and the ladies had betaken themselves to their dressing-rooms, Feversham and Welsted were left alone for the first time since the renewal of their acquaintance ; and now it was that Francis determined to ascertain the real cause, if possible, of the distinguished and distinguishing kindness with which he had been treated by the whole of the family. —The conversation was artfully led by him to the school ; numerous instances of juvenile delinquency and folly were

cited, histories of old times were repeated, till at length
Fanny came on the tapis;—but even *she* at the moment
was not the subject most desired.

" I remember Fanny Rodney quite well," said the Viscount. " She was a nice good-natured little thing, when
I was at school : how has she grown up ?"

" She has improved very much latterly," said Welsted.

" She was very kind always, and I flattered myself
rather fond of me," said Feversham jokingly.—" It would
be extremely improper to boast of young ladies' favours,"
continued his Lordship; " but Fanny Rodney's marks of
affection consisted chiefly, if not entirely, of presents of
fruit or sweetmeats, or some other little articles of *bon-
bonnerie*. I recollect, by-the-by, we used to call you and
Fanny, man and wife."

Welsted's manner and appearance at hearing these
words, convinced his noble friend that he had unconsciously touched upon a tender point; and he immediately changed the tone and character of the conversation to a more serious inquiry into the real state of the
case, at present.

" Lord Feversham," said Francis, " unintentionally, and
weakly, perhaps, I find I have betrayed my secret. But
to be candid, I regret it the less, as the kind interest which
you, and all your family indeed, have evinced for me,
tells me that I should have no secrets, no concealments,
from you. The unexpected development of my feelings
towards Fanny, at all events, gives me the opportunity of
explaining most satisfactorily to you, the reason of my
quitting my excellent friend and patron so strangely and
so suddenly."

" That you should feel an honourable affection for a
sweet, amiable girl," said the Viscount, " is neither unnatural nor disreputable, my dear Welsted, and all I feel
amazed at is, that you did not sooner make me your con-
fidant. That your attachment to Fanny should have
driven you from the house of her father, I certainly do not
understand ; for in point of comfort and respectability,
what can be more suitable than your marriage ?"

" She is engaged to another, my Lord," said Wel-

sted ; " and engaged not only with *my* consent, **but at**
my desire."

" And yet you love her?"

" Better than my life," replied Francis : " but the proposal which has been made to her is in every point of
view so much more eligible than any I could have made,
that I felt it my duty to subdue my affection, and surrender my own hopes of happiness, in order to ensure
hers."

" You are a very extraordinary person," said Feversham ; " but what did Fanny say to your conduct? young
ladies, I am apprehensive, are inclined in general to regard
such heroism with very different eyes from those of
admiration."

"I trust," said Francis, " *she* thinks I have treated her
unkindly. She confessed her affection for me, and I,
overcome by my feelings, owned my love for her,—but I
fled precipitately, and left her ignorant of my destination ;
for, fixed as are my principles, thank God ! and decided as
I am in the conduct I have determined to adopt, I really
believe I could not have endured the pangs of separation."

" And do you mean seriously to say," asked Lord
Feversham, "that you, loving Fanny, and Fanny loving
you, you have given her up eternally?"

" Eternally, my Lord," said Welsted, firmly.

" And who may *he* be," said his Lordship, " to whom
you have thought it thus advantageous to Fanny to surrender her?"

In answer to this question Welsted, delighted (as lovers
always are) to speak on the one subject, after so long a
silence necessarily enforced, detailed the name, condition,
rank, and title of the lover, and indeed all the circumstances which transpired before Francis left Rodney;
which, although new to Lord Feversham, are already
known to the reader.

" If that be happiness for Fanny Rodney, I am mistaken," exclaimed the Viscount, when Welsted had completed his statement of facts; " old Brashleigh is an
acquaintance of my father's, and, to say truth, I think **the**

Earl hates him as cordially as every body does who has any concern with him : my sister, Anne, I believe, once stood very high in his estimation ; at length, however, he presumed upon her good-nature, and seemed seriously to think of placing his goodly person at her Ladyship's disposal, as a husband; but the young ladies communed and conspired together, and had a great laugh at the veteran's expense, notwithstanding which he generally dines here once or twice during the season, bore as he is."

Welsted could not fail to be stricken with the very different ways in which the importance of his Excellency was treated by his old patron and his young friend ; and indeed, in the progress of conversation, Feversham detailed so many meannesses (almost barbarisms) of the tyrannical commander, that Welsted, animated by the wine, with which the labours of oratory had been relieved, began to feel quite chivalrous, and to believe that, whatever might be his duty to old Rodney, a more imperative duty was to rescue his innocent daughter from that, which those only could consider likely to be productive of happiness, who were ignorant of the facts and circumstances, with which he had just been made acquainted.

To speak truth, those facts and circumstances which related to the General's pride, meanness, suspicion and tyranny, powerful as they were in themselves, received new importance from the manner in which the young Viscount developed them ; and as he seasoned all he said on the subject with something like ridicule of disappointed swains, and jilted lovers, Francis gradually felt inspired with hopes, and thoughts, and wishes, wholly inconsistent with his past conduct, or his proposed career ; glass succeeded glass, and each inspiring draught added new energy to his feelings ; and when he parted from Lord Feversham, it was in the firm resolve of starting next day for the academy, bursting in upon the family circle, and like the master of Ravenswood, seeking from the lovely bride herself, an account of her real sentiments respecting the approaching marriage

The arguments ot Feversham, aided by the Earl's
claret, had this powerful effect upon the novice : the chord
had been stricken, the dormant feeling awakened, and
after the silence he had been compelled to keep, in mixed
society, the licence to speak of Fanny and of love had
been so sweet and soothing, that as he proceeded homewards, his whole mind was occupied with renewed hopes
of happiness with *her*, and as I have before said, a determination to snatch her from the altar, and that, which he
now believed, to be perdition.

Elevated and enlivened by the society in which he had
passed the day, his eye, accustomed to magnificent apartments and splendid furniture, his ears filled with the
sweetest sounds, and all his senses pampered by the enjoyment of modern luxury, Francis entered the dingy,
ill-smelling smoky-looking coffee-room at the inn, with
disgust ; the rude plebeian laugh of some beer-drinking
guests, the noises in the street, the narrow benches, the
sanded floor, the low ceiling, the flaring tallow candles,
and the sight of a great healthy farmer supping ravenously
on a huge leg of cold underdone roasted pork with pickled
cabbage in a saucer, made him absolutely sick ; and when
the pale waiter brought him a letter which had arrived per
post, he sought a release from all his surrounding miseries,
by calling for his candle and retiring to his sleeping-room.

I have somewhere else observed upon the effect produced by a return from splendour to what had before
seemed even comfort ; the size and appearance of rooms,
the accommodation procurable, like every thing else in the
world, are judged by comparison ; but the force of that
comparison is not so great when we first behold the
splendid and magnificent, as when we go back to the place
whence we came, and there revert to that which we have
last quitted.   How beautiful in the mind's eye does that
village look where first we loved, and "laughed the jo-
cund hours away."   How gay and joyous seems in memory, the venerable city which once held the adored object
of all our affections ; how sweetly blooms the bower which
sheltered those most dear to us from scorching suns or
angry storms ;—visit them when the bright vision which

once illumined them is gone—the association of ideas may remain, and even hallow the spot, but the places in themselves appear, alas! how changed; and yet in truth, not changed at all. The whole tone of Welsted's character had been altered in three short days; and he who just before, like the prince in the valley, had bounded his prospects by the nearest surrounding objects, and who, doomed as he was to lead the humble life for which alone he felt himself prepared, sat and regaled, and refreshed, and reposed, in his lowly hostelry, content and satisfied, now felt a new ambition; he had moved in good society, had seen that in this happy country there exists no bar, no prescriptive limit which talent and virtue may not pass; and admitted on equal terms to share the friendship of the great and good, began to cherish something like ambition; began to feel that there was no reason why he should not marry Fanny Rodney, and, conscious of at least an average share of ability, wondered how he could tamely have consented to surrender the object of his affections, and with what now appeared to him a primitive simplicity, make a sacrifice which, as his noble friend had plainly hinted, the circumstances of the case assuredly did not require; which as it affected Fanny's happiness was extremely doubtful in its effect, and which, above all, would entail upon him the ridicule and contempt of the *world*— the world of that village in which alone, as yet, his name was known.

In this temper of mind he opened the letter which had arrived by the three-penny post, from Hackney—It ran thus:

Hackney,——— 18—

" Mr. Tickle has applied, according to Mr. Welsted's directions, to Mr. Rodney—the answer which he has received is highly satisfactory.

" Mr. Welsted will therefore please to be at Montgomery-place Academy, on Saturday next, by seven o'clock in the evening;—stages go every hour to Hackney, from the Flower-pot, in Bishopsgate-street, by which Mr. W. may send his trunk with safety."

9

It is impossible to describe the contempt and rage with which Mr. W (as his patron called him) tossed from him this flattering acceptance of his services, this gratifying appointment to office, which, but three days before, he had been so anxious to procure ; the trunk, and the stage, and the Flower-pot, all flashed into his mind, accompanied by the melodious harp of the Lady Maria Rutherford, and the syren notes of the lovely Lady Anne, whose graceful figures and aristocratic features were instantly contrasted with the round fubsy forms of the Misses Tickle ; while the unaffected grace of the well-bred ladies of fashion was, at the same moment, most unsatisfactorily compared with the awkward, giggling, and affected finery of the vulgar damsels of Hackney.

But yet his poverty was forced to consent to all this. Feversham, of course, had felt that it would be indelicate to make any inquiry into the state of his old friend's finances, and Welsted would have starved rather than allude to the subject : his stock of cash, like the days of Mrs. Barbauld's beggar, was now " dwindled to its shortest span," and he therefore felt the necessity of reconciling himself to a fate which he could not avert—unless, indeed, in the course of the night he should finally resolve upon the great project of invading the Rodney family, and inducing the garrison of Somerville-house to surrender at discretion.

He was more irritated, however, by one part of the affair at the present moment, than he would have been at any other :—I mean the silence observed by old Rodney : he had not answered the letter which Francis addressed to him, but merely replied to Mr. Tickle's inquiries after " his character."   There was something like needless neglect in this, and my hero did not take time to consider the present state of affairs at the academy, nor calculate upon the bustle and worry incidental to the stay of the General in the domestic circle of such a family as that of his patron.

Most true it is, that the resolution of Frank was greatly shaken, his mind completely unsettled, his estimate of the advantages of the sacrifice he was about to make, considerably depreciated, and, overwhelmed by worldly feelings, he fell asleep very soon after he had retired to bed.

" Nature's soft nurse," as the divine Shakspeare has it, having in the course of a few hours restored his bodily strength, the agitated young gentleman arose in the morning, with feelings no calmer, and a mind no more at ease, than they had been on the previous night. He had been foiled in his attempt to extract from his young friend the real cause of the attentions which were paid him by his family, a circumstance (so deeply involved had all his thoughts been with other subjects) which had never occurred to him during the evening ; and in his present unpleasant uncertainty of the extent of his deserts from that source, he appeared likely to remain, since, when he separated from Lord Feversham, no arrangement was made for any other meeting, and on the Saturday following he was to assume the ushership of the black rod at Montgomery-place.

It was all in vain that he endeavoured to soothe his mind, or to anticipate, with any thing like complacency, his future career in life : the words of Feversham rang in his ears, and he recurred with shame to what now appeared a mean and pusillanimous defection and surrender of Fanny to a man, his superior in rank, but whose possessions or expectations, as affecting Fanny's future comfort, were by no means extensive or flattering ; and for three hours did the young man remain communing with himself, as to the measures he should now adopt.

He was convinced, let what might have happened, that the " stage effect" of his personal appearance would carry the day with his devoted Fanny ; and he naturally concluded that the General, with such a forcible and unequivocal proof of a pre-engagement, as his practical avowal of affection for Fanny before his eyes, would gladly relinquish all claim upon her hand ;—but where then were all his own professions and protestations? where the firm resolve of his strong mind? where the aid of which he boasted ? where that PRINCIPLE upon which he had

relied, and which sustained him at a still more trying
moment than the present, when the beloved object of his
heart, almost senseless in her grief, clung to him for support? Still it seemed that Nature was to prevail; and,
under the guidance of PASSION, he proceeded to the
coach-office adjoining the inn, and secured his place in
the Pool mail, which passed through the village in which
the academy was situated, and where he would be punctually and securely deposited, between two and three
o'clock the following morning.

Having taken this strong preliminary measure, he felt
himself in some degree relieved, and proceeded to consider what answer he should send to Mr. Tickle's brief, but
sterling address. It would be foolish and indelicate, if
not impossible, to refuse obedience to its contents, until,
at all events, he had ascertained the probable result of his
expedition into the country. He thought it, therefore,
wisest and best to acknowledge the receipt of the letter,
express his pleasure at finding that the testimonials from
Mr. Rodney had proved satisfactory, and announced his
intention of obeying the " order to join," which it contained.

The hours seemed to wear away heavily through the
tedious day, until dinner-time, when Francis, hardly able
to endure the *desagremens,* with which he now felt himself surrounded, went through the forms and motions of
eating and drinking, literally to satisfy the *auri sacra
fames* of the hostess, rather than any appetite of his own.
Having concluded his hasty repast, he again revolved in
his mind the important step he was about to take;—again
considered the results of his enterprise,—the trials to
which he should expose poor Fanny,—the deliberate
violation of his promises to Rodney,—the distress his
appearance would occasion, and, above all, that, which
he dreaded most, the malediction he should bring down
upon the innocent object of his love.

All this passed in his mind, and more than this, the
actual state of destitution, in which he individually was
at the moment. It was true the Earl of Farnborough
had graciously given him his countenance, his conversa-

tion, and his claret; but, spite of what the poets say, he could support Fanny as a wife neither upon looks, nor smiles, nor wine, and, most assuredly, *not* upon forty pounds per annum, his promised stipend at Hackney. What ther was he about to do? faulter in a good determination, fai' in the maintenance of high character, and expose, to even greater calamities than if he had at first avowed his deter mination, the creature he best loved on earth.

A man possessing a feeling like this, for the comfort and happiness of a girl with whom he is convinced he alone can be happy, sometimes gets the discredit either of insincerity or coquetry; but the principle, however it may be misunderstood, is not dishonourable; and *he* who truly and disinterestedly loves, will pause, will suffer wretchedness himself, before he makes a declaration which, if favourably received, must necessarily involve the object of his affection in perils, in necessity, and all the precarious embarrassments of an uncertain life. Francis pictured himself and his Fanny domesticated, perhaps, in some wretched lodging, ill furnished, and ill served, in a miserable and obscure part of the metropolis; discarded and branded as ungrateful and unnatural rebels by her parents; existing on the casual labours of his mind, and depending even for those, upon the possession of health and sanity; and, while existing thus unknown and unnoticed, poor and friendless, giving being perhaps to children, accursed by their angry relatives even before their birth. He trembled at the scene he had painted to himself;—he laid his head upon his open hands, and covering his eyes prayed for support in this hour of trial.

The appeal was conclusive. Morality and honour were already combined to check his progress; but when Religion came to his aid, and he considered that, in the sight of his Maker, his conduct could not be reconcilable with the duty he owed to Rodney; when he remembered that, to gratify his own passions, he was about to induce her, whom he fondly loved, to violate a still more sacred duty than that which it had been in his contemplation previously to infringe, he felt the strengthening glow of confidence in himself, which bade him live and hope, but yet to do to others, as he would they should do unto him.

He raised his burning forehead from his open palm, and gazing round the room, found himself alone ; a few tears trickled down his manly cheeks, but he was firm ; and, though his heart beat, it was true to virtue and himself, and he faintly invoked a blessing upon *her*, for whom he had thus resolved to yield up all his future hopes of happiness on earth, when the shrill blast of the horn announced the approaching departure of the coach in which his place was secured.

In seven hours he would be near her ;—see the light beam through the window where she slept ;—pace again the well-known church-yard path ;—again see the pale moon glitter in the rippling stream. He would stand in the presence of his beloved—would snatch her from the altar, even at the moment when else she would become another's wife-—in those few hours she would be *his* eternally, or be lost to him for ever. The horn sounded again to summon the loitering traveller :—he moved not ;—his teeth were clenched, and his hands clasped :—the moments seemed to linger :—would his resolution fail him now ?— He heard the guard inquiring for " the inside passenger:" —he rose mechanically, took his hat,—paused for a moment, looked towards the door——

The waiter appeared to tell him, " that all was ready;" —the porter held his portmanteau in his hand, the guard hastened the coachman,—the horses pawed the pavement.

" Now, Sir," said the guard to Francis.

He again paused for an instant, and then said, faintly yet firmly, " I am *not* going."

An oath or two at the needless delay which he had occasioned, followed, and in an instant the mail rattled like thunder beneath the gateway. Francis ran to the front window of the coffee-room :—he saw the coach pass rapidly ;—he watched it as far as the bay of the window allowed ;—he listened to the horn as it pealed through the air, and to the noise of the wheels as they rolled along the pavement;—the carriage disappeared from his sight, and the sound died away.

Francis gazed vacantly on the street for a moment; then sinking on the bench before which he had been standing, covered his face with his hands, and shed a flood of tears. It was indeed a struggle;—but virtue and honour had gained the victory, and PASSION was subdued by PRINCIPLE.

CHAPTER IX.

'Tis a very fine thing to be father-in-law
To a very magnificent three-tailed Bashaw.
COLMAN THE YOUNGER.

WE left Sir Frederick Brashleigh, as the reader may remember, just commencing a round of rural gaieties with the family of his betrothed. In the anxiety of Rodney to do honour to the visit of his future son-in-law, he had recourse to a measure which many of my readers, perhaps, will join with most of his supporters, in thinking extremely unwise. It was neither more nor less than *making* a vacation at an unusual time of the year; promising, of course, to omit the Bartholomew-tide holidays, which, in the hope of its being somehow assimilated with public schools, were always kept at Somerville House.

This arrangement, strongly remonstrated against by many of the parents whose children were under his care, proved as inconvenient to *them* as it was agreeable to himself; parties made months before, were all to be unmade; proposed excursions were to be postponed or hurried over; in short, the results of this unexpected removal of the boys were most disagreeable, and even distressing; as we shall discover in the sequel; the lads, however, were packed up, and sent per chaise and per coach, to their respective homes. Their dinner-hall was to be fitted up for the reception of the gay party, to be invited to a *déjeuner à la fourchette*, and the school-room decorated and prepared for a dance, which Mrs. Rodney had long prom sed to give the neigh-

bouring young ladies, and which never could be more seasonably afforded than at the present moment, when Sir
Frederick would be delighted by the splendid exhibition of
rural beauty, which he had been taught to expect.

As for Sir Frederick himself, all the symptoms of distaste for the society of the Rodney circle, which his Excellency had early exhibited, gradually increased every day;
and nothing but the respect he felt for Fanny's feelings and
his own dignity, induced him to postpone the ceremony,
which was irrevocably to make her his own.

At Mrs. Ewebright's dinner his Excellency was compelled to give a succinct account of the origin of the Order
of the Bath, and was moreover requested by some of the
old ladies to be good enough to take off his star (which it
delighted him much to wear), that they might look at it,
and it was actually handed round the room like a musical
snuff-box, or any other indifferent trinket. The innumerable questions which arose out of this extraordinary exhibition, the incalculable quantity of nonsense which the
admiring fools talked, had nearly roused the tiger; and if
his Excellency had (as he felt very much inclined to do)
favoured them with an exhibition of his temper when irritated, it is not improbable, that even the ambition of Rodney itself would have given way to the apprehensions for
his daughter's happiness, which such a display could not
fail to excite.

But it was *not* to be; and every thing was destined to
go on smoothly and pleasantly; the countenance of the
broken-spirited, broken-hearted Fanny, was the only one
unlighted by the smiles and happiness which beamed
around her: in the gaiety of the younger ladies, it must be
confessed, something like envy mingled; and the signifi-
cant glances cast upon the cowslip-coloured Commander-
in-chief, by those, who, matured in the rural recesses of
their father's farms and manor-houses, felt that any one of
themselves would have been a much more suitable wife for
such a man as Sir Frederick, than Fanny; were too clear
in their import to be for a moment mistaken.

Fanny had never been told by her father that the sacrifice which she was about to make for *his* sake, would not

avail him under the circumstances, in the manner which
he at first imagined it would ; had she known the real
state of the case, the chances are, that she would have
contributed to the utmost to divert the affections of her
captive from herself, and assist in their transfer to some
more ambitious fair ; as it was, she felt that she was
doing a duty, and resolved to perform her part with becoming firmness and resolution.

In the midst of these determinations, the kind, sweet
spirit of female affection stole in ; she had, at first (since
I must be candid), been a little piqued at Welsted's sudden abdication ; she knew his heart well enough implicitly to believe all he had said the night preceding his
departure, and was convinced that her future good was
the real object he had in view ; but she felt agonized
when she found he had actually gone without leaving one
line, or one word of remembrance for her : nor was it till
she saw—and may I reveal it ?—not with the curiosity so
idly and unfairly attributed to her sex, but with an interest deeper than those who never loved can understand—
had read the letter which her lost Francis had written to
her father—that letter which, in the hurry of the old gentleman's gaieties, not only remained unanswered, but was
even incautiously left loosely amongst ordinary papers on
his writing-table. From *that* letter Fanny learned the
place of residence of her beloved ; by that letter she first
ascertained his safety ; by that letter she discovered what
were his future prospects ; in that letter she heard that he
had been kindly received by the Rutherfords ; all of which
were deeply interesting points to *her,* who had no care
for any thing on earth but him, whom she was never more
to see. And what of these ?—they soothed and consoled
her—she knew he was well, with a prospect of employment, with an increasing, honourable connexion ; these,
watchfully alive to every thing which could benefit him,
tended doubtlessly to appease her apprehensions and calm
her mind. For, since the arrival of the General, not one
word had passed between Fanny and her father on the
subject of Welsted ; and though his name was introduced
and alluded to, upon every possible occasion, by Mis

Rodney, information concerning him she had gained
none, until his well-known writing accidentally caught her
eye, and she (almost unconsciously) had read the contents
of his neglected letter to her parent.

Had she read only *that* part to which I have already
referred, the effect produced by it might have been only
what I have supposed ; but, alas ! she read one paragraph
more—and read that one paragraph a thousand times, till
terrified at the sound of approaching footsteps, she hastily
concealed the letter in her bosom, and ran to her own
room to read again and again the same fatal lines—They
were few and short.

"I pray to God," said the beloved writer, "to strengthen
my resolution, and heal my wounded spirit. I trust you
have allowed my poor Fanny to remain ignorant of the real
cause of my abrupt departure. Teach her, my dear Sir,
to hate me, if possible. Let her never know the force and
intensity of my affection for her: that Heaven may bless
and preserve her, through a long and happy life, is my
prayer night and day. He, who is destined to possess her,
must be blind to every earthly attraction, every exalted
quality, if he appreciate not her virtues and her merits.
She will not, I think and trust, inquire about *me*. I have
doubtlessly offended her by my sudden departure ; indeed,
as I told you, I could not endure a separation—it was
better it should happen as it did."

This fatal disclosure of Welsted's *real* feelings, the undisguised declaration of his unmixed devotion, inflicted, if
possible, a deeper wound than any she had yet received :
she sat transfixed, cold, and almost lifeless, when, for the
last time, she had devoured the welcome wounding letter
with her eyes ; to find herself adored by *him* she dearly
loved—on the eve of eternal separation from him—and,
worse! involved in a new engagement too deeply to recede!
What a situation for a young creature, full of feeling,
of tenderness and affection ; without a friend or relation to whom she could confide her sorrows, or from whom
she could seek advice. Had she at this moment known
that her father's hopes of relief from pecuniary difficulty
would not be realized by the dreadful sacrifice she was

about to make, I sincerely believe she would have decided at once, and at all hazards, to declare her dread of, and aversion from, the marriage with Sir Frederick, and have thrown herself upon the mercy of her parents, and the generosity of her intended husband; but that fact, as I have just said, Rodney had assiduously concealed from her, well aware that she would make it a plea for discarding the General; a measure which Rodney, who thought the connexion overwhelmingly and awfully magnificent, could by no means, and under no circumstances, now endure; and thus, at the tinselled shrine of vanity, did he persist in offering the sacrifice which filial affection had laudably resolved to make for the nobler purpose of relieving a parent's necessities.

Fanny considered and reconsidered her future conduct, and decided, perhaps unwisely yet naturally, that she would avail herself of her knowledge of Welsted's residence in London, to address a few words to him of a nature which might at once assure him of her gratitude for the disinterested devotion he had manifested for her welfare, and of her unshaken resolution to fulfil the engagement she had entered into, while at the same time she might convince him of her continued regard. A theme like this in the hands of a girl who fondly loved, was difficult perhaps to manage; and since she realized her intention of addressing him, it will perhaps be as well to give her letter as she wrote it.

" That you will be surprised at receiving this from *me*, I can easily imagine; and if I knew or esteemed you less than I do, I should begin by excusing myself for doing *that* which, with ungenerous minds, would most probably expose me to censure.

" I write to you, Francis, as from the grave; for we are parted, so far as regards *this* world, as decidedly and definitively as if I were in my coffin. I have obeyed your counsel. I have fulfilled my father's commands, I have accepted the proposal to which you alluded; and I should have gone to the altar more undisturbed, perhaps, had not circumstances, to which it is needless to recur, put me accidentally in possession of your real feelings towards me.

" To have deserved your affection is my greatest praise, and I thank God that I possess it ; and since the love I feel for you is unalloyed by one single interested consideration, and as I find myself comparatively happy since I have known that it is requited, I cannot but believe that you will more contentedly resign yourself to the eternal separation which must necessarily result from my completion of the engagement which *you* advised, and which *I* believed to be merely an act of filial duty on *my* part, after this declaration of my sentiments.

" I have told you, in the sincerity of my heart, that I could have been happiest of the happy, had it been decreed that we should share a cottage, and the limited comforts of humble life together ; I still feel that I spoke wisely, as well as candidly when I said so :—but *that* is past, and I have followed the example which you so generously set.

" That you should imagine it necessary to make me forget or hate you, in order to induce my compliance with the commands of a parent, under such circumstances, surprises me.   I can never forget you ; I never wish to forget you : nearest and dearest in my heart of hearts will I cherish the recollection of *you*, and of those past scenes of happiness in which our early lives were spent ; but I hope and trust, nevertheless, that I shall fulfil my duty in the state of life into which I am about voluntarily to enter. I shall do my future husband no more injustice in oarding up the recollection of Welsted, than in treasuring the hallowed remembrance of my beloved brother.

" Believe me, dear Francis, it is more essential to your future comfort to forget *me*, than to *my* future respectability to forget *you*.   The die is cast, as far as I am concerned ; and at the altar I put off all thoughts of worldly love, except that of love for my husband.   It will be the study of my life to make *his* happiness ; and if it please God I should be successful, I shall be truly grateful : but the love I bear towards *you* is unearthly, and not of this world ; and whatever might have been the danger which you apprehended from the encouragement of such a feeling, while we were in the habit of constant association, there can be neither sin nor peril in nurturing that affection, which it is my pride, even at the moment of making this sacrifice, to own I feel for *you*. But with you it is vastly different : you are unmarried, and free to choose a woman who shall form your happiness ; the sacrifice you have made is but negative ; you have yet before you the wide world whence to select a partner such as you deserve ;—let me implore you, then, marry. A wife, as every hour proves, gives comfort and respectability ; her tender influence guides, while it seems to yield ; her presence cheers the hours of sorrow, and gives new brightness to the day of joy. Had it been *my* lot to have shared your fate, as I have already said, I should have asked no more : but next to *that*, is my hope for your happiness without me ; to ensure which, it is necessary that you should banish every thought of me, except as a sister. I have taught my heart to lie still when your name is mentioned ; I have instructed myself to speak of you to my mother without trembling or blushing ; I have subdued the strongest feelings of my nature ; I have changed the character of my affection, because it was my DUTY to do so :—if you will condescend to take a lesson from a poor weak girl, follow my example, Francis.

" Let me entreat you, take no notice of this : do not attempt to answer it ; never allude to it in any correspondence or conversation with my father. I feel at this moment so terrified, lest it should be known that I have written to you, that I apprehend even this last adieu is improper :—yet surely it cannot be so ! the Power that knows my heart, and sees my thoughts, will acquit me of any thing but a desire to say farewell to the companion of my youth, the playmate of my childhood, and to assure him, that till the hour of my death, I shall continue to love and esteem him as a brother.

" Adieu, then, dear Francis !—the chances are greatly against our ever meeting again : we shall be but a short time in London, previous to sailing ; and *there* I would

not wish to meet you; at least not so soon :—no—let me
entreat you, seek no interview! In a place so large as the
metropolis, I know we might accidentally see each other:
that cannot be helped, if it happen; but the trial would
be more, perhaps, than *we* could endure ; therefore, let me
conjure you, do not purposely attempt a meeting! Friday
is the day fixed, on which I leave this —— ."

Here some tears had fallen upon the lines and blotted
them. Friday was the day fixed for the wedding;—and
here the letter abruptly closed.

Whether poor Fanny had been interrupted in her task,
or whether nature triumphed for the moment, and she
hastily terminated her studied farewell to her beloved, lest
her resolution should fail; I know not. It was sufficient
for Francis, whose poignant grief was by no means diminished by the knowledge he thus gained of her still ardent
affection for him; and he now began to feel, that however
correct *his* conduct had been towards Rodney, her sub-
mission, under all the circumstances, had not been so
imperatively demanded as she appeared to think; because,
knowing Rodney's love for his child, and *not* knowing the
extent of his pecuniary embarrassments, or their connexions with her proposed husband, he was convinced,
that, if she had withstood the marriage firmly and reso-
lutely, it might even then have been averted. Still he
gave her every credit for filial obedience, and resolved to
console himself with the virtuous affection she could honourably bestow, and the assurance that they had both
acted from the purest motives and the best intentions;
either of them sacrificing for the other their hopes of comfort, and submitting themselves to those laws which nature
and religion have established for the regulation of our
feelings and passions.

The coincidence was unpleasant, by which he was to
take possession of his office at Hackney on the very day
succeeding his dear Fanny's marriage ; the certainty that
his whole heart and mind would be occupied in imagining
and depicting to himself the gaieties and festivities of the

village; the lovely bride decked out, like a sacrifice for the altar—the smiling parents, and the gallant bridegroom, —was any thing but agreeable; and again for a moment he repented that he had abandoned his intention of snatching his Fanny from her lover's arms. But again recurring to what he felt he owed her father, he again soothed and satisfied himself with the reflection that he had, above all things, DONE HIS DUTY.

Whatever might have been the anticipations of Francis, as to the gaieties of the village upon the important occasion, they were greatly exceeded by the reality. Embarrassed, and almost distressed, as Rodney in truth was, the accession of some ready money received from the parents of the children, who had been untimely returned upon their hands, and who, in consequence, had paid their bills, and removed the pupils; was hailed with infinite delight by the poetical schoolmaster; and, taking advantage of the trifling influx of cash, he resolved to make the nuptial celebration as gay as he could. All the respectable persons in the neighbourhood were invited to the *déjeûner à la fourchette*, and the night of Thursday, which preceded the important day, was nearly consumed in decorating the different apartments destined for the reception of the company. An artist of eminence from London directed the exertions of the rural labourers; fruits from Lord Springfield's grapery and pinery arrived to grace the board, and while these proceedings were had in regard to the higher order of guests, equal attention was paid to the preparation of more substantial comforts for the lower classes of his neighbours; in short, elated by the splendour of the connexion with Sir Frederick, in raptures at the accession of honours to his family, and of title to his daughter, the poor "single-minded" Rodney struggled with all his might to produce a *fête*, which, while it astonished the natives, should satisfy his magnificent son-in-law that he *had* a taste, and that, when left to himself, he could, to use a colloquial phrase, "do the thing in proper form."

At length the auspicious morning dawned, and the church-bells rang a merry peal; but the sky was overcast, and strong gusts of wind, accompanied by fleeting showers

of rain, unseasonable at the time of year, threw a gloom
over the gaieties which had been so assiduously prepared;
the garlands with which the village girls had decorated the
church porch, were thrice blown away, and the temporary
treillage with which the London artist had taught the
rural labourers to cover the walk leading from Rodney's
house to the church-door (the favourite walk of Fanny
and of Francis), was swept from its foundation by the
unusual tempestuousness of the weather.

The pert and smirking Miss Amelrosa Ewebright (whose
brother's name I have before mentioned) was appointed
bridemaid to poor Fanny; a proof, if any were wanting
after what I have already said, of the scantiness of her
female acquaintance; and the boisterous mirth of the
under-bred village belle was heard resounding in the hall,
and on the staircase of the academy early in the morning
of the bridal day.

Sir Frederick was on the ground betimes, dressed, to the
amazement of the rural spectators, in full uniform, and decorated with all his various orders, clasps, and crosses.
The family of Willows were in attendance; and Mrs.
Rodney herself, after having bustled through every room
in the house, to watch the progress of the preparations,
appeared with her lovely daughter leaning on her arm, at
the head of the staircase. Miss Ewebright followed; and,
at the foot of the stairs, the company was joined by Mr.
Rodney and his future son-in-law.

Lord and Lady Springfield, and several other specially
favoured persons, were already in the library; and at a
few minutes before ten the party proceeded, led by the
Rector, towards the church.

As Fanny passed along the well-known walk, her
thoughts strayed sadly from the object of the day; and
when she entered the porch, she looked around wistfully,
and almost wildly, and with a hope, I fear, that she might
yet be spared, and that her Francis, even now, would
rescue her from her impending fate. Certain it is, that
her eye was attracted by the appearance of two men, enveloped in travelling-cloaks, who, although at a distance
then, seemed to regard the procession with deep interest;

and who were evidently quickening their step towards the church, as the gay *cortège* entered it.

The betrothed lovers reached the altar;—a pause ensued while Mr. Willows was assuming the proper vestments for the ceremony;—Fanny trembled, and as the bridegroom took her hand, he felt it icy cold :—his eye met hers;—it seemed to flash fire;—something apparently had irritated him—what, she knew not; she leaned on her fair friend, and was ready to sink into the earth. Again she cast a longing look behind, still hoping something might occur. She saw the strangers enter the church;—they passed into the side aisle, and approached the altar. The service began;—Rodney was visibly agitated, and Mrs. Rodney was assiduously engaged in arranging the folds of Fanny's dress, so that they might fall gracefully as she knelt;—the storm without, seemed to rage with new violence, and hail pattered against the windows, and thunder rolled in the air. The Rector proceeded, nevertheless, with the ceremony;—the moment approached;—the question, the deciding question, was put, the affirmative answer given, and Fanny felt the mystic symbol press her finger. More she knew not: she had fainted, and remained unconscious of the remaining forms with which the service concluded.

Sir Frederick's temper, already inflamed by some unknown cause, threatened a dreadful irruption; and when Lady Brashleigh awoke from her trance in the library at her father's house, neither his words nor conduct bore evidence of the gentlest feelings, or the most tender solicitude.

Indeed, to say truth, the day at this period did not seem likely to pass off with *éclat*. The General retired, and changed his dress; so did the bride: and when Fanny was alone with her *temporary* friend Miss Ewebright, the first question she asked was, whether she had seen the strangers, who were present during the ceremony?

" I saw them," said Miss Ewebright; " and I cannot think what they did there."

Fanny paused;—in her own mind she fancied that one of them was Welsted, and the other Lord Feversham; yet, it mattered not now; nor could it have been, for surely

Francis would not tamely stand by, and suffer that cere-mony to be performed, which was to deprive him of his beloved for ever ; and which, now that it actually was concluded, she was still more than convinced, had decided her wretchedness eternally.

This little incident shows how apt those who are in diffi-culty, danger, or distress, are to connect with themselves and their views and desires, the commonest circumstances of every-day life. The truth is, that the persons who en-tered the church, and witnessed the ceremony, were two passengers by one of the stage-coaches, which, to use the technical expression of the public papers, " breakfasted in the village," and who, attracted by the interesting novelty of a country wedding, devoted the few minutes they had to spare, from the hasty reflection, to an attendance upon the bridal pageant.

But whatever nervousness or anxiety Fanny might have felt in the trying situation in which she was now placed, they did not exceed, in poignancy or effect, the continued trepidation and alarm in which her father existed during the stay of his illustrious son-in-law beneath his roof. He was from morning till night of each day in a state of breath-less expectation, that his better half would (as she actually had once or twice been on the point of doing) favour his Excellency with an elaborate detail of the departure of Welsted, *just* previously to his Excellency's arrival, and illustrate the narrative with her own considerations of his conduct, and her individual surmises as to the real cause of his sudden departure.

Had Mrs. Rodney been *entirely* trusted, the probabili-ties are, that Fanny never would have been, as we find her at the present moment, the wife of his Excellency. How-ever, by dint of continual interruptions, rapid changes of conversation, sudden introductions of new subjects, and constantly remaining in her presence, the anxious parent succeeded in keeping down any discussion of the subject. Thus the thoughts of his Excellency (who was in his na-ture both jealous and suspicious) were never directed to-wards the young absentee, nor drawn by circumstances into the right channel ; else certainly the combination of the many confirmatory trifles, to which Shakspeare so well refers, might have led him to some disagreeable conclusion ; as it was, he knew nothing of Welsted ; did not even recollect his person, and when his grandson spoke of him and his removal, he listened as he would to the history of the dismissal of a footman or groom, or any other indifferent topic, reserving the energies of his mind for the greater objects of his life, and the necessary arrangements preliminary to his assuming the important command of Old Woman's Island.

On the bridal morning, however, the secret so long, and carefully kept, had nearly been divulged. In the midst of some discussion in the drawing-room, while Fanny was changing her dress above stairs, a reference was unfortunately made by Rodney himself to the portrait of his daughter, which heretofore had graced that apartment, when search being made for the likeness, it was not to be found.

" I'd lay my life, Francis has got it," said Mrs. Rodney.

The General, who was present, appeared to attend to this suggestion. A fiery look from Rodney nearly annihilated his wife, who saw an order for immediate silence conveyed in the angry glance.

" Well, my dear," said he, " if *Frances* have borrowed it, we must send and beg her to return it."

Mrs. Rodney was about to explain, that it was Welsted she meant, who had carried off the likeness, when having in this ingenious manner averted the coming evil, by availing himself of the similar sound of the male and female names of Frances and Francis, the agitated father familiarly taking his great son-in-law by the arm, led him to another part of the room, and requested that whenever the signal for attack should be given, he would do him the honour to lead the Countess of Springfield to the breakfast-table.

At length the lovely bride, reattired in a simple morning dress, made her appearance amongst the guests, and, lighted up by the animation which the novelty of her situation produced, her countenance looking winningly beautiful, her eyes sparkled, and her cheek was flushed;—alas! not worse evidence does the snow which shrouds the volcano give of the eternal fire which rages within. Her look wandered over the visiters, and all the preparations made for their entertainment, but it rested only on objects identified in her mind with Welsted; and when Lord Springfield gracefully advanced to lead her to the banquet, her eyes filled with tears, as he took her hand, because she remembered at the moment, how kindly he had spoken of poor Francis in former days. What a tone of feeling, what a temper of mind for the bride of his Excellency Sir Frederick Brashleigh!

Assembled at the lengthened tables, the joyous party performed their most skilful manœuvres upon the Perigueux pies and Italian salads, the white soups, and various entrées which systematically succeeded each other, under the inspection of the London artists; and nothing in the world could go off so well—the bells rang merrily, the band stationed in the boys' eating-hall played appropriate airs, and the festivity was continued till nearly four o'clock, when preparations were made for dancing by the younger branches, and the happy couple quitted the crowded assembly amidst the cheerings and congratulations of the elated guests; for of the innumerable ladies then present, those to whom the sparkling champagne, which deluged the board, was a novelty, formed a large majority; and *they*, led on by the agreeable curiosity of tasting several glasses of the fascinating beverage, became more than ordinarily lively; while the females of the lower classes, who, with their husbands, brothers, and sweethearts, were feasted below stairs, made similar attacks upon unlimited issues of milk-punch, of which they drank at discretion; contenting themselves somewhat indiscreetly, with the assurance that nothing professing to be made of milk could be very strong.

Thus the joyousness and hilarity were universal, and the only heart not gladdened by the surrounding gaiety was hers, for whose sake the gaiety was excited. When the carriage drew up to the door, a flood of tears relieved the sorrow of the bride, which the General suffered to flow, unnoticed by any harsh remark, feeling that it was natural for a girl parting for the first time with her parents, even for a happier life, to mourn the separation; but his temper *did* show itself a little in the manner in which he declared the impossibility of Miss Ewebright's accompanying them. Fanny ceded the point with the best possible grace, for Miss Ewebright was neither friend nor favourite of hers: but Miss Ewebright herself received the intelligence very differently; she had imagined that her official station necessarily entailed upon her the pleasure of a journey to the metropolis with her *principal*, and had actually prepared every part of her travelling apparatus, in order that she might fulfil the duties of her appointment. It was therefore to gratify *her* feelings, and not her own, that Fanny ventured to suggest that she should accompany them to London; it was the first favour she had asked of *her husband*—it was, indeed, the first evidence she had given of any thing like an interest in passing events, and she pressed her point somewhat earnestly. His Excellency argued against it, determined, from the first, not to present the gawky hoyden to his London connexions as the chosen friend of his new wife. Her demerits were not so glaring to poor Lady Brashleigh, who, unused to the ways of the world, endured her little *gaucheries* with patience and complacency; but different, indeed were her feelings towards her new-married husband, when after listening to a really winning and artless solicitation in behalf of her anxious friend, his Excellency was pleased to declare, with an oath of the coarsest nature, that he would suffer himself to be consigned to eternal perdition, rather than permit the vulgar creature to be of their party.

An oath, new to the ears of poor Fanny under her paternal roof, where decent manners, and the necessity of good example, utterly banished the odious habit of swearing; abstractedly, and in itself, terrified her; but when she recollected that it came from the lips of him, with whom she was destined to pass the rest of her life—that it was uttered to strengthen a denial of the first and only favour

she had ever asked of him, and that it was delivered with
an expression of countenance perfectly infuriated, her
thoughts instantly reverted to the mild tenderness and
affectionate gentleness of her beloved Welsted ; her mind
was in a moment filled with anticipations of the most horrid nature, and she saw nothing before her but distress
and misery : of course she proceeded to acquaint Miss
Ewebright with Sir Frederick's determination ; but she
was even then too much alive to her duty, to betray the
needless violence of her husband, or the manner in which
he had fulminated his pleasure, or rather his displeasuer,
upon the important subject, to her temporary friend.
Her bridemaid riveted an inquisitive look upon her
pale countenance ; she saw her eyes damp, and her lip
quivering ; and declared in a tone of decision equally
strong, and in language nearly as elegant as that of
Sir Frederick's, that he was a " horrid old monster !"
hoping to receive from the said horrid old monster's bride
something like encouragement, in the censure she was
pleased to bestow upon him ; but no—Fanny merely
replied, that much as she lamented the disappointment
of her friend, she of course was bound to obey her husband.

    " Obey!" said Miss Ewebright. " Oh! Fanny, Fanny
why didn't you run away with Welsted ? If I had known
you intimately ;—if *I* ——"

    " Stay," said Lady Brashleigh. " Forgive me if I en-
treat you not to utter another word upon past occurrences.
I tremble to think how I must have subjected myself to
observation, since even my ordinary acquaintance seem to
have made it a business to examine and comment upon
my conduct. I am grieved to the heart, that you should
have been provoked to say what you have just said ; it
conveys unintentionally the bitterest reproach to me, and
I leave my home, the most unhappy of human beings,
conscious how frivolous and unworthy my behaviour must
appear. Oh! if you knew my heart," continued Lady
Brashleigh ; " if you knew *all*, you would acquit me of
folly or inconsistency :—it is now decided, and the line is
for ever drawn. I know my duty, and pained as my heart

is at this moment, I will perform it punctually, faithfully, and honourably."

" Lady Brashleigh, Ma'am, where, in the name of wonder, have you got to?" exclaimed the General, in a loud voice, from the hall below.

" My husband calls," said poor Fanny tremblingly, her beautiful eyes overflowing with tears.

" Lady Brashleigh, Ma'am I say!—where the devil is she?" again resounded in the same tone. Luckily his Excellency did not enter the apartment, or perhaps there would have been a *scene:* he proceeded towards the library, whither Fanny, having kissed her fair friend, dried her own tears, and in some degree composed her feelings, followed him. He stood talking with her father, evidently out of humour, and when he saw her, he reproached her with her childish delay, and unnecessary tardiness.

" Come, Ma'am," said his Excellency, " if *you* are ready I am ; the horses have been waiting these two hours, and punctuality is the soul of my existence,—without it, a soldier would be ruined : and so, good b'ye, Doctor— good b'ye, Mrs. Rodney !"

" Good b'ye, Sir Frederick," said the old lady ; " take care of her, Sir Frederick ; she's a good girl, and only wants kind treatment to be every thing you wish—I'm sure I hope nothing will happen to make either of you uncomfortable. To be sure, the voyage is dangerous and long, and the climate you are going to, is very bad ; and, you know, she is rather delicate, and you, you see, Sir Frederick, are no chicken ; and, I dare say, *we* shall never set eyes on either of you again, but——"

" I dare say very differently, Ma'am," said Sir Frederick, who was anxious to shorten the equivocal benediction of the matron.

" I augur much brighter things!" exclaimed Rodney ; " the bright beam of hope, beautiful in its radiance, and ever springing in the ardent imagination —"

" ——Have you got your cloak, Ma'am," said the General to his bride, turning away from his father-in-law, who had just pitched his voice to the true poetical twang,

and was evidently about to commence a lecture upon the
pleasures of anticipation, which, as the subject has already
been worked threadbare, by all sorts of writers in all ages,
and as all to be said upon it is contained in the seven words
of the pithy proverb, which tells that " While there is
life there is hope," His Excellency had not the smallest
curiosity to hear.

This was the first moment since the connexion had been
en train, at which poor Rodney felt the full force of
Fanny's griefs, or the weight of his obligations to her.   To
be married to a man who had no taste for poetical imagery,
who was not alive to the attractive beauties of figure and
allegory, was indeed a misery which he had never before
anticipated for his daughter ; for while he was only a
suitor, His Excellency had listened patiently to the innumerable *platitudes* of his worthy host, heard him laud to
the skies the " virid intellect and refreshing newness" of
half the blockheads in the county, given the most careful
attention to his trite and everlasting descriptions of the
" rising sun gliding the horizon," or " the setting sun
couching his radiance in the briny deep," or " the blue
waves lashing with their foam, the adamantine rock ;" or,
the " still lake reflecting Heaven's firmament in all its glorious splendour, while the refulgent moon throws her silvery
beams on the far-spreading landscape, and the curling
smoke, rising as it were, pyramidally, marks the lowly cot,
beneath whose humble thatch industry and happiness
dwell peacefully and joyously together," until the poet
raved of his taste, feeling, and judgment; indeed Rodney's respect for listeners was as great as that which is felt
by the herd of *diners-out,* the only difference between
whom, and the hireling mountebanks of the common play-
houses, is, that the well-dressed witling of the drawing-
room wears not the merry-andrew's jacket of the theatre,
and is paid for his pleasantry in *vol au vents, fricandeaux,
Silleri* and *Lafitte,* instead of receiving the wages of
tumbling, in pounds, shillings, and pence.

Rodney, although only a provincial performer, and, from
the absence of dinner-giving neighbours, constrained at all
times to be an amateur; was never so happy as when he

could obtain silence, and hear himself lecture. This partly arose from conceit, and a desire for dictation, and partly from habit :—to keep his school-room silent was the great object of his life, and so accustomed was he of course to be attended to, and "heard out," that the abrupt left-wheel of Sir Frederick upon the present occasion, absolutely astonished him ; he stood with his brows elevated, and his eyes widely opened, as if in amazement lost, and had actually proceeded through six words of a beautiful simile between a travelling carriage and the trident of Neptune, before he fully felt and perfectly understood the extent of his son-in-law's rudeness.

Thus it is, that a wound inflicted on the *amour propre,* cuts more deeply and keenly than graver assaults upon more important points; thus it is, that a personal reflection or an injury done to a man's vanity, is felt more seriously than an attack upon his character or morality. Rodney of course saw the disparity between his daughter's age and that of Sir Frederick ; he had witnessed occasional indications of ill-temper on his part ; he was aware of the devoted attachment of his child to Welsted ; he was conscious of his own want of caution in having suffered their connexion to exist and continue so long ; he was aware of the injustice he was doing to a young man for whom he had always professed and felt the warmest affection ; he saw he knew that for *his* sake, Fanny was about to sacrifice herself ; and yet, never until this little apparent (but probably unintentional) neglect of Sir Frederick's, did he once really feel as he ought to have felt with respect to the marriage ; he might have seen, nay he *did* see, the absurdity of such an union, and all its concomitant discrepancies, yet none of these were sufficient to work him up to a decision whereby he might have rescued his daughter's happiness and ensured his own ; whereas, on the contrary, such was his emotion at the present moment, that had the same circumstance previously occurred, and his Excellency been sufficiently careless and incautious the day before, to turn away n the middle of a simile, a figure of a flourish, I verily believe Rodney would at all risks have broken off the match. In truth he was grievously annoyed and greatly irritated, at the unexpected display of what he considered his Excellency's bad taste and bad breeding.

The moment of separation at length arrived, and when the bride and bridegroom departed, it was more like a funeral than a wedding. Fanny wept bitterly and loudly; while her mother kept encouraging and consoling her, by desiring her to " look at *her*," " and see that *she* was married, and none the worse for it," in the same manner that Freemasons argue with youngsters, who, anxious for initiation, still fear the requisite ceremonies; for the old lady attributed all her daughter's agitation to alarm and apprehension, mingled with a seasonable share of natural regret at parting. Rodney, however, roused by the abrupt and *brusque* manner of Sir Frederick, gazed on his child with a look of compassionate interest as he handed her into the carriage, and in the following moment his large unmeaning eyes were suffused with tears: this was not unnoticed by his Excellency, who, not particularly partial to weeping beauties, male or female, made it a rule to set down every crying man for a blockhead.

" What! are *you* crying too, Doctor?" said his Excellency: " Ugh! you old fool!" (this was muttered aside,) " I'm mighty sorry, good people, to see you all so much dejected;—it really grieves me to think that I have caused such distress amongst ye—so good bye t'ye.——"

Saying which he shook Rodney by the hand, who at that moment would almost have given his life to recal the events of the past fortnight, and snatch his child from what he now saw pretty plainly must be a perpetuity of misery.

Mrs. Rodney, who was no poet, and whose vanity had not been hurt by the innumerable cutting things which his Excellency had said to her during his stay, and who was not the least conscious that she had been his Excellency's constant *butt* in every place to which they had been invited; saw no difference in his manner, nor in the merits of the marriage then, from the view she had always taken of it; and returned to her guests, who were as merry and gay as good cheer and good spirits could make them; hoping *this* one would not get cold, and that the punch would not disagree with *that* one; praying that the dancing might not break down the floor of the school-room, and that no accident would happen to the *young* couple on their journey.

Her fears for *them* were needless. After travelling an hour or two, his Excellency, who had indulged himself in a violent *tirade* upon the ill-breeding of Miss Ewebright, and in expressing his astonishment at the selection of such a person to accompany Fanny to the altar, swore vehemently, that there was some horrid smell in the carriage—something unbearable; what it *was* he could not conceive; —but he *must* discover the cause of the inconvenience.

The carriage was stopped, the servants were summoned; —it appeared that the odour which so disgusted his Excellency, arose from a basket of sandwiches which poor Mrs. Rodney, in the simple kindness of her "virid mind," had with her own hands stowed away in one of the pockets, deposited in a small basket, and covered with a nice clean damask napkin. The moment the objectionable packet was discovered, his Excellency desired to know who had presumed to load his carriage with such filth as that.

" Mrs. Rodney, Sir Frederick," said his man, " put them into the carriage herself."

" Then throw them away, Sir," said Sir Frederick, " I'll have no such stuff here. Why, Ma'am," said the bridegroom, while the servant was yet standing at the carriage door, " your poor old mother must have a very odd notion of modern travelling, Ma'am;—throw them away, d'ye hear, Sir."

" Yes, Sir Frederick," said the man; and knowing his master's temper and character better than her ladyship did, immediately scattered forth the carefully selected viands by the road-side.

" There," said his Excellency, " shut the carriage, Sir; some passing beggar will be glad enough of them, I dare say—shut the carriage."

" Yes, Sir Frederick," said the man, and bang went the well muffled door; up jumped the servant, and away rolled the barouche.

Sir Frederick did not even turn towards his bride; but

throwing himself back against the cushion, exclaimed in a tone of subdued phrensy, " Infernal greasy filth !"

A fly, or a feather, or a fan, may be the subject of the hottest quarrel ; and although a basket of sandwiches be no romantic object whereon to ground the bitterest feelings of regret and sorrow ; true it is, that this discussion about a paltry collection of eatables, was at once the cause and effect of innumerable sorrows and disappointments.

That it was the cause of sorrow, who can doubt ?—Poor Fanny beheld in silence and with an aching heart, the kind, yet homely attentions of her poor fond mother rejected with disgust and contempt by her husband; and *she* that tried to do her best to please and comfort those she loved, held up as an object of ridicule to her daughter's servants, in their mistress's presence ;—to a simple unsophisticated girl, this must surely have been cutting and wounding.

That the discussion was the *effect* of disappointment, there can be as little doubt ; the truth is, that Sir Frederick had determined not to leave Europe unmarried, and having seen Fanny once or twice, and without any intimate knowledge of her connexions, plunged at once so far into the engagement, that he could not, when he found himself grievously mistaken in the " sort of people," to whom she belonged, retrace his steps somewhat too rashly taken ; the spirit once awakened, the disposition once excited, every thing added to his displeasure and disgust ; and now that he had done what he considered his duty, and fulfilled his very foolish intentions, he felt that he had a right to find fault, and manifest his sovereign contempt for all the exertions which had been used for his amusement and entertainment, and by proving the greatness of the sacrifice he had made for Fanny's sake, ensure her gratitude, and excite her admiration.

How all this is to end, of course I cannot here pretend to guess ; or, at all events, let my readers know ; certain it is, that when, to use the figurative language of our friend the schoolmaster, " night threw her sable veil over the lovely face of nature," and the bride and bridegroom were safely housed at Hartford Bridge, where the eccentric Commander-in-chief at Bombay chose to lodge on that special occasion, there were excited in the hearts of the newly-married pair, none of those joyous feelings which leave the bosoms of more ardent lovers.

Rodney retired to rest at the academy, wearied and distressed in body and mind; while Welsted, after watching the hours by the coffee-room clock, at the Bell and Crown, in Holborn, until eleven, repaired for the last time to his bedchamber in that inn; and having placed the letter and portrait of the now Lady Brashleigh beneath his pillow, laid himself down to enjoy the misery of contrasting his own situation, at the moment, with that of his Excellency the Commander-in-chief at Bombay.

CHAPTER X.

What though no gaudy titles grace my birth—
Titles, the servile courtier's lean reward,
Sometimes the pay of virtue, but most oft
The hire which greatness gives to slaves and sycophants,—
Yet Heav'n, that made me honest, made me more
Than e'er a king did when he made a lord.
ROWE.

SINCE custom and propriety have combined with fashion and delicacy, to require the temporary seclusion from society, of ladies and gentlemen in the interesting situation of Sir Frederick and Lady Brashleigh, I am compelled to quit the happy couple at the door of their selected *domicile* at Hartford Bridge, and bring the reader back to the proceedings of Mr. Francis Welsted, who was doomed, on the morning subsequent to the day on which we revisit him, to assume the divisional command at Mr. Tickle's. He rose from the feverish, fitful repose, which he had attempted to enjoy; refreshed neither in body nor improved in spirits; and, although he was conscious that the conduct he had adopted during the struggle with his feelings was, without dispute, the most correct and honourable, still, now that the event was beyond recal, and *he*, assured of the certainty of Fanny's loss, he could not entirely suppress the sigh of regret for what was past.   Nay, he even reproached himself with needless timidity and delicacy; and read over and over again the "last words" of his adored Fanny, till the blood thrilled in his veins, and the tears stood in his eyes; but there is a proverb which says quaintly enough, "What is done cannot be undone." And, although the "doing" of this marriage was the certain "undoing" of his happiness, the knot was now tied, the blow was struck, and it was irrevocable.

From Lord Feversham, Welsted had not heard for several days; indeed, not since they parted in Grosvenor-square; for the Viscount had followed his father, by his Lordship's desire, into the country, where the Earl, the newspapers said, was enjoying the sport of fishing with a numerous party of fashionables; whereas I believe the fact to have been, that his Lordship was making the amiable to a select body of free and independent electors, whose interest he was particularly anxious to secure, and of whose rights and immunities he intended hereafter, that his said son Feversham should become the parliamentary guardian and representative.   If I be mistaken, and it were a fishing party after all, the Viscount's presence was, at all events, considered necessary to the sport; and accordingly he quitted town for the purpose of giving his assistance. The consequent absence of his animated friend had decreased most palpably the social enjoyments of Francis, who found no pleasure in the gaieties which playhouse lobbies and smoking pot-houses afford to the small fry of clerks and apprentices, who, in these days, frequent the metropolitan public places of amusement, and subsequently discuss the merits of a player, or the virtues of a singer, over their pipes and potions of punch or brandy-and-water, with as much ardour and eloquence, as if either the one or the other, were of the slightest importance to society.

It was, to say truth, *not* so disagreeable as might have been expected to Welsted, to be obliged to change the scene, and commence his domestication at Hackney on this particular day. In all societies there is something worth observing, some novelty of manner or character, whence amusement, if not instruction, may be culled, and the very difference which he anticipated in the Tickle family, from any thing he had been accustomed to, and from the forcible contrast their circle must naturally afford to scenes and characters recently most familiar to his eye, he hoped to receive something like consolation, derivable from a change which it was, at all events, absolutely necessary he should make, and to which he trusted he should soon become reconciled.

Having defrayed, therefore, his expenses at the Bell and Crown, and having eaten his last dinner, and paid for it with his last guinea, my adventurous hero, implicitly obeying the order of his superior, removed himself and all his personal property to the Flowerpot, in Bishopsgate-street, whence, after numerous delays, incidental to the long journeys of short stages, he was conveyed in safety to the door of Mr. Tickle's magnificent seminary, and, in a few minutes, found himself actually in the presence of that important personage himself, who suggested that it would be no bad opportunity for him to present himself to the boys at prayers, which would be performed immediately after their supper. Then Sunday intervening before any actual business was to be done, would afford him an opportunity of becoming acquainted with the boys' names, persons, and different standings in the academy, upon which subjects he would be still further enlightened by the hints derivable from Monsieur Ronfleur, the French master, and Mr. William Dixon, the English usher; to whose use, in common with the Latin assistant (Mr. Francis Welsted), was appropriated a small, yet convenient apartment, from whence they were nocturnally summoned to supper in the parlour, a place they were not expected to visit, without such special invitation; indeed it was a proneness to violate this rigid regulation, which first excited the suspicion and ire of the heads of the family, in the case of the departed Mr. Stevens.

Accordingly, at prayers Frank made his appearance : his desk, having previously been introduced to his Fren and English colleagues; and having, as might be expected, attracted the whole attention of the boys from the duties which they were mechanically performing; he repaired after the service, by invitation, to the sacred parlour, whence, to his surprise and admiration, he was conducted by Mrs. Tickle herself, attended by a bright shining housemaid, as tall as a grenadier, and as grave as a judge; to a neat apartment, overlooking the garden, cleanly papered and carpeted, which the lady, with a wonderful show of urbanity and amiability, informed him was " destined for his dormitory." Overwhelmed with the kindness of *Madame*, the young man accompanied her on her return to the parlour, where supper was prepared, and the young ladies *en attendant*, who thought it necessary to a display of good breeding, not to take the smallest notice of Welsted, but to remain in a corner, whispering and tittering, evidently making fun of somebody, in a tone of voice which left each individual of the party in doubt whether *he* was, or was not, the immediate and special subject of their mirth.

The supper consisted of *hot fish* and cold roasted beef, a huge dish of pickles, and another of potatoes, with an immense fruit-pie. The effect produced upon Welsted by the substantiality of the repast was evident to Mrs. Tickle, who assured him, that much as there seemed upon table, there was plenty of mouths to eat it, for as they dined at two, their appetites were sharp enough before ten, which, on Saturday night was the hour appointed for the present meal.

" You can play a good part at the English roast beef, can't you, Mounsheer?" said Mrs. Tickle, addressing herself to the French master.

" Play wid de beef, Madam?" said Ronfleur; " I no play, I eat; ha, ha! I declare—I like rosbif—eh?"

" Yes, Mounsheer," said Mr. Dixon, " we know you do, Sir."

" Well, you ought to work double tides sometimes, Mounsheer," said the lady of the house; " for you see, Mr. Welsted, Mounsheer is a papist, and they fast more than we do."

" Yes, Ma'am," said Welsted ; who thought tne ladys' manner of alluding to the French gentleman's religion somewhat abrupt.

" Fast, indeed !" said Tickle, " and pretty fasting it is too. Why, Mounsheer, don't mind a cod's head and shoulders and potatoes, with oyster sauce and a few pancakes, and an omelette into the bargain, by way of starvation, besides soup maigre, like what our boys get on high days and holidays, and a dish of maccaroni to wind up with. Come, never mind, let us sit down ; this is no fast, —is it, Mounsheer ?"

" No,—I declare," said Ronfleur, " we no fast—ha, ha ! plenté to-day,—I declare."

In a few moments Welsted ascertained that the poor Frenchman was the butt of the family, and the good-natured simplicity with which he displayed his gallantry towards the young ladies, and the manner in which they received it, excited a feeling of compassion for an old man in a strange country, compelled to labour in the decline of life for his bread, and to earn his pittance mixed with scorn and ridicule. But his pity was wasted ; *vive la bagatelle* was the motto of Monsieur Ronfleur, and he saw not, or if he saw, felt not, the irksomeness of his situation, or the degradations to which he was forced to submit.

" Come, Mounsheer," said Miss Tickle, as they were preparing to seat themselves, " come here, and sit next me ;" and she said this pointedly, and illustrated by action, in order to express her horror at the idea of getting next the new usher. Harriet sat on the opposite side next her mother, and next to *her* the smirking Dixon, whose hair was extremely well powdered, to do honour to the festive board ; while the contrast, its snowy whiteness afforded to his dingy neckcloth, was decidedly disadvantageous to the effect of the drapery.

" What will you have, girls ?" said Mrs. Tickle.

" I'll have some fish, Ma, please," said the elder.

" And I," said the younger, " will have some of the beef, Pa ; where it's most underdone, please, and a pickled onion or two, please, Pa."

11

" To be sure, my dear," said Tickle, who was as tender
as a dove of his own progeny.

" Mr. Welsted, what will you take ?" said Mrs. Tickle,
—" you are the stranger."

" I'll take a little of this beef, ma'am," said Welsted,
making up his mind to do at Rome as Rome does.

" La ! Ma," said Miss Tickle, in a sentimental tone,
with a large flake of fish upon the point of her knife, " I
wonder where poor Mr. Stevens is now :—don't we miss
him ?"

" Oh," said Tickle, " I dare say he's home before this,
my dear."

" Poor Stiffens," said Ronfleur ; " I declare—I like
Stiffens ; he plaisant, good, gentil man. I sorry he go."

" La ! so we all are," said Mrs. Tickle.

" Ah !" said her elder daughter, helping herself to some
thick melted butter.

" You saw him here, Mr. Welsted," said Tickle, " the
day you dined with us : he was your predecessor."

Welsted assented : and forthwith a whisper, sent across
the table to her sister, by the elder Miss, produced an exclamation from the younger, of, " Oh, la !" and a subsequent horse-laugh.

" Be quiet, Harriet," said Mrs. Tickle ; " he'll hear you
presently :" which, if *He,* meant Welsted, he certainly did,
and noticed at the same moment that the younger Miss
Tickle had not the faculty of aspirating the H : a calamity
producible at times of very comical results.

" Stiffens," said Ronfleur, who was eating salad, and
who seemed determined to recur to his favourite subject,
" Stiffens, he draw very well : I declare—eh ? his draw-
ings were superbe, Sir, eh ?"

" Yes," said Mr. Tickle, " he had a great genius that
way."

" Ah !" sighed Miss Tickle again involuntarily.

" What's the matter, dear?" said her father.

" Nothing, Pa," said she, sighing more deeply.—" A
glass of ale, Sally, if you please."

These words, addressed to the monumental maiden before mentioned, produced a foaming tumbler full of " heavy wet," which the delicate and despairing damsel easily despatched.

" Some hale for *me*, Sarah," said her younger sister.

" Yes, Miss."

" What beer do you take, Welsted ?" said Tickle, in a tone of mingled familiarity and patronage.

" I'll take some ale, Sir," mechanically answered the young man ; and stretching out his hand to receive some, which the maid was handing about ; his ears were saluted with another whisper across the table, from Miss Tickle to her sister.

" Harret,' said Elizabeth, " Ring !"

" Hay," said Harriet in the same tone.

" Look," said her sister emphatically ; directing with her eyes, Harriet's attention to a ring, which Welsted happened to wear on one of his fingers.

" Betsy, *ao* be quiet," said Mrs. Tickle. " I desire you will."

" Ah, Madame," said Monsieur Ronfleur, " she has so much *gaieté*, so much very fine spirit, dat you no keep her quiet, eh ? I declare."

" There are times for all things, Mounsheer," said Tickle gravely, who had overheard the whisper, and saw too that it had not escaped Welsted. " Won't you take cheese, Mr. Welsted ?"

" None, Sir, thank you," said Welsted.

" Try my radish, Sare," said the Frenchman goodnaturedly, during a squibbing conversation, which was carrying on between the mother and daughters at the top of the table. " My radish, I declare, is superbe.—I keep," continued he, bowing gracefully, " tanks to my excellent patron dere,—a little jardin, where I make grow des epinards and les onions, and de radish you know. Dey are large, ha ! ha !—but fine—not pipi, nor olow, I declare."

" You are very kind, Sir," said Welsted, really feeling obliged for the trifling attention of the stranger ; and, having out of civility taken, and subsequently bitten, the fiery produce of Monsieur Ronfleur's horticultural pursuits, was, as one of the young ladies humorously observed, bitten in his turn, by the hottest specimen of the vegetable perhaps ever tasted by mortal man ; the mirth his little distress occasioned was excessive, and nobody seemed at all annoyed at the result, except poor Ronfleur himself, who made a thousand apologies and protestations, that the mishap, as far as he was concerned, was perfectly unintentional.

"Upon my word," said Tickle, "Mrs. T. I am ashamed of your daughters—they really do not know how to conduct themselves."

"La, Pa," said Harriet, "we only laughed to see how ot the radish was."

"I am afraid,—I declare," said Ronfleur, "dat poor Mr.—Mr.—Bedsted is——"

What, it is impossible to say, for the shout of laughter which followed this blunder in my hero's name, was so long and so loud, that Miss, who was at the moment concluding her light evening repast, with the ripe part of a huge Cheshire cheese, having unfortunately overfilled her mouth just previously to its occurrence, was seized with a choking fit of coughing, and was led out of the room in a sort of semi-convulsion, by her affectionate sister, her mother, and father.

A general feeling of alarm was expressed, which, however, was somewhat allayed by an assurance on the part of Mrs. Tickle, who returned for some water, that Betsy would soon be better ; for which assurance she gave most efficient reasons, not necessary here to repeat, and which to Welsted's ear, even with his knowledge of Mrs. Rodney, seemed at the moment almost superfluous.

That poor Francis was now doomed for ever to be called by the name innocently appropriated to him by Monsieur Ronfleur, must be pretty evident to my readers ; and it must be confessed, that the experience of the past hour was not very likely to reconcile a mind agitated as his was, to the prospect before him.

It was quite amusing to see (and perfectly characteristic) the anxiety of Ronfleur to obliterate, by every possible civility and attention towards Welsted, any impression of rudeness which the mistake in his name might have conveyed; and while the young lady was getting better in another room, he did not resume his seat (for all the party had risen in alarm), but came over to Welsted (whose manner soon convinced him that he was not in the slightest degree offended), and assailed him with offers of snuff; and half-whispered observations in praise of the family. which, during their absence he thought he might, advantageously to all parties, throw in.

" Very fine young woman, Miss Tickle," said he, " good head—clever—I declare—quick—*piquante*, you know, eh?—draws, eh? sings, and pinches;—oh, I declare, Ma'mselle pinches beautiful."

" Yes," said Welsted, wrongly imagining his French friend to allude to some of the young lady's little endearing ways, instead of simply, with the French idiom, recommending her performance on the harp.

" And Miss Harriet is an uncommon nice girl, Sir, when you come to know her," said Dixon; " of the two, she's the most lively."

" Ah!" said Ronfleur, " Ma'mselle Betsé—you know —eh?—I tell some other time, Mr. Bed—— psha? Well —eh? tell me, eh?—Welsted, eh?"

" Welsted," said Francis.

" Welsted? I assure you, Mister Welsted, I never shall be guilty to forget him no more."

At this juncture the family group returned to their places, and supper being removed, a plated stand of bottles, jugs of hot and cold water, sugar, and glasses in abundance, made their appearance.

" Now, Welsted," said Tickle, who was in truth annoyed at the rudeness of his girls, and had taken the opportunity of leaving the room to express his disapprobation of it,—"what mixture do you take?"

" I—seldom ——" said Welsted.

" Let Harriet mix you some hollands and water; you'll find it excellent," said Tickle.

" If you please," answered Welsted.

" Ollands? Mr. Welsted," said Miss Harriet, inquiringly.

" Thank you," bowed Welsted.

" Ot or cold, Sir ?"

" Cold," said Frank, merely because he did not know how to repeat the word she had just uttered, so as to express its real meaning, without practically correcting her mode of pronouncing it.

" *With* sugar ?" continued Harriet.

" No, I thank you," said Frank.

" You are no friend to the grocer then," said the smiling girl, who, having been directed to make the amiable, determined to show off, in some of the pleasantries of middling life.

" Ma, what will you have ?" said Elizabeth.

" I'll take some of the dark brown, my dear," said Mrs. Tickle ; " it a'nt genteel for ladies to ask for brandy, you know, Mr. Welsted : he ! he ! he !"

" Mounsheer, what will you have ?" said Tickle.

" Water, Sare, water, if you please," said Ronfleur, " with a leetil bit of sugar, if Miss Harriet will be so kind."

" There, Mounsheer," said Harriet, pushing towards him a bumper of the pure element, sweetened to his taste.

" Shall I pass you a spoon, Sir ?" said Miss Tickle to Welsted, endeavouring, after her younger sister's example, to atone for her rudeness by overstrained civility.

Welsted bowed, and accepted her offer.

" Now, Dixon," said Tickle, " you'll brew for yourself."

" If you please, Sir," said the grave arithmetician, who proved himself in the performance a perfect master of mixed quantities.

" How's your throat, child ?" said Tickle to Elizabeth.

" Oh, quite well, Pa, thank you," said she ; " it was only a bit of the hard rind of the cheese that stuck."

" Ah !" said Mrs. T——, you *will* always eat the rind, let me say what I will—you never remember how many nasty dirty hands it has been through."

" I suppose Miss Elizabeth feels *Ticklish*," said Dixon, who was a punster.

" Ha ! ha !" said Ronfleur, with all the simplicity and *bonhommie* imaginable :—" So many times you say dat

joke, every body laugh always, I declare—him so good,
ha! ha! ha!"

" Any news in this evening's paper, Mr. Dixon?" said
Tickle to his usher, who always went to a neighbouring
public-house, to glean intelligence from the Globe.

" I see there is a little change in the ministry, Sir," said
Dixon.

" Can't be for the worse," said Tickle. " What is
it?"

" Lord Farnborough is appointed Postmaster-Ge-
neral."

" What!" said Tickle, " he that was Rutherford?"

" Yes," said Dixon.

Frank's ears tingled—and his heart palpitated at the
sound of his kind friend's name, but he said nothing.

" Farnborough!" said Mrs. Tickle, " that was them as
was down at Worthing, last year—don't you remember,
Betsy?"

" To be sure I do," said Miss Tickle; " it's them Lady
Rutherfords that never wears shoes but once, and dresses
four times every day."

" They can afford it, my dear," said Tickle, " so long
as we pay taxes to support them."

" They are a very onappy family," said Harriet; " I
don't believe e lives with his wife at hall,—at least I saw
a long haccount of 'em hin the ' Fashionable Magazine,'
or ' Igh life hexposed,' and *there* they give a very onfa-
vourable description of the ole of 'em."

" Unfavourable!" said Tickle, " how should it be otherwise?—a parcel of lazy, useless lords, living upon our
labour, like drones, and doing no kind of good whatever
to the state."

" I believe," said Welsted, unable any longer entirely
to restrain his feelings, " you are under some mistake
about Lord Farnborough's family."

" Oh dear, no, Sir," said Miss Tickle, snappishly;
" Miss Bacon, which we knew at Worthing, last year,
was very intimate with a gentleman who was acquainted
there, and was sometimes asked there to dinner; and I

know from *her* that there used to be such pieces of work
in the house between the father and the mother, that the
daughters were obliged very often to shut themselves up
in their rooms for whole days together."

" That is very surprising," said Welsted.

" And the son, which is at Hoxford," said Harriet; he
is a reglar gambler, and as lost is heye sight with sitting
hup and drinking.   Miss Bacon said he never was sober
from morning till night; besides, there was many skits
about 'em in the papers."

" I really think," said Welsted, gently and diffidently,
" you must be mistaken ; I happen to know something of
the family, and——"

" Oh!" said Mrs. Tickle, bursting into a fit of laughter,
" if *you* know them, why there is no more to be said : —
come, girls, let us be off, I did not know we had such
great folks at table, he! he! he!"

" I may state," said Welsted gravely, " that I *do* know
the family, and know most assuredly, that for the greater
part of it, the history you have heard is wholly ground-
less."

" But, la, Sir," said Miss Tickle, " it's all in the
Fashionable Magazine, all about their lace veils, and the
poor woman and the soup, and the windmill, and the one-
horse shay, and all the story of the young lord and Miss
Biddy Arlyne, of the Liverpool theàtre."

" Come, come," said Tickle, " I dare say Mr. Welsted
knows what he is talking about; and, at all events, you
are rather too young to be a judge of such matters, and a
little too noisy into the bargain, Miss Betsy."

" It's the ot grog, Pa, as as got into her ead," said Harriet, comically.

" Come, Mrs. T. come," said Tickle sharply, " it's time
for us all to go to bed. Dixon will you have the goodness
to light the candles ?"

Dixon did as he was desired ; and, after a brief cere-
monial at parting, the ladies retired, and by their immo-
derate laughter in the hall, loudly proclaimed their utter
disbelief in Welsted's knowledge of the Farnboroughs,

and the conviction of their own correctness as to the history.

"Those are noisy girls of mine, Sir," said Tickle to Welsted, when they had left the room.

"I am only sorry," said Welsted, "that they should have formed so erroneous an estimate of Lord Farnborough's family : because, in the first place, it is manifest injustice to an excellent and exemplary set of people ; and in the second place, it too plainly indicates the unfortunate influence which the ignorance, or misrepresentation of panders to the rage for scandal, really has over the public mind."

Tickle saw that Welsted was vexed, and appeared interested in the dispraise of the noble lord, and therefore, with all the inherent cunning of a vulgar clamorist, shifted his ground from an attack upon one particular object, to a sweeping satire upon the whole British Peerage.

"Why, to speak truth," said Tickle, " we are no great lord-lovers in this family, Mr. Welsted ; we owe them nothing, and we neither look for their favour nor their smiles ; all my pupils are from the truly respectable part of society ; the happy mean ; which, in th s country, i. we were but fairly represented, and only had our rights, would show themselves to our own honour and the admiration of the world ; as *your* countryman says, Mounsheer, our nation is like our porter, froth at the top, and dregs at the bottom, but the mean—literally, the golden mean, contains the strength and spirit."

"My contreman !" said Ronfleur, somewhat indignantly, " what has my contreman to do, Sir, wid your porter ?"

"Voltaire, Sir," said Tickle, " the immortal Voltaire."

"Ha, Voltaire, oui—I declare," said Ronfleur, " ha ! ha ! vous avez raison,—great man dat, Sir,—great rogue too ;—dat is what fault I find with de English Monsieur B. C. Ouelsted (dat is right, eh ?)—yes, I declare, Welsted, dat dey print too much, not de truth—you know what I mean."

" Print too much, Mounsheer!" said Tickle, who, six
months before, had recovered three hundred pounds
damages for a libel on his school, published in a respectable
literary magazine. " What! restrict the liberty of the press?
—Sir, ' it is like the air we breathe, if we have it not we
die.' "

" Press! eh! yes," said Ronfleur.

" I don't think," said Dixon, sipping his half-and-half,
" that Mounsheer knows what our liberty of the press
means."

" Don't I, Mr. Dixon?" said Ronfleur; " ha! ha! I
declare—I suppose I don't, eh?"

" Why," said Welsted, " it is not exactly understood
in France."

" No, tank God," said Ronfleur, " it is not known, I
declare, in ma belle contree."

" Thank God, Mounsheer?" said Tickle, interroga-
tively.

" Yes," said Ronfleur; " de liberté of de press is de
liberté you always quarrel for, and which is no more nor
less than to take poor devil men out of dere house and
famille, to fill your ships to fight, wether dey will or no
—eh?—dat is your liberté of de press—and beautiful
liberté he is too, I declare,—eh?"

" I thought he did not know, Sir," said Dixon, addressing Tickle.

" If he don't, Mr. Dixon," said Tickle, " I am afraid it
is too late to make him understand it now."

Whether the Major-domo intended this observation to
refer to the period of Monsieur Ronfleur's life, or the time
of night, I know not; but immediately after the observation, Dixon looked at his watch, and, finishing his grog,
rose, exclaiming with surprise, " Dear me, Sir, 'tis half-
past eleven."

" Never mind," said Tickle, " it is Saturday night, Mr.
Dixon, all holiday at Peckham, Sir; it comes but once
a-week, you know; and besides, we have our new officer
aboard.   Come, Welsted, take another glass to our better
acquaintance."

Welsted, who saw that the political principles of his

new commander were diametrically opposed to those of
poor Rodney, whose respect for the aristocracy was such,
that he could never stand upright in the presence of a
great man, and in whose implicit devotion to his superiors, Welsted, at times, believed his own prejudice
against his betters had in some degree its origin; and
moreover, being anxious, if possible, to go to rest with a
better opinion of Mr. Tickle than he had been able to
form from Mr. Tickle's self-display, acceded to his invitation to continue the *sederunt ;* and, accordingly, his
companions again replenished their goblets, and Monsieur
Ronfleur made himself another jorum of *eau sucré.*

" Have you been long in this country?" said Welsted,
to Monsieur Ronfleur.

" Ah! oui, Monsieur," said Ronfleur, sighing, and laying his snuff-box emphatically on the table.

" Yes," said Tickle, " Mounsheer's is a hard case."

" Oui, he vary hard, Monsieur Tickle," said the old
man, drawing his hand across his eyes; " but never mind
—'tis of no use to complain—for myself I care nothing.
When de Revolution—you know, Mr. Wel—Welsted ?
yes,—before your time, Sir—when dat come, I was officer of de king; my poor wife, Madame Ronfleur—ah,
me! good, noble woman, God bless her memorie!—she
was to meet me, from Paris, and fly with me from my
chateau; but, ah! no, no, no! dat was not to be;—she
was killed—yes, Sir—while I, who would have died with
her, was away;—and her head—mon Dieu!—which has
repose on dis bosom,—ah! ten thousand times,—was
shown for triumph to de peuple. Ah, me! ah, me!"
Ronfleur paused for a moment, and no one felt disposed
to break the silence, and he resumed. " My poor boy,
Henri, my one child, was escape; after his mother's
death I left him safe, safe, safe. I travel all night to de
coast; when I was gone ten,—oh, more dan ten league,
and in de middle of de night, I hear a little faint cry, like
my poor child's voice. I say to myself, nonsense dis,—
it cannot be; but again I hear de same; I call postilion to
op,—I look, and behind de voiture, dere was my poor
retty little Henri half asleep, but oh! so he was crying.

When I go away from my chateau, he follow me, mount
behind de berlin, to take part of his fader's fate; nobody
saw him, he came wid me all dat way.   If I had try to
bring him wid me out of France, we should both have
been dead : I was, by compulsion, forced to leave him at
the next poste.   Poor boy, poor boy! brave garçon that
was!   I never saw him no more from dat long day to
dis; but oftentime, in my sleep, I hear his little cry
still."

Ronfleur again paused a moment, not half so much
affected as his new auditor! for the story had been often
told to the others.

"Well," said the old man, refreshing himself with a
pinch of snuff, "well, Sir, I come to dis contrée seven-
and-twenty years ago, from my chateau in Brittany;—
ah! beautiful place!   I declare—at first I know not what
to do; I am here alone in all de world,—but I must eat:
I declare, eh? dere was one English Lord who give me to
live, but it could not last so always.   I was but French
gentleman; I know little but de tongue of ma contrée,
and little use I found all else I did know; till, at last, I
came to take place in de neighbourhood of London, dere I
live ten, perhaps twelve, year in de one place.—I never
heard from my poor boy, never thought to see ma belle
France no more.   At last your contree restore les Bour-
bons, I return to ma belle France;—ha, ha! I declare!—
I go to find my chateau in Brittany—no, he is gone—all
gone—my trees cut down—my vines all perish—my house
all burn—every thing lost to me,—and my poor child
dead;—ah, dear! ah, dear!"

"But *now*, Sir," said Welsted, "under the present
regime, your restoration would be certain."

"Thereby hangs a tale, Sir," said Tickle, in a whisper.

"Ah, sacre! sacre! sacre!" said the old man, striking
his forehead thrice with his hand. as he uttered the words,
"fool I was—I did not know—I cannot help him now—I
was receive at de Tuileries—I was receive by my King—
I wore de white cockard—I put lilies to my coat, and sing
through de streets fo Paris ' Vive Henri Quatre,' till I was
a horse."

" Well," said Welsted, smiling, " after such signal marks of loyalty, Sir, why return hither?"

" Ah, mon Dieu ;" said Ronfleur, " I was fill with follie and ambition, peut-être, fear, perhaps. Juste as I was fix—I declare,—eh?—Napoleon return to Paris ;—I don't talk of it much—I was fool, although I tought myself wise ;—he offer me to be Prefet, you know,—eh?—I accept him—sacre !—den came des Allies. I declare—Napoleon go—I run like divil-man to get to my old home again ;—here I come—I find Mr. Tickle, he give me roof to put over my poor old head, and now, Monsieur Ronfleur, very good gentleman, ha! ha !—I declare—he never shall go to his belle France no more."

" That, Sir," said Tickle to Welsted, with more sharpness than consideration, " is a history of Blighted Ambition."

" Strange !" said Welsted, looking at the old man, and contemplating his gray hairs, and drawing an imaginary parallel between his relative conduct and condition, and those of an Englishman similarly circumstanced.

" Never mind, Sir," said Ronfleur, his face suddenly brightening from a deep cast of pensiveness into an expression of perfect gaiety, " I beg pardon for my storie— it is doll, very doll, and stupid—I declare—bad times, eh? mon brave Dixon ; no good to cry ; I shall never cry no more—non mes amis—chantons—chantons—

> " J'aurai bientôt quatre vingt ans,
> Je crcis qu'à cet âge il est temps
> D'abandonner la vie ;
> Je la quitterai sans regret,
> Gaiment je ferai mon paquet,
> Bon soir la compagnie."

And at the conclusion of this verse (which he sang to the air of " Maris jaloux vous avez tort"), suiting the action to the word, he rose from his seat, and moving in a sort of dancing step towards the table, whereon the chamber candlesticks were ranged ; selected one, and after lighting the candle, shook hands with Mr. Tickle, and " le brave Dixon" (as he called him), and bowing gracefully and

gaily, yet somewhat grotesquely, to Welsted, slowly
quitted the room, repeating, *sotto voce*, " bon soir la
compagnie."

But after he had shut the door, and nearly crossed the
hall, they all heard him sigh deeply.

" That's a strange old body," said Tickle; " isn't he,
Mr. Welsted ?"

" Of a happy disposition, Sir, at all events," replied
Francis.

" And such a favourite with the boys," said Dixon,
" they'll do any thing for Monsieur Ronfleur; he makes
little paper bird-cages for them, and plaits hair watch-
chains and purses, and carves little figures—and——"

" Well, Mr. Dixon," interrupted Tickle, who thought
he perceived the effects of the " half-and-half," in the
fluent familiarity of his assistant, " I think we had better
retire, it is just twelve o'clock—so along, as Mounsheer
would say ;—by the way, you know your room, Welsted ?"

" I do, Sir," said Frank, " thanks to Mrs. Tickle's
kindness." — " To-morrow," continued Tickle, " *Mr.*
Dixon" (he was now speaking officially and magiste-
rially), " you will be good enough, Sir, to take charge of
the boys to church, although it is not your day; Mr. Welsted will go with *us;* it is better the boys should be more
used to him, before they are all turned loose upon his
hands."

" Of course, Sir," said Dixon, " I will take care of *that*
Sir."

" To-morrow, Mr. Welsted," continued Tickle, " we
breakfast at half-past nine ; on other days at half-past
eight, in the summer ; and so good night :" saying which,
he urbanely shook hands with his new usher, and led the
way up stairs, Welsted being followed in the march by
Mr. William Dixon, aforesaid ; who (such was the talent
he possessed for satisfying himself in grog-making) was
excessively well pleased that there were ballisters, by which
he might " hold on" during the ascent to his bedchamber.

CHAPTER XI.

A gentle wife
Is still the sterling comfort of man's life ;
To fools a torment, but a lasting boon
To those who—wisely keep the HONEY MOON.

TOBIN.

THE reader, perhaps, will hardly be prepared to hear that the blissful seclusion to which I so properly and delicately consigned the new-married couple at Hartford Bridge, was of such brief duration, that the afternoon of the Sunday on which Welsted first saw the morning dawn in Tickle's house, gave to the wondering eyes of Lady Brashleigh the important metropolis of our happy Island.

To endeavour to describe the solemn dulness of the Saturday passed in the silent recesses of Mr. Demezay's once well-frequented inn, would be vain ; nor is it necessary for me to detail the causes which led to the abbreviation of his Excellency's stay in his " bower of bliss," since the effect is all that is absolutely essential to the conduct of my narrative.

Suffice it therefore to say, that his Excellency, after breakfast on the Sunday, having whistled and walked about the room for some time, and after having cut and pared, with the most minute attention and scrupulous precision, every nail which decorated the long yellow fingers of his shrivelled hands, broke a lengthened, and else perhaps endless silence, by abruptly asking her Ladyship if she wasn't deucedly tired of the place.

What to answer she did not exactly know, nor was she quite alive to the question, seeing that her thoughts were at the moment occupied with subjects utterly foreign to the present scene, and the principal character thereon ; her hesitation, however, met with one of those gentle rebukes, to which she found it was right and fitting she should as speedily as possible accommodate herself, and she answered, that she was quite ready to do whatever he pleased.

"I hate that sort of indecision, Madam," said Sir Frederick; "in God's name have an opinion; if it agree with mine, well and good, and if it don't, Ma'am, why then it will, at all events, give us an opportunity for discussion."

"Really, Sir Frederick," said Fanny, who finding that he much admired the frequent repetition of his newly-acquired title, less to please *him*, than from a feeling of acquiescence in the common usage of the family, constantly adopted it in speaking to him, "I *can* have no choice on the subject, for, as I have never seen London, how should I know whether I shall prefer it to this?"

"How should you know, Ma'am?" said his Excellency; "why, surely, a sillier body than you might make such a discovery as that, without working a miracle London is a city, Ma'am, Hartford Bridge is a single house, Ma'am; can't you give an opinion between a country life and a town one—between crowded streets and a solitary inn, eh?"

"Whichever *you* prefer," said Fanny, "I am sure I shall like."

"And pray, Ma'am, how are you sure of that?" asked Sir Frederick; "my taste mayn't assimilate with yours —I ask, Ma'am, do you find this dull?"

What a question !

"No—I—"

"I dare say you do," said his Excellency; and if *you* don't, Ma'am, I do."

"Then pray let us go on to London, where your friends and ——"

"*My* friends, Lady Brashleigh," interrupted Sir Frederick; "I would rather go and tiff at Saugor; my marrying has offended them so confoundedly, that I sha'n' go near them,—I shall go to some hotel, at all events, in the first instance."

"All I can say is," said Fanny, smiling, "and unconsciously, yet somehow archly, laying hold of the lapel of his Excellency's coat, "whatever you wish, I am ready to do."

"That is exactly what I hate, Ma'am," said his Excellency, withdrawing himself from her hold, not in the gentlest or most courteous manner; "I hate implicit compliance—I hate your bending twigs;—willows are only fit to make baskets of, Ma'am;—I like people to have opinions of their own, else, as I have just said, one is robbed of the pleasure of arguing;—however, Ma'am, for once, I'll think for you—we *will* proceed to town to-day, for I have much to do, and many preparations to make, and, at all events, we shall be livelier there than here." Saying which, he stalked across the room, and ringing the bell, summoned his servant to his presence.

"Order the carriage immediately, with horses to Bagshot; see the bills paid, and desire her Ladyship's woman to get ready forthwith; d'ye hear, Sir?"

"Yes, Sir Frederick," said the man.

"Stay a moment, Sir," said his Excellency: "Would your Ladyship like tiffin?"

"Fanny, who knew enough of his Excellency's orientalisms to understand his meaning, was again on the point of leaving to his decision the important point of luncheon; when, resolved not to irritate her sensitive spouse in the presence of the servant, she answered decidedly in the affirmative.

"What, hungry again, Ma'am?" said Sir Frederick. "Well then, Sir, if your Ladyship wants tiffin, order some; desire them to be quick with it, d'ye hear, Sir?"

"Indeed, Sir Frederick," said Lady Brashleigh, "I don't wish for any thing, if——"

"If you don't wish for any thing, Ma'am, in God's name, why d'ye ask for it?" exclaimed his Excellency. "Go, Sir, and do as *I* order you."

"Yes, Sir Frederick," said the man, and vanished.

Lady Brashleigh, during the last part of this dialogue, had walked towards the window, and was looking out at the moment the Southampton Independent was changing horses. Sir Frederick walked to another window, and saw two or three gentlemanly men, who had, it seemed, dismounted from the vehicle, standing in a group below; one of whom was evidently attracted by the appearance of

Fanny. Her tearful eyes, however, were fixed unconsciously on the carriage, and she saw not the continued
gaze of the admiring stranger. The perception of his
Excellency Sir Frederick Brashleigh, however, was considerably quicker; he stepped back a pace or two from
the window which he had been occupying, and still Fanny
remained where she was. Worlds would not have convinced a man of *his* disposition, that she was not pleased
with the appearance of the individual, and gratified by
the look of approbation which he had noticed. The tiger
was roused.

"Come from that window, Ma'am," said he, in a tone
of grating discordance; "it is only women of loose character and improper habits who show themselves at windows, in the civilized world, Ma'am."

Poor Fanny, who was wholly unconscious of the extent
of his Excellency's meaning, obeyed the command as a
child would obey a parent, and immediately quitted her
place.

"Was he an acquaintance, Ma'am?" asked Sir Frederick, see-sawing himself backwards and forwards in the
chair he had just taken possession of; his face exhibiting
one of those sneers, which ere now has paralyzed a subaltern, or exterminated a commissary.

"Who?" said Fanny.

"The beau in the white hat, Ma'am," answered Sir
Frederick.

"I saw no beau," said Lady Brashleigh, smiling.

"I don't want to argue just now, Ma'am," answered
her spouse; "only I beg you will cure yourself of the
vulgar habit of standing at windows."

Such was the purity of poor Fanny's intentions, and
such the innocence of her heart, that she could not comprehend why her irritable partner should be so much
agitated, as she evidently saw he was, by so unimp rtant
an occurrence. His Excellency, however, cooling rapidly.
when he again saw a tear ready to start, added, "Don't
suppose I am angry, Ma'am, I am not; I know you are
guileless, Ma'am, and unworldly, but we are always to
consider appearances, Ma'am, and I don't wish to be
laughed at, even in mistake."

All this was Greek to the novice; and considering it was but the third day of their union, perhaps, the subject for conversation might have been better chosen; because, pure and innocent as Fanny really was, she could not help considering, and calculating in her mind, in order to discover whence could possibly arise the ridicule to which her husband appeared so sensitively alive; what it was he meant by being laughed at; and why he was so desirous that she should not be seen; few eyes had glanced on her rural charms save Welsted's, and the pure flame which beamed in those, was little likely to impart a feeling other than virtue herself might approve.

Luckily, at this juncture, the luncheon appeared—and a profusion of eatables graced the board.

" Lady Brashleigh, Ma'am," said his Excellency," some cold lamb ?"

" None, I thank you," said Fanny, who had forgotten that luncheon was ordered by her desire; and whose appetite was effectually satisfied by the asperity of her commander-in-chief.

" What *will* you take, Ma'am?" said Sir Frederick.

" A glass of wine-and-water is all I wish for," said Fanny.

" The devil it is, Ma'am!"—the waiters who were in the room started,—" then may I ask, why you chose to order tiffin, Ma'am ?"

" I mean, Sir Frederick," said Fanny, endeavouring to smile, " all I wish for, before I eat."

" Eat!—I have no desire, Ma'am, to force your appetite," said he ; " here, Sir, take away the tiffin."

" The what, Sir Frederick ?" said the principal waiter.

" The tiffin, Sir," repeated his Excellency, in a voice of thunder.

The waiter ran his eye over the table, and touched every article thereupon, from a cold round of beef down to the salt-spoons, looking inquiringly at his Excellency, to ascertain what he might possibly mean by tiffin.

" D'ye hear me, Sir?" cried Sir Frederick : still the man stood and stared.

" Sir Frederick desires you will remove the luncheon,"
said Lady Brashleigh.

" Sir Frederick desires no such thing, Ma'am," said
her husband ; " I flatter myself that Sir Frederick knows
what he is about, without taking lessons from your Ladyship,—I say, sirrah, take away the tiffin."

" I really beg pardon, Sir Frederick, but I don't
know——"

" Don't know !" exclaimed his Excellency, in a tone
of ferocious contempt, and looking daggers at the unhappy varlet, who stood trembling, and as pale as death
before him ; then collecting and composing himself a
moment—" ugh, I forgot, you never were in India ; well,
take away these things, Sir, and get me some chit paper."

The waiters looked at each other with an expression of
the most romantic astonishment: the first, who had undertaken to inquire and ascertain the meaning of tiffin, had
no disposition to push his researches any further ; and the
second, to whom the latter command was specially addressed, had been so terrified by what had occurred, that
he did not think it quite prudent to begin his; he answered,
" Yes, Sir Frederick," and got out of the room as fast as
he could.

" Well, Ma'am," said his Excellency, " there you are,
—at the window again ? upon *my* word !"

Poor Fanny had again repaired to the window, to hide
those tell-tale tears which ever and anon would fall ; she
retired tacitly, and sitting down, sipped the wine-and-water
which his Excellency had prepared for her.

" I am afraid," said her Ladyship, " the waiter did not
understand that you wanted some note paper."

" So am I, Ma'am," said Sir Frederick ; " but I care
very little about it. I would have sent a chit over to Sir
Archibald Gregson, while I was in this part of the country, if they had brought me the paper ; as it is, the carriage, I see, is coming round, and the less time we lose the
better, for I never was more heartily sick of a place in all
my life."

Poor Fanny mechanically rose, and was proceeding to
her room to make preparations for their departure.

"And pray, Ma'am, where is your Ladyship going *now?*" said Sir Frederick

"To put on my shawl," said her Ladyship, "and see that my maid has got every thing ready."

"See that your maid has got every thing ready!" ex claimed Sir Frederick; "that cannot be necessary, Ma'am, if she know her business; and if she know it not, she has no business with you, Ma'am; besides you are *going*—whither? along the public passages of a public inn?—Ring the bell, Ma'am, for some of your servants, and direct that your woman may be sent for; how do you know that she is in your apartment? consider your character, Ma'am, and the necessity, as *my* wife, of a deportment vastly different from that which was suitable to your father's rank in society; let me never hear of your coming here, and going there, and doing this, and doing the other, without proper attendants, Ma'am."

Lady Brashleigh commanded her feelings, and rang the bell as she *was ordered to do.*

When the waiter appeared, Lady Brashleigh did not know exactly what she ought to say, and her spouse thought proper to say nothing.

"Did you ring, my Lady?" said the man.

"Yes," said Lady Brashleigh, "Sir Frederick wants— my—that is ——"

"Sir Frederick, Ma'am," said the General, in the same tone of voice (which, by the way, closely resembled that of a player of the name of Cooke, who, several years since, used to act Richard the Third, and Sir Pertinax Mac Sycophant, at one of the London Theatres), "Sir Frederick wants nothing, Ma'am;" and then turning to the waiter, said, "Her Ladyship, Sir, desires to have her woman sent to her."

"My Lady's maid, Sir Frederick?" said the waiter.

"Maid, Sir, if you choose!" repeated Sir Frederick, sneeringly. "I thank you, Sir, for setting me right.— You'll please to do as you are ordered, Sir, and make no comments; and, sirrah," said he, calling the man back, who was actually gone,—"be quick about it, Sir."

"Yes, Sir Frederick," said the waiter, and again disappeared.

"You should always be prepared, Ma'am," said his Excellency to Fanny, "before the moment we are starting; —however," added he, chucking her under the chin, with an air of fondness, "we shall know each other better before we die, Ma'am :—come—here is your woman – go and get yourself ready."

Poor Fanny, hardly knowing whether she lived or not, and half worried to death, repaired to her room, attended by her maid, and shortly returned, fully equipped for the journey.

"Twelve minutes and a half, Ma'am, are more than I can allow for beautifying;" said his Excellency, as she entered the room : "however, when we get to London, you will be forced into activity ; we shall have no time to spare there — come — is the woman ready ?"

"Yes, Sir Frederick," said Fanny, "we are quite ready now."

"We! Ma'am," cried his Excellency, "who are we, Ma'am ? your maid and yourself, Ma'am —upon *my* word, an agreeable association ! I desire you will learn better to appreciate the distance at which circumstances have placed you from the poor ignorant creature who curls your hair and pins on your neck-kerchief ;—We, Ma'am !—recollect the station which you will be called upon shortly to fill ;— We, indeed !—poor girl !—but. come, you mean no harm, I dare say !—Why, Lady Brashleigh, Ma'am, you have been painting yourself !"

Fanny stared with astonishment at the accusation.

"I, Sir Frederick ?" said she.

"Surely you have," said he ; "come hither, Ma'am, come to the light — umph, no—it isn't paint," added his Excellency, rubbing her cheek at the same moment with his hand,—"you are flushed, Ma'am—has any thing alarmed you ?"

"No, Sir Frederick, I—I—"

"Are you sure, Ma'am ?" said he, "*quite* sure ?"

"What *should* alarm me ?" asked his Lady.

"I don't know what *should* alarm you, Ma'am," replied he slowly, and half sneeringly; "but I do not at all approve of your wandering about public inns by yourself, Ma'am—where's your woman?"

"Here am I, Sir Frederick," said the maid.

"Umph!" said his Excellency, "very well, that's enough,—I dare say I am wrong, only see that this is amended another time; come, Ma'am, let us be off." Saying which, with an air of gallantry, he offered his arm to his trembling bride, and descended the staircase.

When he reached the hall, he had the particularly good taste to inquire whether the gentleman he had seen standing at the door wearing a white hat, was gone on towards London.

"No, Sir," said the landlord, "the gentleman you mean, is staying here."

"Umph," said his Excellency, "thank you, Sir;—come, Lady Brashleigh,—step into the carriage, Ma'am;—I—I—wish you good morning, Sir:—staying here—umph!" Saying which, the amiable bridegroom followed his lovely Fanny into the barouche, and the door being closed, "all right" was given as the signal for starting, and away they rolled towards the great metropolis.

I have no doubt that this *sketch* will appear to many of my readers too coarse, and almost unlike nature; especially to those who are young, ardent, and full of love for some bewitching object with whom they picture the uninterrupted enjoyment of happiness, whenever stern guardians shall relent, obdurate parents soften, rigid aunts unbend, and Hymen bless their propitious loves; but it is really no caricature; dominion, rule, and authority were the idols of Sir Frederick's heart, and now that he had married the girl (why he hardly knew, and since their union less than ever), and she was necessarily subject to his commands and whims; the chief pleasure derivable to him from the match was to show his power and control, and rehearse, as it were, in his domestic circle, the dictatorial conduct, which he intended to display upon more important occasions and a larger theatre in the East.

It will be recollected, that I warned my reader what to

expect from him ; if, as a young man making his way
the world, married for love, and domesticated with a
charming creature of a suitable age, he was remarked for
being morose, petulant, and coarse ; careless of his Amelia's charms at one moment, and furiously jealous of her,
at another ; raving about his rights and privileges, while
they were safe and unattacked, and bartering his most important and delicate interests, when he could do so, for
personal advancement ; what was to be expected from him
in after-life, when *he* had become in turn the great man
and commander, and when from a sudden whim, or rather
as I believe a pique (taken at an unqualified refusal which
his offers had just previously received in London), he had
united himself to a creature young enough to be his
grand-daughter, of whom, judging by past circumstances,
it was clear he would be continually suspicious ; from
whose conversation he could receive no gratification; since
she had never been in India (of which alone he loved to
talk), and whose inexperience, while it was a perpetual
source of uneasiness and irritation to *him*, rendered her
wholly unfit for the *dignified* station she was destined to
fill ; his Excellency having at the same time the most
sovereign contempt for her parents; whose names he never
mentioned without accompanying the words with gestures
indicative of dislike, and even disgust ?

In addition to these evident drawbacks to his perfect
felicity, he felt, now that he had completed the engagement which he had rashly and intemperately entered into,
the most sensitive alarm at her Ladyship's approaching
visit to London, and a positive disinclination to introduce
her to his friends and connexions, all of whom he knew
were quite ready to find fault, and condemn his taste and
judgment, even were his bride perfection ; but who now,
having some tenable ground for satire and observation,
would doubtlessly open the most furious batteries of ridicule and reproach upon him for having united himself to
a girl whose mind was uncultivated, and whose manners
were unformed ; for although Fanny was young and beautiful, and kind and tender, and versed in all moderate and
becoming accomplishments for a rural nymph, she knew

not **how** to exhibit herself after the fashion of opera girls
in French dances, nor whirl the giddy round " in man s
embrace." Of Italian, the soul-subduing language of
love, she knew nothing; of chemistry she was hopelessly
ignorant; she had never drawn from the antique, nor attended lectures on natural philosophy;—and what would
Mrs. Brashleigh, his Excellency's daughter-in-law, who
was deep blue, think of such an ignorant creature as this?
and how would Miss Diana Chicherly, and Miss Ellen
D'Aubigny, his cousins, endure the society of a creature
so ungraceful and so unenlightened ?

The fear of ridicule, which keeps many men and women
right, drove Sir Frederick from his original purpose of
proceeding direct, and in the first instance, to his daughter-
in-law's residence ; and his thoughts were occupied during
the progress from Hartford Bridge to Bagshot, in considering whither, when he reached Hounslow, he should direct the boys to drive.

Between Hartford Bridge and Bagshot, his Excellency
spoke but few words ; in passing through Blackwater, he
desired her Ladyship to draw down the blind on *her* side
of the carriage as the sun glared in his eyes; the sun
was *not* on that side of the road, but there were various
groups of students belonging to the Military College,
whose youthful figures and animated countenances, set
off to advantage by the gay uniform of the establishment,
appeared to his Excellency, likely to produce unpleasant
reflections and comparisons in the mind of his youthful
bride.

Poor Sir Frederick !—little did he think how far from
him, and the straggling youngsters of the Military College, were seated the thoughts of poor Fanny. She
seemed to herself, since her marriage, to have been in one
continued dream, and *that* not of the most agreeable nature. Her eyes rested on passing or surrounding objects,
but she saw them not ; words rang in her ears, of which
she scarcely knew the import. She leant back in the
carriage, pale and abstracted, and, as she felt it was her
duty to do, mechanically obeyed the directions of her
husband, as she had heretofore obeyed those of her father;

she felt for *him*, whose *wife* she was, all the respect due to his age, mingled with the awe which his conduct excited ; he was shrewd enough to see the external symptoms of her mental disorder, but still attributed her dulness and abstraction to the separation from her family.

As the carriage rolled down the hill into Bagshot, his Excellency, after gazing, unnoticed by *her*, for a few moments upon her pale cheek, took Fanny's hand, and inquired if her head ached ? The question startled her, and the answer was a flood of tears.

" Don't cry, Ma'am," said his Excellency, withdrawing his hand : " My first wife was a weeper, Ma'am ; and I *did* hope to have escaped a second. However, it seems you are come of a crying family. I hope I shall see less of this hereafter—I excuse it now—it's natural perhaps —as for myself, I never *could* cry at any thing, so I cannot say from experience."

" My head *does* ache violently," said Fanny ; who of course could not explain the real source of her sorrow, and therefore was compelled to be disingenuous.

" I dare say, Ma'am, you feel the effects of the wine-and-water you drank, said Sir Frederick ; " you are not used to that sort of wine, Ma'am ; Madeira is stronger than the currant wine of Somerville House ; you must take care to remember *that*, when you get into good so· ciety, Ma'am."

A reply to the insinuation conveyed in this speech, or an observation upon the ill-natured allusion to the home-made wine of the academy, Lady Brashleigh felt neither strength nor inclination to make ; and therefore assented to the remark with a forced smile.

The carriage reached the inn, fresh horses were hurried out, the servants remounted, and away they went again. As they left Bagshot, his Excellency called the attention of his Lady to two Lodges near the turnpike.

" That, Ma'am," said his Excellency, " is the Duke o Gloucester's house ;" after saying which, he drew up the glass on *his* side, and by no accident uttered another syllable, until within a mile of Hounslow.

" Are you asleep, Ma'am ?" then said his Excellency,

"No, Sir Frederick," said Fanny; "but I thought *you* were."

"I never sleep in a carriage, Ma'am," replied Sir Frederick, "and hate a companion who doesn't talk."

"I was silent, because I was afraid of disturbing you,' said Fanny, in a tone of affectionate regard.

"Umph!" said his Excellency; "thinking of Miss Amelrosa Ewebright and the academy, I fear—no matter, Ma'am—we can't command our thoughts."

"No," said Fanny: what *she* thought at the moment it is impossible to guess; and it would be extremely improper to tell, even if I knew.

"I am puzzling myself whither to order the boys to drive," said his Excellency; "Ibbotson's is the best hotel in London, and extremely reasonable, but they don't take ladies; Long's is too noisy for us, and besides——"

Here he paused.

"I am sorry I am not able to assist you in the selection of a residence," said Fanny.

"I should wonder if you were, Ma'am," said his Excellency.

And at this moment, such was poor Lady Brashleigh't idea of London, its accommodations, and the number of its hotels, that her Ladyship was silently praying that his Excellency might not select the same place of residence as her dear Francis. Unsophisticated Fanny! to see his Excellency, the commander-in-chief at Bombay, with his Lady and suite, enumerated amongst the fashionable arrivals at the Bell and Crown, in Holborn!

At Hounslow, his Excellency having summoned "Master Charlton," as he was pleased to call him, into the sinister parlour of his inn, adorned with the print of Ceyx and Alcyone, and its companion, communed with him long and seriously touching the hotel to which he should be driven.

It may seem extraordinary that a personage so great and self-willed as his Excellency Sir Frederick, should solicit the opinion of an innkeeper, upon a point so nearly allied to his comfort and arrangements; but he was a true Indian, and although he had passed years in active service on the continent, and had resided in various parts of his own country since; early habits predominated, and he entered as little into the manners or customs of home, as Mr. Charlton of the Crown Inn at Hounslow, would have entered into those of Bussy-Gusserat, or Sooragepore. In London, his Excellency had resided but little, except in the very height of the season, and then always at Ibbotson's; for in those days the Indians had not taken club lodgings on the first floor over an upholsterer's shop in Grosvenor-street; nor had they any particular place of rendezvous, except the coffee-room of the hotel in Vere-street; and therefore, under the guidance of mine host of the Crown, his Excellency resolved on transporting himself to Mivart's, whither the boys were accordingly commanded to drive.

To a man of different character and disposition from Sir Frederick, the next stage would have produced matter of much interest; the display and explanation of the approach to the metropolis, to one who, though new to the scene, was perfectly adequate to the enjoyment of receiving information upon points which, considering the locality, must necessarily be more or less connected with persons moving on the great theatre of life, and upon which, as matter of tact, if not of good-nature, it would have been wise to enlighten his bride as much as possible, ought to have given him pleasure; but not a syllable did his Excellency utter in the way of conversation, until having passed the turning to Isleworth, Fanny, attracted by the light fantastic modern entrance to the grounds of the venerable Sion, ventured to ask what place it was? to which his Excellency replied, that it was Sion House, but that she had better restrain her inclination for asking questions, which, if strangers were in her society, would at once declare her *newness*, in what he again was pleased to call the " civilized world."

In passing towards Kensington, the appearance of Holland House, struck Fanny particularly; it had a venerable and even romantic air, and reminded her of the family place of the Springfields; and although she was ignorant of the literary and political classicality of it-

damp smelling apartments, she felt that she should like
very much to make some inquiries concerning it, of her
important spouse; but she repressed the rising inclina
tion, in compliance with his former hint. As tyrants
themselves, however, cannot control looks, poor Fanny
gazed somewhat earnestly on the venerable pile, and while
thus employed, her husband observed her.

" What are you looking at, Ma'am?" said he.

" I was looking at that old house, Sir Frederick," said
Fanny.

" That *old* house," repeated his Excellency. " Do you
know what house it is, Ma'am?"

" Not I," said Fanny.

" Then what interest can you possibly have in looking
at it?" said Sir Frederick: and if you don't know the
name of a place, why don't you ask, Ma'am? That is
Holland House, Ma'am."

Fanny, who had never heard of Holland House, was
resolved to ask no more about it; seeing that she now
perceived it to be a matter of more difficulty than even
she had apprehended, to meet the views or suit the disposition of his Excellency, who having only half an hour
before, commanded her to abstain from interrogatories
lest she should betray her ignorance, now chid her for not
endeavouring to cure her want of knowledge by asking
questions.

They passed through the town of Kensington, and entered the Park; the novelty of the scene, the appearance
of numerous horsemen, and a crowd of carriages drawn
up opposite the gate of Kensington Gardens, the lengthened promenade, and the general gaiety, attracted poor
Lady Brashleigh, and she roused herself from her waking
dreams to gaze on the motley crowd.

" This, Ma'am," said Sir Frederick, " is Hyde Park,
the resort of the gay and idle on a Sunday, where you'll
find the peer and the pickpocket jostling each other, and
where," added he,—observing that her Ladyship's notice
was attracted by the splendid uniforms of two dandy
lancers, " above all things, Ma'am, ladies never lean out
of their carriages either to show themselves or look after

other people, except, indeed, such ladies as are in the habit of standing at windows when they are at home, Ma'am."

Fanny felt a chill of dread, of something almost like hopeless horror, at the prospect which presented itself of future life, when she heard this needless observation ; the recurrence to the event of the morning, proved that his Excellency's rage was not only brilliant and flashy, at the moment of its first corruscation, but that when the bright flame had subsided, the vindictive feeling still lay smouldering in his heart, ready to blaze with the first gust which might unfortunately chance to blow upon it.

She drew back and resumed her former attitude in the barouche.

" Well, Ma'am, said Sir Frederick, " what are you hiding yourself for ? Are you ashamed to be seen, or are you displeased with being detected in such society ? There is a medium, Ma'am—a happy mean, which I trust your Ladyship will study to attain ; it is not because I dislike the exposure of your person like the sign before a house of public entertainment, that I wish you to seclude yourself, as if you dreaded to meet the public eye : pray, Lady Brashleigh, once for all, let me entreat you to consider that I am much older than you are."

Her Ladyship needed no jogging on this point.

" And that with *my* experience, whatever I suggest is for your advantage. When folks are married, Ma'am, their interests are identified : although I may have my own respectability and comfort in view, in whatever counsel I give, neither comfort nor respectability can be supported or sustained by *me*, without your participating in both."

To this lecture Fanny made no reply, but obediently raising herself into such an attitude as she hoped she might be suffered to maintain without offence, recommenced her silent observations of the *beau monde* from Leadenhall and Whitechapel, transplanted for the day to the promenade of Hyde Park.

The only object his Excellency pointed out to her Ladyship, in their progress towards Brook-street, and per-

haps the only object of which he could give her a true
description, was the residence of his illustrious chief; to
that, he pointed as the home of him, whose splendid
deeds have placed our country on the proudest eminence
amongst the nations of Europe, and of which his Excellency Sir Frederick Brashleigh felt the most enthusiastic
admiration; the ardour of his sentiments being by no
means damped or deteriorated by the recollection that *he*
individually, and personally, owed his distinctions, deco-
rations, and command, to the success of those stupendous
operations in which he had, it is true, borne a share, but
which were so gloriously conducted by the immortal subject of his praise.

Fanny gazed on the edifice with an interest to her
wholly new in its character; she had read of WELLING-
TON, and of his triumphs, and she thought of him as the
hero at the head of thousands, marching over the field of
victory, and commanding the destinies of the world; but
to see the house in which he dwelt, the very room in
which, perhaps, he was then sitting, excited an extraordinary feeling, and seemed to mark more distinctly than
any thing which had yet occurred, the change which had
so suddenly taken place in all her views and pursuits, and
which brought her, as it were, into immediate contact
with those, of whom, in her humble retirement, she had
only read or spoken.

The carriage, although delayed for some time in its
progress along the " drive," at length cleared Grosvenor
Gate, and rolled rapidly through the square, to the hotel
destined for their reception; where in a short time, they
were installed in an admirable suite of apartments, dinner
was ordered, and the happy couple perfectly domesticated.

The restless disposition of an Indian, however, soon induced his Excellency " just to walk to Ibbotson's, to see
if there were any letters, and perhaps he might call at
Mrs. Brashleigh's while he was out; dinner was to be
ready at seven, but he would be home long before that,
—and away went his Excellency, having previously recommended her Ladyship to lie down and repose herself
after her fatigue; the said recommendation having been

accompanied with a " chaste salute" upon her Ladyship's dexter cheek.

Lady Brashleigh did as she was bid, and rested herself for an hour or more ; when, Sir Frederick not having returned, she repaired to the drawing-room, and found that it was considerably past six o'clock. She seated herself on a sofa, not daring to go near the windows, one of which was thrown up, lest she should be detected by his Excellency in the commission of the heinous offence of looking into the street, contrary to his Excellency's special orders.

Foreigners tell you that the quintessence of earthly dulness is to be found in a Sunday in London, where the habits of the people, and the regulations of the police, close every shop and place of amusement, and where the graver duties of religion are not, as in Popish countries, dismissed in the early part of the day, and the evening devoted to gaiety and mirth. To Fanny, although no foreigner, nothing ever appeared so *sombre* as the afternoon of her *debut* in the " civilized world." Town was getting thin, and not many carriages were moving about ; the hour at which she rose was one at which people are getting home, first to recover from the fatigues of the morning, and then to prepare to dress ; sounds she heard few, and not daring to look abroad, sights she saw none ; and she remained communing with herself, and thinking over the events of the past week, reconsidering her letter to Francis, trying to imagine where he was at *that* moment, fancying, perhaps, that he might be near her, and even passing through the very street in which she was residing, until nearly half-past seven.

The butler appeared, and inquired if the servants should put down dinner, or if her Ladyship expected Sir Frederick. She answered in the affirmative ; and while the discussion was going on, his Excellency appeared, attended by a personage to whom he was anxious to introduce Lady Brashleigh as early as possible. Her Ladyship was startled at the appearance of a stranger ; but when his Excellency desired Mr. Binfield the butler to have two additional covers laid, she was absolutely overwhelmed,

—to have to preside at table with strangers, to make her first appearance without any preparation, and so soon after her marriage;—it altogether appeared as extraordinary as unfeeling on the part of his Excellency, to invite a party on the day of their arrival.

"Lady Brashleigh," said his Excellency, "this is Captain Macaddle, Ma'am;—allow me to present him to your Ladyship—he accompanies us to India as one of my aides-de-camp, and I hope he will be fortunate enough, Ma'am, to make himself acceptable to your Ladyship."

Fanny, startled at the kind and almost respectful tone in which she was addressed by her husband, curtsied and smiled—Captain Macaddle bowed lower than ever Captain bowed before, and then stepped backwards two or three paces from her Ladyship.

Scarcely had this ceremony been performed, when the servant announced Major Mims; and forthwith there entered the apartment a small, freezing personage, looking like a well-preserved Egyptian mummy just taken out of its wrappers; who bowed profoundly to his Excellency; and then, conducted by his Excellency to Lady Brashleigh, underwent precisely a similar ceremony to that performed by the Captain; of whom, at this juncture, the Major took no kind of notice whatever.

"This, Lady Brashleigh," said his Excellency, "is Major Mims, Ma'am, my military secretary—a most worthy person, I can assure your Ladyship; and one who has highly distinguished himself, as I can affirm from personal knowledge."

Major Mims bowed again, but said nothing.

"Bring dinner, Sirs," said his Excellency, turning to the servants. "My dear Lady Brashleigh," continued he, addressing her Ladyship, "I fear I have kept your Ladyship waiting; but having so little time to remain here, I was desirous, as soon as possible, to present these gentlemen to you, and therefore waited to catch the Major when he came in to dress."

"Your Excellency was extremely kind," said Mims, without moving a muscle of his face; looking as if he were dead and dried, and as if he had rather been in his

grave than where he was.   Captain Macaddle had, on the
arrival of the Major, retired to the extreme edge of the
second window, where he stood waiting to be called into
play.   As for Fanny, she was overcome by wonder :—
the tenderness of manner assumed by her husband before the new comers; the mute respect with which they
appeared to treat both him and her, struck her still more
forcibly ;—he was not like the same individual—he seemed
even to wait her commands, and pause in his proceedings
for *her* decision.

Another thing attracted her attention, and very forcibly
too; which was the excessive ugliness of the two new vi
siters—the one as a *blondin* and the other a *brunet.*
There never had, as she thought, been seen in any one
place, two such hideous persons; and it was not until
they had been in the room for some time, that she com-
prehended whether they were acquainted with each other
or not, for it was not till after Sir Frederick approached
her Ladyship with an endearing air to inquire about her
head, that the two worthies ventured to speak.   When
his Excellency made that movement, they communed together at the other end of the room, with perfect gravity,
and in the softest whispers ; looking as if they expected
every minute that the world would fall into pieces.

Dinner announced; Sir Frederick offered his arm to
Lady Brashleigh, and joked, as they passed along, upon
the old-fashioned customs of men and their wives ; and
Captain Macaddle and Major Mims followed, after having
bowed to each other at the door, for some time, with infinite ceremony.

When they reached the dinner-room, the aide-de-camp
and secretary were posted at the head and foot of the
table ; and Sir Frederick sat on one side, and her Ladyship on the other—a disposition of forces highly acceptable
to Fanny, who was thereby relieved of all embarrassment
as to doing the honours.   Little did her poor unsophisticated Ladyship then imagine that the principal duties of
military secretaries and gallant aides-de-camp, consist in
carving at dinner, and sending round the wine after it !

" Lady Brashleigh, Ma'am, some soup ?" said his Ex-

cellency ; " do, my dear girl ; come, it will do you good :
give her Ladyship some soup, Major."

The Major, with the most solemn air, did as he was bid.
Sir Frederick took soup—so did the staff.

" What wines have you there, Sir ?" said his Excellency
to Binfield the butler.

" Madeira, Sir Frederick,—Hock, Barsac, and Champagne, Sir Frederick !"

" Is the Champagne iced, Sir ?"

" Yes, Sir Frederick."

" Far short," said his Excellency (whose mouth was
filled with soup), addressing Major Mims—" far short, Sir,
does the ice of this country fall of the saltpetre of our
Obdars—ice, Sir, is a very good substitute for saltpetre :
but you cannot cool wine in England, Sir, and that is the
truth of it."

A dead silence followed this observation, and nothing
was heard for some moments but the noise which the uncivilized Captain Macaddle made in eating his soup.
Captain Macaddle apparently was hurrying the operation
in order to help the fish under his charge. His Excellency
saw the dilemma.

" Don't hurry yourself, Captain," said his Excellency ;
" all in good time, Sir. Major, a glass of Madeira after
your soup, Sir ?"

The Major bowed affirmatively, but spake not.

" Your health, Sir," said Sir Frederick.

The Major bowed again, gratefully.

" Lady Brashleigh, shall I give you some turbot," said
Captain Macaddle, in a half whisper, those being the first
words *he* had uttered.

" Her Ladyship don't eat fish, Sir," said his Excellency,
in a tone which indicated that it was not for an aide-de-
camp to presume to ask her. " My love, you will take a
patty in preference, I know :—nobody can eat fish in this
country—they talk, Sir, of their turbot, and their salmon ;
but there is no comparison between those and our fish in
India, Sir."

" None, Sir," said Major Mims, in a whisper.

" Won't your Excellency take any ?" said Macaddle.

" Not I, Sir," replied Sir Frederick ; " I'll take a patty —I cannot manage fish here."

His Excellency took a patty—so did the Major—so did the Captain—and the turbot was removed untouched. In the midst of his Excellency's invective against fish, the Major and Captain discovered that the patties were made of lobster; of course they said nothing.

" A glass of Champagne, Lady Brashleigh?" said his Excellency gallantly.

" I —— ——"

" Oh! Ma'am, I must not be refused," said Sir Frederick ; " give her Ladyship some Champagne, Binfield."

The Champagne was poured out ; handed to the Major and Captain. Fanny was evidently affected by the intense cold ; so decidedly had they chilled it. Captain Macaddle was taken by surprise; and Major Mims, whose teeth were not of the first order, was instantly afflicted with a violent twinge.

" How capital, Sir, that wine would be," said his Excellency, " if it had but been cooled by an Obdar!"

" It—makes a—very great—difference, Sir," said Major Mims, actually crying with pain.

The dinner then proceeded as mutely as it commenced, except that Sir Frederick occasionally made a kind observation to his lady, who occasionally made a reply.   As the feast wore on, his Excellency entered upon a dissertation, touching the merits, or rather demerits of Port wine ; and appealed to the military secretary for a corroboration of his censure upon that powerful and popular liquor.

" I think, Sir," said the Major, scarce opening his lips, and looking as if the fate of an empire depended on the expression of his opinion ; " one glass of Port, Sir, is agreeable after cheese."

" Cheese !" exclaimed his Excellency, " and who, Sir, in the name of decency, ever eats cheese? the sight, the smell, the knowledge that cheese is in the house, makes me sick.   What d'ye mean, Sir, about ' after cheese?'"

At this moment cheeses of sorts were paraded.

" Lady Brashleigh," said his Excellency, " I presume *you* don't eat cheese, Ma'am?"

" Not I," said her Ladyship.

" *I* never eat cheese, Sir," said Captain Macaddle.

" I very seldom taste it," said Major Mims, sighing deeply.

" Jou, Sir," said his Excellency, " take it away !"

And accordingly the cheese disappeared untouched.

The dessert and wine having been put down, his Excel lency, after two or three agreeable compliments to his lady, began to talk ; and continued talking, while the members of his family did little but nod their heads in as- sent to what he said, like Mandarins on a chimney-piece ; until his Excellency finding that Lady Brashleigh evinced no disposition to move, kindly discovered that she looked pale, and would, perhaps, like to retire to the drawing- room, " Whither," said Sir Frederick, " I shall follow your Ladyship shortly."

At this signal, away flew the Major to the door, and the Captain to the bell ;—the Captain scrambled back and picked up her Ladyship's gloves ;—the Major stooped and caught up her Ladyship's pocket-handkerchief ;—his Ex- cellency stood solemnly erect during the ceremony, and the servants lighted her Ladyship to the drawing-room.

As soon as Lady Brashleigh had retired, his Excellency filled a large glass of claret, and drank " The ladies :" after which, he leaned his head on the back of his chair, and fell fast asleep ; from which slumber he awoke after a nap of three quarters of an hour, during which period, neither Mims nor Macaddle had spoken one single word, or stirred one single inch :—the Major having finished the bottle of claret, which stood near him, together with a large plate of wafers; the Captain having swallowed the whole remnant of the dinner-Madeira, and a side-dish of almonds and raisins; for as neither of them dared to move, lest he should arouse the slumbering commander, either determined, like provident cattle, to feed, at least to the length of his tether.

" Captain Macaddle," said his Excellency, stretching himself and yawning into wakefulness, " ring the bell, Sir, and see if her Ladyship has ordered coffee."

Captain Macaddle rang the bell, and when the servant

came, made the inquiry as commanded.   The answer was in the negative.

"Take coffee to the drawing-room, Sir," said Sir Frederick : and up he rose—up rose Major Mims, and up rose Captain Macaddle.

"I'll take one glass more of that claret," said his Excellency.

"Claret, Sir!" repeated the Major in a tone of dismay.

"Or, no! stay—a glass of Madeira, as a *finale*," said his Excellency.

"Madeira, Sir!" said Macaddle, with a look full of horror.

"Where is the wine, Sir?" said Sir Frederick.

"I believe it is finished, Sir," said Macaddle.

"Umph!" said Sir Frederick. "No matter, Sirs; I'll trouble you for the water then, if you please."

Saying which, his Excellency drank some of the pure element ; and without taking the smallest further notice of his staff, opened the door, and proceeded to the drawing-room.

After a short debate, the unhappy satellites agreed to follow their great leader, and accordingly proceeded to the presence of Lady Brashleigh.

During the next half hour, and during the ceremony of drinking coffee, his Excellency remained seated on a sofa next his bride, paying her the most marked and amiable attentions, while Mims and Macaddle remained in a distant window, in the softest possible conversation.   At length it appeared to the poor sufferers that they might possibly get away, and therefore they began to move gradually towards the door.

"Are you going, gentlemen?" said his Excellency.

"Unless you have any further commands, Sir," said Macaddle.

"I have none, to-night," said Sir Frederick ; "but I wish, Macaddle, that to-morrow morning early, you would step down to the Tower, and see the Colonel ; and while you are there, you might just as well go to the London Docks, and get a list of those cases ; and then if you were to come up to the wharf of the Paddington canal, and inquire about the Manchester boats, I think it would be wise. At all events, don't forget to be at Tattersall's to look at the horses at two; and then, as you come back, call at the Horse Guards for an answer to the letter I mentioned; and then, it will not be out of your way to look in at Ransom's, to see if the money be paid in; and if you call there, you can go to the Quadrant and get us an opera-box for Tuesday."

" Yes, Sir Frederick," said Macaddle.

" And Mims," continued his Excellency, " we really must find that man to-morrow, Sir. Put yourself on the top of a coach, Sir, and see about it; there will be no difficulty whatever in finding him; his name is Smith, and he lives somewhere in Buckinghamshire; *that* I know; however, you must contrive to be back in London before dinner; because, although I shall not dine at home, I may have something for you to do in the evening.

" Certainly, Sir," said Mims, bowing.

" Good night, then," said his Excellency.

" Good night, Sir," said the gentlemen.

" Good night, Lady Brashleigh."

" Good night," said her Ladyship, kindly holding out her hand, which the departing functionaries could not well avoid taking; in short, her Ladyship shook hands with both of them good-humouredly, and they disappeared.

Scarcely had the door closed upon them, when the sweet placidity and amiability of his Excellency's countenance suddenly changed to the most furious rage.

" Are you mad, Ma'am?" exclaimed his Excellency " or has the Champagne got into your head, Ma'am?"

" What have I done," said Fanny, " to induce you to think either?"

" Why, Ma'am, you shook hands with those persons," said he.

" Well?"

" Well!—do you consider *who* you are now, and *what* you are?—the lady of his Excellency the Commander-in-chief at Bombay shaking hands with her husband's aide-de-camp, on a first interview!"

" I really was not aware——"

" Aware! how should you be aware, Ma'am?" cried the commander. " In your father's line of life, Ma'am, his usher is as good as himself, and he need not be ashamed of allowing his wife or daughter to shake hands with him; but *I* stand in a very different position, Ma'am. My staff are drilled to know their places, Ma'am; to do their duty, and put up with every inconvenience, even to the swallowing of stale eggs, and eating the drumsticks of turkies; but there is an end of *that*, Ma'am, if such liberties are allowed them as you have been pleased to afford these gentlemen to-night."

" I really——"

" You really, Ma'am, have taken too much Champagne," said his Excellency; " it is a wine you are not used to, and you should not drink it."

" You pressed me, Sir Frederick," said Fanny. " I——"

" Pressed you!" cried he. " So you allow a man to prevail with you if he press you, Ma'am! Umph—you should have refused—I did not wish *my* people to see what sort of person you are; nor did I choose to lecture you upon the different qualities of wine before my servants; but I was surprised to see you drink so much of it."

" I am extremely sorry," said Fanny; " another time I shall know better: I——"

" No, you won't know better, Ma'am," said Sir Frederick; " there are no rules without exceptions—there are no fixed principles for conduct in civilized society, Ma'am. You will see persons at *my* table with whom you *must* drink wine if you are asked: there are times and seasons when one thing ought to be done, and times and seasons when another thing ought to be done; we must consider our station and dignity, Ma'am, or else what do we live for?"

" I am sure, Sir Frederick, I had no intention——"

" Intention, Ma'am!" said his Excellency, his face absolutely crimson with rage; " what has intention to do with it? what difference does it make to me, whether my bungalow is burnt by a knave or a fool? my loss is the same."

" I really do not understand," said Fanny.

" I am sure you don't, Ma'am," interrupted Sir Frede-rick; " therefore I must instruct you. What must those men think; where must they imagine you to have been bred; whence to have come; how to have been educated? b..t I am not angry, Ma'am, I am only vexed and morti-fied—you must be more cautious for the future."

A short calm succeeded this storm, and Fanny was by this time sufficiently aware of his Excellency's disposi-tion, to know that an escape would best be effected during a *lull;* she therefore expressed her desire to go to rest.

" Certainly, Ma'am, by all means," said his Excel-lency; " I quite forgot you had been travelling, Ma'am. I conclude you will wish to write to your family to-mor-row: if you get your letters ready early in the day, I will see and get them franked."

" Her Ladyship's woman, Sir," said his Excellency to the servant who answered the bell.

" I have much writing to get through myself," conti-nued his Excellency to his bride, " and shall not get to bed for some time; however, go you, and I have no doubt sleep will set you all to rights; and to-morrow *perhaps,* I may present you to my daughter-in-law."

" I shall be extremely happy to make her acquaint-ance," said Fanny, with something more like firmness of manner than was usual in her deportment; as if she felt, considering their relative positions, that if her dig-nity *were* to be maintained, it ought to be maintained towards her husband's relations, as well as towards his dependents.

Her Ladyship's maid having arrived, her Ladyship re-tired; and his Excellency, having called for the undigni-fied beverage in which he nocturnally indulged after all observers were gone; namely, brandy-and-water, betook himself to writing and sipping alternately, in which mingled pursuits he remained until past two o'clock,

when, overcome by drowsiness, he glided slily and softly
to bed.

And this day was the day upon which Welsted attended
church at Hackney with the Tickles, partook of the homely
roasted beef and puddings of the numerous establishment;
and, after tea (and prayers) was furnished by Harriet
Tickle with the corroborating testimony of the " Fashionable Magazine" itself, to prove that Lord and Lady Farnborough were the unhappiest pair upon earth; that the
exemplary Lord Feversham was a sot and a gambler;
and that his unaffected and accomplished sisters were two
of the veriest wantons in creation. Welsted, notwithstanding this potent authority, still had faith in his own
eyes and ears, and stoutly maintained the fight against
the young lady, who was ready to vouch for the veracity of
her statements, in which she was supported by her father;
who, although he knew nothing of the truth of the story,
implicitly believed it upon the general principle which he
uniformly maintained, that as to the nobility it was too
true, not only that bad were the best, but that those
who ought to be the best were decidedly the worst.

And after the conclusion of this evening, after the tur-
moils and sorrows that both Francis and Fanny underwent; separated from each other, and either ignorant
where the other was—what happened to both? At the
same hour they both retired to rest; Fanny's first thought,
when she closed her eyes, was of Francis; and the first
thought of Francis, when he laid his head upon his pillow
was of Fanny.

CHAPTER XII.

Oh, where is the honour safe? not with the living ;
They feed upon opinions, errors. dreams,
And make them truths ; — they draw a nourishment
Out of defamings ; grow upon disgraces ;
And when they see a virtue fortified
Strongly, above the battery of their tongues,
Oh ! how they cast to sink it !—

BEAUMONT.

IF the proceedings of the first evening had excited
feelings in Welsted's mind diametrically opposed to admiration or respect for the family in which he was domesticated, the operations of the first day (and that too a
Sunday), most assuredly did not tend to weaken the impression previously made ; and his thoughts, after having
rested on his beloved for a certain period, wandered (as
they naturally might) to his own condition. It was true,
he was only *on trial*, as it were, in his present situation ;
but of what utility to him would be a change, what advantage was he likely to reap in any similar office, in any
other academy, that did not offer themselves here? Indeed, in the *scholastic* world, Mr. Tickle's was considered a most eligible house for a young man who wanted
an assistant's *place ;* there was always plenty to eat and
drink, a comfortable bed-room, agreeable society, and
forty pounds per annum ; but these, to poor Francis,
were not such allurements as they would have been to
many of his brethren of the birch, and *that*, which to
most of them would have appeared the greatest temptation, namely, the " lively society of the young ladies,"
served, under *his* circumstances, and with his present
feelings, rather as an alloy to the more substantial advantages of the situation.

The ladies, mother and daughters, with a pertinacity
and taste peculiar to their class of life, seemed deter-

mined, whenever an opportunity offered, to recur to the sore subject of the Farnborough family, thinking it, what *they* called *prime* fun, to worry a good-tempered man upon the only topic which was likely to put him out of humour ; this was what the Hackney wags called " getting a *rise* out of him ;" the meaning of which expression is to me unintelligible, and can only be furnished, I presume, by persons in the habit of using it.

It must be confessed, however, that Tickle himself, whose pale face and beetle brows, and sharp aquiline nose, and scrubby head, proclaimed the thorough-paced hard-going radical ; far from appearing displeased with their constant allusions to the Farnboroughs, to Welsted's knowledge of them, and to the folly and vice of the aristocracy in general, followed up the playfulnesses of the female part of the family with more serious denunciations and assertions, and generally wound up the discussions as the Matador puts the finishing stroke to the already bleeding victim of the lighter efforts of the Picadores and Torreadores who have preceded him. The Spanish bull would have had one advantage which the English usher had not : when once the fatal blow was given, there would have been an end of the contest ; after having been cut up, he would have been quietly stewed down into soups or olios, and his torments would have found their termination long before the next day's dinner-hour. Not so poor Francis, for each attack seemed fiercer than the last ; and from the innumerable anecdotes and illustrations adduced by the Misses, it seemed, really, as if they had *read up* to the subject between their meals, in order to display their own eloquence and information, and merit the praises of their levelling parent, by beating down the modest yet firm vindicator of his superiors.

After Monday's repast, an allusion was made to some paragraph in the newspapers, and, as usual, the heroines flew to arms, and became so pointed—pointed I can hardly call it, for the performance was too clumsy to deserve such a character—so abusive, not only of their betters, but of those who had the good taste to espouse their cause, that Welsted, the amiable Welsted, could bear it no longer, and turned round upon his assailants in terms which, if neither polite nor prudent, were at least justifiable, and richly merited by those to whom they were applied. This show of resistance startled Mrs. Tickle, whose vulgar mind was incompetent to the noble art of defence; and who, in her self-importance, was led to consider any opposition to her dictum in *that* house, little short of treason. Tickle took fire at the flame of his wife's anger, and a scene ensued.

"Mr. Welsted," said the pedagogue, "I must beg— nay, Sir, I must insist upon it, that such objectionable topics are not brought forward at my table—and, above all, not argued in such highly reprehensible terms ;—I tell you once for all, Sir, that our principles are diametrically opposite ;—I hate and despise the adventitious advantages of rank ; they are invidious and odious; they are derived from no personal merit, but merely because the last blockhead was father to the present one :—my children have been brought up in the same creed, and as I do not wish them to be converted, I shall thank you to apply your eloquence to some other subject; for although I am convinced they have too much good sense to waver in opinions founded not only upon filial duty, but upon an attentive observation of life and its occurrences, still, Sir, the arguing of such matters is extremely unpleasant. I am, Sir, and I am not ashamed to own it, an advocate for liberty,—I may say, equality ; and I despise the over weening power of authority by which one class of people is permitted to domineer over another, merely because their relative situations in life are different."

"Sir," said Welsted, " I——"

"Sir," said the advocate of liberty and free discussion, "I make it a rule never to allow myself to be *answered* by any of my establishment : without maintaining this sort of deference to the head of a house like *this*, business could not be carried on.

"Perhaps, in explanation," said Welsted, "I might be permitted to say ——"

"Nothing, Mr. Welsted, nothing," repeated Tickle, "I lay down rules, and they must be obeyed; I have ven my opinion of such conduct, and as it is quite right we should understand each other in the outset, let that suffice. We are all lords—of the creation ; and though the king can make a duke, he cannot make a classical scholar by any patent or charter which he has it in his power to bestow—therefore a truce with discussion, for *that* I cannot suffer ; let us drop the business, and change the subject by drinking our noble selves."

" There, Mr. Welsted, what d'ye think of *that* ?" said Mrs. Tickle, glorying in the defeat of the young courtier, as she called him.

" Madam," said Welsted, " I am perfectly contented."

" Ah, now," said Mrs. Tickle to the girls, " now that's very handsome,—very proper indeed—your health, Mr. W."

And thus the party broke up for afternoon business, and Welsted repaired to his duties, determined that more than the month of probation, he would not remain under the roof of a friend of liberty and the freedom of discussion, who refused to hear reason, or listen to any thing likely to overturn his own principles or repel his own propositions.

While the labours of the day were in progress, while Dixon was superintending the writing class who were copying " Virtue is the only nobility," in all sorts of hands, while Tickle was thundering forth, with powerful emphasis, so that Welsted might catch the sound even in his place,

> " Equitis quoque jam migravit ab aure voluptas
> Omnis, ad incertos oculos et gaudia vana;"

and while Francis himself was assiduously employed in correcting exercises touching the blessings of liberty ; the maid-servant, to whom reference has before been made, entered the school-room, and whispered Mr. Welsted that he was wanted. " Who is it?" said Welsted. " A gentleman, Sir." " Desire him to wait," said Welsted ; " I will be down directly." The maid disappeared, and Welsted quite determined not to subject himself to the reproaches of his superior, so shortly after his arrival, and their recent difference, continued his avocations until he had gone through the class, and his time for quitting school for the afternoon arrived.

Meanwhile his visiter had been ushered into the parlour, in which the lady of the house and her daughters were laudably pursuing the mysteries of modern work, which they performed in precisely the same way as their betters, by cutting long slips of muslin, and hemming them, and shutting them up in boxes; and in twisting silk on bits of cards cut star-wise, and in following with the needle little ill-designed inky devices, with the loan of which, some amiable friend had obliged them, and which they had undertaken to copy without the smallest notion of drawing. The Misses Tickle, however, were better supplied than the ordinary run of plebeians; for Stevens had been pattern-drawer to the family, who duly appreciated his designs, and continued, as perhaps we may find in the sequel, to carry on the work which he had begun before his departure, even now that he was gone.

In this circle, however, much to his amusement, was Welsted's friend (whoever he might be) domesticated, and during the three quarters of an hour which he had passed in the society of the happy family, had contrived to ingratiate himself wonderfully with Mrs. Tickle and Harriet. Elizabeth's heart was not hers to give, but her Ma' had determined in her own mind that she had never seen so genteel and charming a gentleman; and as for the second daughter, her eyes spoke plainly, in the Hackney and hackneyed language of their society, her favourable opinion of the person and manners of the handsome stranger.

Elizabeth, whose affections, as I have just said, were not her own, was nevertheless as much stricken as her sister; in short, they had never seen such a visiter under their roof; and although, perhaps, it was done more platonically, Elizabeth quite as particular as Harriet, examined the new-comer, with mingled curiosity and admiration; there was a newness, and a brilliancy, and a freshness in his countenance, his air, and his dress, a perfect ease and good nature; in short, there was *that*, which nothing but conscious superiority and constant intercourse with the best society can possibly give. He entertained them with news of all sorts, flattered the mother, complimented the daughters, and gravely volunteered himself as silk-holder, while Miss Harriet (who did not in the slightest degree appear to dislike the trouble of placing it, in the first instance, over his hands) wound off, I know not how many skeins.

In the midst of this operation, the parlour door opened, and Welsted entered.

" Stop, my dear Welsted," said his friend; " don't speak, I cannot shake hands with you until this young lady has quite done with me."

Harriet's eyes flashed triumphantly at the idea of Welsted's perceiving how securely she had entangled his handsome friend.

" Why, in the name of wonder," said Welsted, " who would have thought of seeing you here, and thus employed!"

" Don't interrupt business," said his friend : " what is life without labour? and the labour we delight in," continued he, looking expressly at Miss Harriet, as the poet says, " physics pain."

" There, Harriet, now have done," said Mrs. Tickle; " I dare say the gentleman and Mr. Welsted have something better to talk of than a piece of green silk."

" Allow me, Madam," said Welsted to Mrs. Tickle, " to present to you Lord Feversham, the son of the Earl of Farnborough, whom you were saying you remembered last year at Worthing."

" Sir !" said Mrs. Tickle, jumping from her chair—in which evolution she was followed by her daughters— " Lord Feversham—dear me, my Lord !" said she, curtseying to the very ground—" I hope you will excuse us —really if I had known, my Lord—Lord bless me, my Lord !—your Lordship must have thought us very rude."

" Rude, my dear Ma'am," said Feversham ; " why rude? you treated me kindly and hospitably; and my fair friend made use of me, for which I am greatly obliged to her ; and as for names, unless men were to walk about the streets with labels round their necks, like decanters on a dinner table, who is to know them?"

"My Lord," said Harriet, actually pale with fear, at the familiarity with which she had previously treated Feversham; "your Lordship—really I——

"Excuse it!" cried Feversham, "my dear young lady, I should not have the slightest objection to serve an apprenticeship to so indulgent a mistress."

"My love," said Mrs. Tickle to Elizabeth, "run and tell your papa, that his Lordship is here—make hase, girl." •

"Yes, ma'," and away ran or rather flew Elizabeth.

"You don't remember seeing this young lady at Worthing, last year?" said Welsted.

"I was not there," said Feversham; "the Countess was there, because my sister Maria was advised to try sea-bathing; but it was a great nuisance, because my father and mother, who are mighty old-fashioned folks, and cannot endure being separated, were unable to be there together,—the Earl was obliged to be almost entirely in London."

Welsted's eyes travelled towards those of Mrs. Tickle and her daughter, who had so warmly censured the domestic differences of the "old-fashioned couple,"—and the ladies were quite conscious of the glance and its meaning.

"But," continued Feversham, "my dear fellow, why did you not write to us before you removed hither—I had no conception you would have been off so soon—you know Lady Brashleigh is in town?"

"Fanny!" said Welsted, "what, already?"

"I saw Sir Frederick yesterday, in a travelling carriage, as I was riding through the Park," said his Lordship, "and with him a young lady, looking pale and fatigued, so I concluded it was her Ladyship, else I confess I should not have recognised her."

At this period Mr. Tickle made his appearance and was presented to the nobleman, who received him with all that frankness and cordiality which characterised his general conduct; the cringing schoolmaster loaded his

14

Lordship with the most servile attentions, and apologized for the remissness of the servant in not informing *him* that somebody wanted to see Mr. Welsted, as he should have instantly relieved him from his duty.

Welsted was anxious now to get Feversham out of the circle, but hardly knew how to propose it, for the novelty of the scene amused the Viscount, and he continued giving an account of a party at which he had been, after the Saturday's Opera (the day of his return to town), which was music to the ears of the girls, who heard matters discussed familiarly, of which they had no notion, but from distant report, or upon hearsay evidence.

" I stayed excessively late," said Feversham, " for *me*— we are such sober, regular, good sort of people, in our family, that we really make it out, best in the country, and I verily believe I should have been later still, had not some foolish fellow proposed play, which instantly drove me off; I have made it a rule, since I knew right from wrong, never to touch card or dice, and the moment I see preparations for such sort of sport, I am off."

Welsted's eye again fell upon the countenances of the family group, and the look was again understood.

" But," continued Lord Feversham, " talking of the Opera, I have brought my friend Welsted the tickets for my mother's box for to-morrow; her Ladyship is gone out of town, and the season is near its close; I thought, as I knew there were ladies in your family, Mr. Tickle, they might be acceptable, and if it be not contrary to all the rules of your establishment, Welsted will show you the way to our box; he has been there before, and the tickets are quite at your service."

" My Lord," said Mrs. Tickle, " really your Lordship is——"

" Indeed, my Lord," said Mr. Tickle, " really your Lordship is——"

" Oh, dear," said Harriet, " how very kind of his Lordship."

" Isn't it ?" said Elizabeth, " Oh, Lord !—my Lord !"

And they proceeded to overwhelm him with vulgar and

awkward acknowledgments, until in order to escape the persecution of their civility, and enjoy a few minutes' conversation with his friend, Feversham, accompanied by Welsted, beat a retreat into the drawing-room.

"Hav'n't I done right?" said Feversham, as Welsted shut the door, "I thought it might, perhaps, please your friends to give them the box."

"Quite right, my dear Lord," said Welsted, "and I am very much obliged to you; but you are by no means aware of the prelude to your visit, nor shall I worry you with it now, but some other time it may make you laugh, —I hear the Earl is appointed to the Postmaster General- ship."

"The Postmaster Generalship!" exclaimed Feversham. "Not he, my dear Francis; where might you have heard such a story as that? he is appointed ambassador to France, which to him, and particularly to my sisters, is, as you may easily believe, a much pleasanter thing; and one of the objects of my visit to this place, which, by-the-by, I discovered with considerable difficulty, is to say that his Lordship wishes for half an hour's conversation with you upon a subject which is of importance to his Lordship, to me, and to yourself; as I am in training for diplomacy, I say no more, nor would it be fair at the moment; but if you will contrive to dine with us on Sunday (we have fixed *that* as a good day for *you*), some sort of carriage shall be sent for you here, and sent back with you at night —it is a proposal, I tell you—not, perhaps, worth your notice, but to *me*, your acceptance of it will be highly gra- tifying. You are entered at Oxford," said his Lordship, "I believe?"

"Entered!" said Welsted, "more then entered; I am sorry the fact of my having taken my Bachelor's degree has been so long lost upon your Lordship—for all of which advantages I am indebted to my excellent friend Rodney, who placed me, in every respect, in the position of his son; and I am now of the same standing as poor William Rodney would have been, had he lived."

"That is even better than I expected," said Feversham; "but I must say, as to Rodney, even to *you*, his general

kindness seems to have failed in the match he has made
for his daughter; there can be no happiness there; and
though saying so may seem cruel, under the circumstances, I never saw any human being look more jaded,
or more perfectly woe-begone, than she, whom I took for
her Ladyship yesterday; by the way, you have got a
good, fine girl in *this* house."

"Which do you mean?" said Welsted.

"Not *my* friend,—the silk-winder," said the Viscount,
"the sober, sad, and serious one; upon my honour, if she
were but a little better set up, and knew what to do with
herself, she would light up uncommonly well; there are
many of the Almack's girls who would give half their por-
tions for such a pair of eyes as hers."

"Pray," said Welsted, "let me ask you a question—
you must not be offended."

"Offended with you, Welsted?"

"Well then, have you, by any accident, ever heard of
a book called, 'The Fashionable Magazine, or High Life
exposed?'" said Welsted.

"Heard of it! to be sure," said Lord Feversham;
"that is the book in which our family is so agreeably disposed of—don't you know the secret?"

"Not I," said Welsted.

"About two years since," said Feversham, "one of our
footmen was caught by the under butler, stealing spoons
and forks, and my father not choosing to involve himself
in the elaborate troubles of a criminal prosecution, informed
him that he was aware of his practices, and dismissed him
his service—of course without a character; in less than
three months we know he was concerned in an attempt at
a burglary, made on the pantry window, which failed, and
we heard no more of him for some time; till we discovered
him to be the editor of the work in question, which I am
told has a large sale, and extensive circulation, and in
which, in order to repay my father's lenity, he has libelled
and caricatured his Lordship and our family, through
thick and thin; but it makes no difference, for, of course,
nobody believes such scurrility, and therefore it *can* do
no harm."

It was not worth while, just at that moment, to undeceive the Viscount, as to the effect produced by falsehoods
and calumnies regularly and incessantly persisted in, in
print; it was sufficient for Welsted to arm himself with an
unanswerable answer, if ever he was again attacked upon
the subject by the Tickles. Had he known human nature
generally, or the class of howling liberty-boys in particular, he would not have taken this trouble. It was now
perfectly needless. The stubborn, high-spirited, independent Briton (such as Tickle professed himself), who
rails and blusters at his betters, and thinks it the birthright
of an Englishman to be discontented, and to proclaim his
discontent at every possible opportunity; is, when the
test is applied, the most fawning sycophant upon the face
of the earth; nay, whenever that portion of the political
world, which is addicted to radicalism and foul linen, can
flatter, or wheedle, or terrify, or induce, by any other
means, an aristocrat to join their ranks, their joy is boundless and unmixed; and the lordling, who would have been
stigmatized as an ass, or a tyrant, had he maintained his
proper station in society, the moment he joins the motley
herd below him, is hailed as combining in his precious
person, first-rate natural talents, with every accomplishment necessary to give full force to his virtuous exertions.

The young ladies, who were no politicians, had assumed
the censorship of the nobility, I presume upon *moral considerations;* but the mother, who thought it "knowing"
to follow her betters while she ridiculed them; aimed at
political par.isanship, in the circles of Mare-street and
Bethnal-green; and set wild by the appointment she had
received of secretary to a female Bible society (for so ano-
malous were her proceedings, that while she ran down the
State with all her might, she professed to uphold the
Church with the most furious zeal), she always took the
lead in any public subscription amongst her associates;
and so general was her liberality, and so confused her notions of right and wrong, that while she was advocating
with her purse and tongue the dissemination of the Scriptures, she was subscribing for the relief of an imprisoned
atheist; and while abstaining from the consumption of

West Indian sugar, to save the poor blacks in the colonies, strongly maintained the necessity of sending naughty individuals of her own sex to the tread-mill in England.

But she, and all that were hers, were at first dazzled by the appearance, won by the manner, and were finally so overcome by the attention and kind offers of the young lord. As to his dissipation, *that* clearly could not be true, said one; as to his eyesight, said another, never were eyes brighter, or fuller of expression; as for affectation, he had none, said a third; and the father of the flock wound up the general commendation, by expressing a belief that his Lordship was an exception to the general rule, the very phœnix of the peerage, and that, for once, the editor of the "Fashionable Magazine, or High Life exposed," evidently must have been mistaken.

" It is not only his Lordship's kindness about the opera-box," said Tickle to his better half—" *that* is amazingly good-natured, but it is the connexion, my dear. What a thing to have hit upon, to get this Welsted here! Now, girls, you see the folly of laughing at people before you know them."

" Well, for *my* part," said Mrs. Tickle, "I really thought, when he said he knew the Lord's family, he was telling tantaradiddles."

" So did I," said Elizabeth, in a whisper.

" But you see you are wrong, young ladies," said Tickle; " and now let me, once for all, beg you to mend your manners to Mr. Welsted; he is a most gentlemanly young man; and consider, as I say, the connexion; this young nobleman will marry, and of course have a family; his children may in time come to Montgomery-place Academy,—who knows? and though I hate nobility in general, this Lord is such a very different person from any Lord I have ever seen before, and—"

What more Mr. Tickle might have intended to add in the way of praise to the already unusual quantity he had devoted to Feversham's person, manner, and qualities, I know not, for Welsted and his Lordship returned to the parlour to take leave of the family; which opportunity his Lordship seized to say, that he hoped it would not break in upon Mr. Tickle's arrangements to spare his friend on the following Sunday.

" Not in the least, my Lord," said Tickle ; " whenever your Lordship, or the noble Earl your Lordship's noble father, wishes to see my young and excellent friend (if Mr. Welsted will permit me to call him so) I shall be but too happy to deprive myself of the pleasure of his society."

" Will your Lordship take anything ?" said Mrs. Tickle.

" Nothing, I thank you," said Feversham ; " I must ride fast to get back in time to dress for dinner."

" I find, my Lord," said Tickle, smirkingly, " that the noble Earl, your Lordship's father, is about to join the administration."

" What !" exclaimed Feversham, " Lord Farnborough ! in what capacity, pray ?"

" Postmaster General, we heard, my Lord," said Tickle.

Indeed !" said the Viscount, " News travels fast and strangely."

" I hope, my Lord," said Tickle, " I have not prematurely broached the subject ; I was not aware——"

" Pray make no apologies," replied the Viscount, "none are necessary ; only that I assure you, however you may have obtained the information, it is wholly without foundation.'?

" Dear me !" said Tickle—" that is very strange. My usher, my Lord, saw it in the newspaper only the night before last."

" That is extremely probable," said Feversham ; " and if you knew the glorious ignorance of facts, in which the newspaper-mongers in general live in this great town, and the perfect facility with which, by a dash of the pen, a plausible falsehood (always at the command of an inventive journalist) can supply the place of real information, you would not be surprised that an editor should occasionally send a cripple fox-hunting, convert an elegant and accomplished equerry into a weather-beaten veteran ; burn a countess to death in the North, before she had admitted fires into her boudoir ; marry a couple who have never been introduced ; or appoint a nobleman to an office in the government which never was intended for him, and which, I can assure you (in the present instance at all events) he would not have accepted had it been offered."

" Dear me!" said Tickle, " that is very strange."

" Not more strange than true," said Feversham ; " but I must be away, it is getting late ; indeed time flew so swiftly while I was under that young lady's commands, that I hardly guessed the hour—so good morning,—I hope in the course of to-morrow evening to pay my respects ; till when, adieu ! "

The whole family rose ; one flew to the bell, another to the door, and the girls to the windows ; the grenadier housemaid darted across the fore-court, armed with the key of the great gate, which speedily creaked upon its hinges as his Lordship and Welsted paced the stone pavement thereunto leading. Tickle remained uncovered on the steps of the house, and the ladies stood gazing at the nobleman in hopes of one " last lingering look behind." They were, however, disappointed, and in a few minutes the gate was reclosed, and the inmates of the house preparing for the family tea.

Those who are skilled in human nature, and have studied minds, I should think, need not be told the subject of the ladies' conversation after his Lordship's departure. Should there be a doubt remaining, it will surely vanish, when I say, that neither of the Misses Tickle had ever been to an opera. The very tickets became objects of curiosity. A Countess's name inscribed upon her own property was to them a wonder. Indeed, such was the anxiety with which the belles sought information upon all points connected with the important subject, that Welsted, who did not on the one hand choose to commit himself by giving wrong intelligence, and, on the other, disliked the idea of betraying his ignorance, was nearly overcome ; for so great a change had been wrought in the opinions of the young ladies, by the occurrences of the afternoon, that Francis was no longer chilled with icy looks, no longer listened to with indifference, no longer helped to tea ungraciously ; he was now " dear Mr. Welsted," and was entreated not to eat *this*

and drink *that*, with an earnestness extremely prevalent
in those circles, where feeding seems to be the sole source
of pleasure, and forcing food down a man's throat the
very *acmé* of politeness.

But when the morrow came, and wore away, the
anxious hearts of the young ladies really palpitated, and
they felt that aching sensation, that nervous restlessness,
which persons of sanguine constitutions and glowing
imaginations are apt to endure on the eve of any great
and interesting event. . A glass-coach was hired for the
occasion ; the multifarious ringlets destined to grace the
young ladies' heads, burst not from their paper buds, but
clustered round their faces in their proper papillotes, even
at the dinner-table ; and every sort of exertion was used
by the damsels, to render themselves as much like the
people with whom they were to be associated as nature
would allow ; although it must be admitted that Gothic
towers would not worse assimilate with a Grecian temple,
than the belles of Montgómery place, with the frequenters
of the first tier of opera boxes.

Mr. Tickle declined being of the party, therefore one
ticket was yet to spare, and even the family under discussion had sufficient tact to leave its disposal to Welsted ;
it is true, the young ladies ventured to recommend two or
three candidates, particularly Miss Harriet, who suggested
that Mr. Biddle was a remarkably genteel young man ;—
however, the proposition was overruled ; he was employed in the post-office, and could not get home in
time ; Mr. Kidney, a *very* nice gentlemanly lad, was also
suggested by the younger sister ; but alas ! ineffectually ;
Elizabeth "named no names," she merely sighed and
thought how much Stevens would have liked such a party,
but even *she*, stricken as she was with Cupid's dart, consoled herself prudently and philosophically for the absence
of her beloved, by the reflection that had *he* been in the
way, Welsted would not have been at the academy, and
then there would have been no opera-box to go to.

Welsted determined in his own mind, very soon after
Tickle had declined going, who should be the fifth of the
party, and I dare say my readers will not be long in

guessing that the honour was designed for poor Monsieur
Ronfleur; to *him*, a gentleman, and a man of the world,
it would be doubtlessly agreeable, and he was, moreover,
unlikely to .commit any of those dreadful solecisms of
which it was by no means improbable that either Mr.
Biddle or Mr. Kidney, in conjunction with the young
ladies, might be unconsciously guilty; and therefore,
founding his request to Mr. Tickle on the acknowledged
leisure of the French master in the evenings, Welsted first
consulted his principal, and under his sanction offered the
ticket to Monsieur, who meant to express his feelings at
length in words—but nature had done more for him in
the way of eloquence, than art; his eyes spoke his gratitude for the kindness of his new acquaintance, and the
old gentleman, who had been for years the constant
object of the young ladies' ridicule, for once found himself
again addressed in the language of kindness, and with an
offer of civility.

The Misses were disappointed at the decision : but such
was the influence which the new usher had suddenly
obtained, that, seeing the different example set, they began
to feel ashamed of their past conduct ; and when Monsieur
Ronfleur appeared at a quarter before seven o'clock, in
the parlour, ready to attend the ladies, handsomely dressed,
his hair well powdered, and his coat decorated with the
cross of Saint Louis, they were startled ; even Welsted
could not help feeling surprise, not unmingled with
pleasure, at the extraordinary versatility of Ronfleur's
character—the humble, quiet, French teacher, slovenly
and almost dirty in his appearance, no sooner was called
into his proper sphere of action, than like the worn
warrior at the trumpet's sound, he rallied from the indifference which his sorrows (lightly as they weighed upon
him) induced, and he came to his place in society, the
gay, the gallant, and the finished gentleman.

When the girls appeared, dressed, Welsted was considerably alarmed—but not for the reasons he had anticipated—he expected to find them not sufficiently ornamented for the part of the theatre to which they were
going; but when he beheld them ten thousand times finer

and more gay than the lovely creatures, whose entrance
into the drawing-room in Grosvenor-square, attired for a
similar visit, was strong upon his recollection, he began
to be apprehensive that they had *overdone it;* but his
feelings upon this point were beggared by those resulting
from the *tout ensemble* of Mrs. Tickle herself, who had
exerted all her skill, and expended almost all the finery of
her wardrobe, to do honour to the scene ;—a yellow and
blue striped silk gown (with a pink stomacher), trimmed
and flounced with three rows of gauze, looped up in fes-
toons ; a yellow silk turban with a preposterous plume of
scarlet feathers, so arranged as to admit of the exhibition
of a tarnished bandeau, adorned her head ; all her neck-
laces were laid round her neck, and all her rings decorated
her fingers ; an imitation shawl reticule, as large as a moderate *sac de nuit*, containing, as Welsted presumed,
pocket-handkerchiefs for the party, hung upon her arm ;
her hair, which according to the established principle of
meum and *tuum* was indisputably her own, was ringletted
more carefully and minutely than that of either of the
girls ; a sort of palampore covered part of her shoulders,
beneath which a large patterned silk scarf was seen in all
its flaunting gaiety ; over all of which, it being then July,
she wore a French grey cloak, lined with sky-blue silk.

This combination of colours, in the full glare of sunshine, which unfortunately betrayed the fact that art had
supplied the rose which nature had withdrawn from her
cheek, was, it must be owned, terrific. Welsted, however
much a novice in London finery (although he unluckily
had formed his judgment upon a comparison which he in-
stituted in his mind between the families of Farnborough
and Tickle), still ventured to imagine that in the theatre,
and by candlelight, the glaring effect might be somewhat
subdued, and thus lived on, in hope : as for the girls
there really was very little to find fault with them ; they
were, it is true, like the Poet's morning, "rosy fingered,"
and the healthy hue of their hands pervading their arms,
afforded a contrast to the tightly-strained white kid gloves,
which only half covered them, somewhat more striking
than agreeable.

All dressed as they were, they all drank hot tea in the sunshine, which Tickle was amiable enough himself to make; upon which occasion the facetious Mr. Dixon observed, that it was not surprising to see the ladies so beautifully dressed, considering "that Mr. Tickle was a *man tea* maker," a joke which actually convulsed Mrs. Tickle, who did not in the smallest degree comprehend it, and made her husband, who did, very nearly angry; such was the sensitiveness of the leveller upon the important point of subordination.

"Why, Mounsheer," said Tickle, "I never saw you wear that cross before,—what is it?"

"It is the Croix de Saint Louis," said Ronfleur, "I receive him from my King—Louis Seize—I declare—ah!"

"Doesn't Seize mean sixteen, Mounsheer?" said Tickle.

"Oui—yes—I declare," said Ronfleur, bowing.

"Why, then, that was he that they guillotined," said Tickle.

"Oui," said Ronfleur, bowing again, silently, evidently not wishing to excite Mr. Tickle upon the subject.

"Good job too, I think," said Tickle.

"Good!" said Ronfleur, with something like agitation, for which this was no time; mingled with anger, for which Mr. Tickle's house was no place.

"Mr. Tickle doubtlessly thinks it good, Mr. Ronfleur," interrupted Welsted, "because, had there been no revolution in France, he would not have the advantage of your services here."

"Ha," said Ronfleur, and he paused a moment, holding his snuff-box perfectly still—then shaking his head, he placed his hand affectionately on Welsted's arm, which he patted thrice, and, sighing, said earnestly, "Thank you, Sir,—thank you."

The tea was hurried, and the ladies all ran up stairs just to look at themselves; and Welsted and Ronfleur being left alone, Ronfleur asked him whether he saw any objection to his wearing the order which had attracted so much notice in the family. Welsted was not likely to be a very good adviser on such a point, but he declared he saw no possible reason why he should not.

"I tell you, my friend," said Ronfleur, "I not wear my cross here—I am poor man—I am in my shop—ha, ha, I declare—but when I am in my Lord Farnbro's box, I am in my place, and I wear to the honour of his Lordship, and of you, dat mark of my poor King's bonté, which himself give to me."

It being clear that Ronfleur was perfectly right in his views, and the ladies having set all their finery in order, the young ones having, *entre nous,* followed the example of their mother and "tinged their cheeks with red," the party stepped into the coach. Ronfleur volunteered to go on the box with the coachman, rather than crowd the ladies, but his offer was kindly overruled, and the belles occupied one side of the vehicle, and Welsted and Ronfleur the other : Tickle saw them off, and after due caution about cold, and handkerchiefs, and wrapping up, and many other important points, away went the happy quintette to the King's Theatre in the Haymarket.

Arrived at the splendid terminus of their journey, the party were soon seated in the Countess's box, where (since the reader has already been to the opera with Welsted, in the course of this story), I shall leave them till the end of the performance, which excited by turns their admiration, laughter, simpering, and dread ; nor were the criticisms of dress, in which the party indulged themselves, the least interesting features of the memorable evening. Ronfleur was all gaiety and pleasantry ; he discussed the merits of the elder Vestris, and the Hillisbergs and Theodores, with the fluency and tact of a *mâitre de danse,* proclaiming, as persons who speak on theatrical matters invariably do, the dreadful falling off in performers and performances, since his younger days.

It is curious enough, that these grumblers forget that by this constant succession of degradations from the days of Quin and Cibber, Pinkethman and Booth, the art and mystery of acting must, in the course of another century, fall utterly into disrepute, never remembering that the difference so perceptible to *them,* arises from the difference in their own eyes, and dispositions to be pleased ; a truth easily ascertained, if they would only condescend to re-collect that their fathers told *them* precisely the same things of the actors of *their* day, and consequently sati-rized and censured by similar comparisons the performers, which *they*, in their turn, now declare to have been so much superior to the present race, which, doubtlessly, will in its turn be referred to by *us*, in *our* old age, with similar disadvantage to the race to come.   Whatever Monsieur Ronfleur remembered of dancers, certain it is, that during the evening in question, he never once recollected his murdered wife, his lost child, his forfeited rank, or his devastated property ; he laughed and chatted, was full of gaiety and anecdote, and no more resembled the French Master at Montgomery-place Academy, than an Irish labourer resembles an Irish Lord.

To Welsted's unsophisticated mind, and who was by no means aware of the vast heinousness of the offence, the fact, that Mrs. Tickle at the end of the opera produced from her huge reticule two large paper bags filled with gooseberries and currants, of which the whole party (not excepting, I fear, my hero himself) partook, was not so distressing as to any man of the world it could not have failed to be ; his apprehensions and alarm were, however, excited, somewhat too late, when Feversham, who made a point of visiting his old friend and new acquaintances, stepped upon some of the discarded coats of the gigantic Lancashire gooseberries, and immediately began to censure and ridicule the appearance of such vegetable produc-tions in his lady-mother's box ; until he perceived, by the distress evident in the countenances of its present tenants, that they had been actually guilty of the irreme-diable offence.   He changed the subject the moment he was assured that they were really the culprits ; but the manner in which Welsted heard him, after he left them, direct the box-keeper to take special care to have the filth properly removed, with a sort of explanation, which his Lordship felt obliged to make, even to the servant of the theatre, touching the slightness of his acquaintance with the criminals, soon convinced Welsted, that to raise one's

arm within the walls of a palace, is not more perilous or
strictly interdicted than, in the present state of society, to
eat gooseberries in an opera-box.

The ballet ended, Welsted endeavoured to retrace his
way towards the crush of fashion, and succeeded to a
miracle; what the next step preliminary to their departure
was to be, he still was doubtful; but, profiting by the experience which he purchased when with the Countess herself, he was inclined to adopt the course which, in point
of fact, was the correct one; still the crowd was such,
that the party remained fixtures, and the young ladies
from Hackney, who had no idea of the spirit of the room,
felt angry and offended as they were pushed to and fro by
the contending factions of fashion ; not aware that being
subjected to such an inconvenience is matter of option,
and more than that, considered by many of the best regulated belles the best part of the opera.

Unskilled in the ways of the world, the Hackney party
declined pushing and squeezing in return, and therefore
remained passively to be pushed and squeezed by every
body else. At length, some very grotesque dress caught
Miss Harriet's eye, and her remark upon it was at once
so odd and unexpected, that Welsted burst into a fit of
laughter, in indulging himself in which, he threw himself
backward, rather further than in such a phalanx there was
room to admit of with security, and accidentally thrust
himself close to a lady who was behind him; he instantly
turned round to apologize for the unforeseen accident,
when, to his astonishment and dismay, he beheld—Lady
Brashleigh !

To have seen Lady Brashleigh under any circumstances
so near him, would have excited ten thousand strong feelings, and ten thousand painful agitations; but to see her
at the opera, in the first week of the honeymoon, he had
certainly not anticipated ; and when he did behold her,
situated as he was, with two laughing, giddy, giggling
girls, over-dressed and decorated, and who had attracted
very much of public attention, hanging upon his arms, his
countenance bespoke his feelings—he turned deadly pale.
Fanny was as pale as death before ; she was leaning on

Sir Frederick's arm.   What were they to do?—I mean
Fanny and Welsted; for, at all events, they must here be
united: the feelings of either were equally agitated; she
felt greatly surprised at his appearance there, and with
such companions; but as Sheridan says,

> " By him they love offended,
>   How soon their anger flies;
> One day apart, 'tis ended—
>   Behold him, and it dies."

The idea of *not* speaking to Welsted—to the being who
loved her better than life, and whom she tenderly loved,
and who had sacrificed everything for her—indeed, the
very circumstance of *not* noticing him, would tacitly
criminate herself, and lead Sir Frederick Brashleigh, if he
chanced to recollect his person, to imagine that there must
be some extraordinary reason for her display of coldness
towards so old a friend.

Welsted felt it would be impossible that they should
meet and part thus without a word; yet resolving to leave
it to her discretion, to take what measure she thought
best, he turned nearly round again, so as to admit of her
addressing him, if she chose.   She struggled with herself
for a moment, and endeavoured to calculate; but calcu-
lation was out of the question, and she cordially and
frankly held out her hand to him; he took it as calmly as
he could.

Sir Frederick said nothing; but opened his eyes to
double their usual extent, at the same time screwing up
his mouth to half its natural dimensions.

Her Ladyship instantly addressed him.

"You don't remember, Mr. Welsted, Sir Frederick?"
said Fanny.

"No!" said his Excellency, staring still more; "I did
not know your Ladyship had any acquaintances in
London."

Fanny whispered his Excellency, that Welsted had
been her father's assistant.

"Very odd situation, indeed, Ma'am, to stumble upon

such connexions," muttered his Excellency; and then turning to Welsted, he made a commonplace inquiry after his health; that being the mode established by the English people for commencing a conversation.

" Lady Farnborough," said Welsted, " was kind enough to lend me her box to-night."

" Farnborough !" said Sir Frederick; " you are acquainted with Lord Farnborough, Sir ?"

" Yes," said Welsted.

" Umph !" said his Excellency: who seemed to think Fanny was more than sufficiently attentive to the observations of Mr. Welsted; " Good night, Sir !" saying which and bowing very graciously, his Excellency pushed his wife forward through the crowd: she again shook hands with Francis, and they parted. He had been unable, of course, to elucidate the mystery of his position between the two Misses Tickle; and as Fanny looked back—for she did look back—he thought her eyes fixed themselves with a strange and doubtful expression upon his female companions.

Francis was wholly unnerved; but such is the command, which even the most timid woman has over herself, that, although Fanny's heart was bursting—breaking— one could hardly perceive upon her countenance the evidence of a more than ordinary feeling; while Welsted absolutely trembled as he stood, and totally lost all recollection of his friends, to whose questions he made the most incoherent answers.

Different, indeed, were the feelings of the Misses, when they saw the cordial greeting of the beautiful girl, leaning on the decorated chevalier: they began to feel a mingled wonder and veneration for their new usher, who certainly would have passed no unpleasant evening, had not his whole mind been absorbed by the sudden and unlooked-for appearance of *her*, to see whom was, in truth, his most ardent desire; but of whom the sight was too much to endure with any thing like composure.

But time wears on, and operas must have an end; so must chapters—and since neither accident nor incident marred the safe return of the Hackney party in the glass-

15

coach, I need only say, that they reached home by half-
past one; at which late or early hour the young divi-
nities satisfactorily proved their humanity by demolishing
a substantial supper of cold boiled mutton and pickled
onions; and when Francis retired to rest, his thoughts
rested, as they generally did, on Fanny; if Lady Brashleigh did not dream of Welsted, it was because, poor
soul, she was unable to sleep.

CHAPTER XIII.

You have so overpowered me
With unexpected kindness, that my tongu
Is mute, and speech too scanty to express
My inward gratitude———I cannot thank you.
TRAP.

WHATEVER unpleasant feelings had been excited in
Welsted's mind, by the extremely *mal apropos* appearance of Fanny at the Opera-house, those by which she
was agitated were by no means more agreeable; nor did
the petulant ill-humour of Sir Frederick, who hurried her
through the lobbies and along the passages, as if apprehensive of losing her, should any eye besides his own
glance upon her beauties, at all contribute to sooth, or
conciliate her, and as they drove back to the hotel from
the theatre, she rejoiced at the silence which his Excellency was pleased to observe, and which, when broken,
was broken only to speak of Welsted.

"That appears a gentlemanly young man, Ma'am,"
said his Excellency, "that Mr. Welsted. I recollect, I
think, seeing him at your house. What induced your
father to part with him, Ma'am?

It was, luckily, dark — and therefore the confusion
which would have betrayed her Ladyship, when she declared that she was ignorant of the cause of their separation, was unobservable.

"He seems to have bettered himself considerably,"

said his Excellency; " he talks of Countesses, and seems the chosen beau of some very fine young ladies, Ma'am."

Who those ladies were, Fanny would have given the world to know; although *her* opinion of their "*finery*" was not quite so favourable as her husband's. The mirthful gaiety of Welsted beyond all else surprised her; nor could she reconcile his apparent liveliness with her own feelings, nor imagine how two persons (and they too of assimilating characters) could possibly be so differently affected by the same causes.

Poor Fanny! she had neither time nor leisure to devote much of her thoughts to the subject nearest her heart She had been received by Mrs. Brashleigh with, first, a scrutinizing glance of curiosity; secondly, with an approving nod; and thirdly, with a patronizing salute on the cheek. The same spirit which the lady evinced in her introduction to her new and youthful *mother-in-law*, characterized all her further proceedings; it was one continued display of patronage and condescension; and to say truth, Fanny needed much advice, in the purchases and arrangements she had to make; and, barring the occasional side-cuts at the academy, and disparity of age in marriages, and young ladies' worldly prospects, which it would have been impossible for Sir Frederick's daughter-in-law to restrain, the time passed quietly until the time of sailing approached.

Never, during the various excursions which Lady Brashleigh was compelled to make in search of essentials or finery, did she enter or quit a shop, never step from or return to her carriage, without feeling a dreadful hope, an alarming wish, that she might meet Francis—but for one moment—to say farewell, and then separate for ever. They had met only for an instant in London, and the meeting was so unsatisfactory, nay, so distressing, that she would have given the world to hear the shortest possible explanation of the circumstances which could have brought him into the centre of all gaiety, with ladies, laughing at the very period (or so shortly after) at which he had represented himself to Rodney as devotedly attached to *her*, and hopelessly wretched in consequence of having lost her.   To seek an interview now, even with the best intentions, would have been incompatible with the duty which she owed Sir Frederick ; but amongst the motives which would have justified her to others, had she suffered her own feelings to get the mastery of principle. was the desire she felt of speaking to Welsted about her father.   She knew enough to be assured that Welsted's talents and influence were in the highest degree important to Rodney's success in his profession ; that to Welsted's exertions an increase of pupils latterly had been mainly attributable ; and besides those natural feelings, which are more particularly applicable to self, her anxiety was great to persuade Francis, if possible, to return to the academy. She would almost have asked it as a proof of his love ; but then, what right had she to seek any testimonial of affection from him, which she knew must never be requited by her ? perhaps the anxiety for her father's welfare might have been heightened unconsciously, by the wish to have some just reason for again beholding Welsted before she bade him what she felt was an eternal adieu ;—but I have no right to say this.

Suffice it, that the difficulties which she first felt, increased with time ; and amidst the constant whirl of business, into which she was forced, and of pleasure which was forced upon her ; day flew after day, and the week at length arrived, in which they were to proceed to Portsmouth, to embark.   She found Major Mims the most gentlemanly little old creature imaginable, ready to trot off the longest distances, on the shortest notice ; Captain Macaddle, though carefully selected by his Excellency for the homeliness of his appearance, was by no means deficient in attention to her Ladyship, and while his Ex cellency was absent, both of these gentlemen made themselves agreeable enough ; the moment his Excellency entered the room, they were like so many sleeping beauties in the wood, all struck motionless, and apparently senseless, in the respective attitudes which they had accidentally assumed before his Excellency's arrival.

Towards his amiable and unoffending Lady, Sir Frederick grew gradually harsher, more indifferent, and less considerate ; and he continued this process of *training* until she took her cue from the *rest* of the staff, and never ventured to mutter a wish or express an opinion in his presence; indeed, an answer to an observation, or a remonstrance against a command, were matches to the mine, and her Ladyship, as well as the officers, became instinctively amenable to martial law.

Fanny, amongst other prejudices, strengthened, if not wholly created by a constant residence in a home like her little ivy-bower at her father's house, had an almost insurmountable dread of the sea; she had read of shipwrecks and storms, and hurricanes, but had never seen the boundless waste of waters upon which she was destined to pass the next four or five months of her existence : when she had visited the huge Indiaman in which her passage was taken, she felt more composed, and reconciled herself with the idea that a vessel so large, and high out of the water, must be safe, and steady and agreeable ; and by degrees, and a constant association with hundreds of those who had made, re-made, and made again and again the same voyage, she became more reconciled to her fate, and it was most fortunate that she did ; not only because her fears and apprehensions could not lessen the danger she contemplated, but because the slightest expression of timidity or anticipation of peril was met by Sir Frederick with the most violent denunciation of folly, stupidity, and childishness, and avowals of contempt and disgust for mingled ignorance and affectation.

Never, to be sure, from the beginning of the affair, until this very juncture, was poor girl so tormented, so completely destroyed as Fanny Rodney. Her obedience in the first instance, rendered her passive in the hands of her parents, and led her to abandon herself completely to their guidance ; and now her inexperience compelled her to rely entirely upon others for advice and information ; so that it may be said more truly than in most cases, that she was led to the altar, a willing sacrifice for the good of others.

At length, after a week of perfect confusion, and a day or two of storms and squabbles, his Excellency and Lady

Brashleigh, the staff, and baggage, were embarked on board the ship appointed to convey them to Bombay ; but as my readers have, in all probability, practically enjoyed the comforts of seaport towns, the agreeable diversity of contrary winds, rainy days, and high seas, wet seats, and damp boat-cloaks, dirty landing-places, bad inns, and exorbitant charges, I shall spare them the recital of all the difficulties, worries, inconveniences, and embarrassments, by which the party were delayed nearly eight days after their *first* embarkation. At last however, the wind shifted a point or two to the northward of east, and away bustled the Honourable Company's ship, his Excellency the Commander-in-chief at Bombay, and all.

And thus was separated from her home, her family, her friends, and Welsted, poor Fanny Rodney ; committed to the charge of her irritable husband, and the more perilous, yet not more uncertain, caprices of the briny deep ; and there was something chilly in the wind, and lowering in the sky, as she stood by Sir Frederick's side at the tafferill, gazing on the lessening hills of England, and watching the ship's wake, which seemed to fly from beneath them with a whirling roar, as the huge vessel cleaved the rising waves. A tear stood in her eye as she contemplated the night closing in upon them ; and when it grew too dark and too cold to watch the horizon any longer, she went down to her cabin with an aching heart, feeling the full force of all her miseries ; the tears then fell, but Sir Frederick came to *sooth* her, and she therefore felt that she dared weep no more.

During the five or six weeks which were occupied by the preparations for their departure, and of which I lament that the space assigned me in these volumes will not permit me to give a more elaborate description, much had been doing in which the future prospects and interests of Welsted were concerned ; indeed it appeared as if he were doomed to meet the reward of his disinterested surrender of his angelic Fanny, in the most unexpected personal advancement. Alas! had the views which dawned upon him at the present moment been opened to his eyes at the time of Sir Frederick's offer, he might fairly and honourably have claimed a pledge from his beloved, and held out the most gratifying prospects to her and her family for the future : but it was fated to be otherwise ; else had the pleasure and gratitude which he now felt, with constant reference to the loss he had sustained, been experienced and enjoyed without the slightest deterioration.

On the Sunday subsequent to Frank's visit to the opera the Viscount's cabriolet appeared at Montgomery-place, to convey the "usher" to the Earl's ; and he departed just before tea-time at the academy, for the dinner party in Grosvenor-square. Arrived there, the same kindness, the same pointed attention marked his reception, and the whole family again seemed anxious to vie with each other in giving evidence of their feelings towards him.

Nothing particular occurred during the early part of the day ; the dinner was a repetition of the last, and the subsequent ceremonies the same as those which followed the former one ; the only striking difference between the events of the two days, was to be found in a conversation which passed between the Earl and Welsted.

After coffee, his Lordship called Francis aside, and told him he wished to communicate something to him which would require his consideration, and proposed adjourning to the library, where, undisturbed by the general conversation, they might "talk it over quietly." Francis followed his Lordship, hardly prepared for what was to be disclosed to him.

" Mr. Welsted," said his Lordship, as soon as they were alone, " I was extremely sorry when I heard that, during my absence from town, you had accepted, what I confess I think, a situation unworthy of your abilities and character ; indeed, that absence, unavoidable as it was, prevented me from earlier explaining myself upon a point which, I own, is extremely interesting to *me*, and which, I hope, may be advantageous to *you*."

Welsted bowed.

" My son," continued the Earl, " tells me that he has communicated to you the fact of my appointment as ambassador to the court of France : connected with that appointment is the subject on which I wish to speak. I find you have graduated at Oxford, of which I was not till very recently aware; and although I may be offering that which it may not be worth your while to accept, if it would suit your views to reside at the University during Feversham's stay there, he would be delighted, and I should feel obliged. The truth is, Feversham is anxious to retrieve lost time, he feels diffident of himself, he has not read so much as he ought to have read, he dislikes committing himself to strangers, he feels (as indeed he well may) strongly attached to you, and it is at *his* request that I have now broached the matter to you."

" Independently of every other consideration, my Lord," said Welsted, " to do *that* which could please Lord Feversham, would be most gratifying to me ; but your Lordship's proposal involves so many pleasures and advantages, that it requires *no* consideration : I most thankfully accept your Lordship's kind offer."

" What !" said his Lordship, smiling, " before you know upon what terms you are requested to do so ?"

" The satisfaction of passing my time with Lord Feversham," said Welsted, " in pursuits which, while gratifying to my own inclinations, may be useful to him, will be quite sufficient."

" Indeed !" said the Earl ; " and so, my dear Mr. Welsted, the best return I can make you for saving my son's life, and preserving the hopes of my family, is to request you to quit a situation in which you are fixed, to reside at Oxford at your own ' proper charge,' merely to oblige *me*, and gratify my heir ?"

Save his life? thought Welsted—what does his Lordship mean ?—convinced at the same time, that however unconsciously he must have done the deed, or have been supposed to do it, it was no doubt, the spring and cause of all the kindnesses and attentions which he had received from the family, crowned at length by the present most delightful proposal.

" No, Mr. Welsted," continued Lord Farnborough,— " talking of money to a gentleman is always disagreeable, but, as the world goes, it is absolutely necessary to do so;

theiefore I break the ice on which your delicacy would not permit you to tread. I am not a very niggardly father, as Feversham will tell you; I am perfectly convinced, that to allow a young man a sufficient income to maintain his station in society, without profligacy or extravagance, is the surest way to prevent his falling into either. There exists, I trust, that sort of confidence between Feversham and myself, which ought to subsist between man and man; while, as a father, I have never since his childhood been called upon, by any circumstance of his life, to reprove or correct him;—that being the case, you may be sure I never object to the fair use of money, and I believe one of the principal reasons why I never have occasion to make an unpleasant remark is, that I place a reliance on his honour, which he feels a pride in never violating: as I intend you to be his companion, and as you have been his preserver, to be his friend, upon that footing only will I accept the services which you must inevitably render him by your association with him; and to support that character, I must insist upon your allowance from me, during your residence at Oxford, being the same as *that*, which I consider sufficient for *him*."

Welsted was completely overcome by this unexpected offer, and the extraordinary liberality of the remuneration; he essayed to speak, but the Earl again interrupted him; " I must hear nothing," said his Lordship; " I am resolved upon *my* course—you have simply an Ay or No to give as to the offer."

" I ——-" said Welsted.

" You accept it," said the Earl, " and I consider that *I* am the person obliged; it is my intention that Feversham, and of course yourself, should pass the vacations, or whatever portion of them you may choose, with us at Paris, until *he* shall have concluded his university, or *I* my diplomatic career; of these arrangements we can talk afterwards:—before his return to Oxford, you will find apartments here always at your service."

" I really do not know how to repay your Lordship's kindness," said Welsted.

" I know," said Lord Farnboro

high feeling and delicate mind, a recurrence to past services is, perhaps, unpleasant,—but to a father, speaking
to *him* who has preserved his only son, it may be permitted again to assure that person, that nothing he can
do to mark his gratitude is sufficiently important to deserve thanks : as for future prospects, I think it may be
hereafter in my power (not that I can venture to hold out
any thing like a certainty), should you determine to take
orders, to be of use to you ; but I cannot pledge myself
to any thing specific, although I think the measure of
ordination could do no harm, but on the contrary, must
be advantageous : as far as securing *that*, there will be no
difficulty :—however, we have now discussed our business sufficiently, and your new home, Mr. Welsted, is
open to you, whenever you feel disposed to come to it."

Welsted, delighted as he naturally must have been with
such a princely offer, and such cheering prospects, told
his Lordship that, notwithstanding the splendid change so
suddenly effected in his circumstances, he felt it his duty
to remain at Hackney until the expiration of the time for
which he had engaged himself; nor did he, by the avowal
of his intentions on that point, at all lower himself in the
opinion of his new and munificent patron.

" Let us send for Feversham," said the Earl, and communicate your acceptance of the offer; his pleasure will
be as great as mine, although his delicacy prevented his
mentioning the subject; indeed, I did not trust him with
the whole of my plan."

Saying which, his Lordship rang the bell : a message
was despatched for the Viscount, who shortly joined the
council, and the expression of his feelings, when the result
of the deliberation was made known to him, was perfectly
unequivocal; and the manner in which Welsted found
himself thus extraordinarily rewarded for an action which
had even escaped his memory, was on every account most
gratifying, and nothing, as I have just said, existed to mar
the brightness of the scene before him, but the recollection that, if all this had happened a few weeks earlier he
might have looked forward to eventual happiness with his
Fanny.

That it did *not* happen before was mainly attributable to the selfishness of Rodney, whose character was a most extraordinary compound of kindness and meanness, avarice and liberality. It will hardly be believed, that immediately after the event, upon which, in fact, all Welsted's good fortune turned, Lord Farnborough, then the honourable Mr. Rutherford, had in a letter to Rodney most warmly expressed his feelings towards the preserver of his son—and expressed a wish to forward his interests in the world, as a proof of his gratitude and that of his family. At that period William Rodney was alive, and such was the jealousy of the poetical parent, that he suppressed Mr. Rutherford's letter, and answered it evasively, returning thanks in *Frank's name* for the liberal offers it contained, but at the same time refusing them ; and this was the man who had brought up and educated the orphan of his friend, but who yet could not endure to see the child of his bounty so suddenly, and so far surpass his own son in the race of life.

It is strange, yet highly characteristic of the chivalrous kindness of poor Francis, that he had actually forgotten the day when young Rutherford, while bathing, had sunk in very deep water, and risen for the last time, unseen by any of his schoolfellows. Welsted caught sight of the perishing boy, and without a moment's doubt or hesitation, plunged into the water with his clothes on, and at the hazard of his life, dragged the exhausted sufferer to the shore. When he returned home, and changed his dress, it seemed as if he had put off the memory of his intrepidity with the habits he wore ; he never mentioned the circumstance; and as there was no one present, except the boys to tell the tale, it fell ineffective upon Rodney's ear. Young Rutherford described the accident in a letter to his father; and the family, whose hopes were centred in their darling child, felt all that gratitude which Mr. Rutherford forthwith conveyed to Rodney, to whom he was personally known, and whom he thought the properest person to address, being also the surest channel of communication with the usher ; but the head of the house, having heard nothing of the affair from the hero of it, thought

it had been exaggerated by young Rutherford ; **and that**
at all events it was not of sufficient importance to say any
thing about to Frank, since it appeared likely to induce
some display of family gratitude, which might at once give
his protégé precedence in the world of his son, and probably rob him of his assistance, of which at last, as it
turned out, he was deprived by a sacrifice to what he considered the worldly interest of his daughter.

Welsted would not have believed this history of the
conduct of his patron in this matter, nor would he ever
have been likely to know it, had it not been for his accidental meeting with Feversham ; but, when sufficient of
the *dénouement* had been displayed to recal the oblite-
rated rescue to his mind, he naturally felt, although he
could not of course express, surprise that the conduct induced by so strong a sentiment of gratitude as the family
now openly acknowledged should have been so long delayed.   The truth, however, was disclosed to him, and
after all accidentally ; for when he was expressing to Feversham his acknowledgments for the favours conferred by
the Earl, the Viscount told him explicitly, that his acceptance of the offer had greatly surprised him ; and that his
own unwillingness to speak to him on the subject arose
from a desire not to be refused, and a fear of offending
him ; of which anticipations had been created in their
minds by what they had all along considered a silent and
almost ungracious refusal of thanks ; in fact, an uncivil
mode of denying them the pleasure of evincing their feelings towards him.   All this it was, that when the Earl saw
Welsted, and saw the urbanity and good taste which characterized his conduct and conversation, determined his
Lordship, now finding him unemployed, to fulfil, if his
son approved it, the intention which, in fact, he formerly
had of making him his tutor.

Had Rodney acted with common fairness, Welsted
would have been Lord Feversham's tutor at Eton ;—that
would have opened prospects to him which might have
been realized, he might have become the happy husband
of Fanny, and the respectable successor of her father ; or,
if better things had turned up, through the influence of

his pupil's family, have filled a station in the Church, honourable in its character, and sufficiently lucrative in its emoluments to have rendered him and his wife perfectly comfortable, and her parents truly blest. But differently were things to turn out : and while the manly exertion of humanity, the exemplary performance of every duty, and the fulfilment of every right principle led, in spite of meanness and artifice, the unassuming Welsted into honours and prosperity, the dirty ambition which could barter independence of feeling for a little transitory rank—fail in the honest duties of society, to gratify a little personal pride— and suffer the paltry pomps and vanities of this world to keep down merit, and even break the strongest ties,— was doomed to meet its just reward in poverty and disgrace.

From the marriage of Fanny with Sir Frederick, Rodney might with security have dated his ruin, even by anticipation. The parents of his pupils, disgusted with the absurd trickery of " making holidays," sent their sons elsewhere ; Welsted's departure, as poor Fanny well foresaw, threw the classical department altogether upon the old gentleman, who was not equal to its conduct ; and moreover, as I anticipated at the time, the holder of the securities, whose enmity to Sir Frederick, for having, as he said, robbed him by sycophancy of a considerable part of his birthright, was easily transferred to his Excellency's father-in-law ; began a series of applications for payment, and in less than six weeks the bewildered poet received a warning and summons together, to discharge the obligations at the termination of the following half-year.

Then it was, and in his distress, that he turned to Welsted in imagination ; then it was that he repented the unnatural match which he had so imprudently made up for his child, robbing himself at once of the aid of Francis, and the society of Fanny ;—how to recover the former he knew not, and how to retrieve his own affairs without some such measure he was ignorant ; from his matter-of-fact helpmate he could gain neither advice nor consolation : he therefore resolved to go on as long as he could, " watching for a bright ray of hope, which might beam through the darkness of the clouds, and light him eventually to some secure and peaceful haven."

His tranquillity, however, was not mucn contributed to, by the continual questions of Mrs. Rodney, as to why one boy didn't come back? and why another boy was taken away? and why other boys did not come? because, as she wisely, but needlessly observed, " if some more don't come than are here now, why, Mr. Rodney, we must shut up shop!" and " do you know, my dear," added his soothing spouse, " as if Old Nick had set his cloven foot in the house, all the nice, little delicate, peaking, pudding-and-milk children are going away, and none remain but the huge bumpkins of farmers' sons, who eat their own weight of mutton every month: who's to pay the butcher's bills, if things go on this way, I'm sure I don't know."

Nor did Rodney : and when occasionally he opened the door of the room which had been Welsted's, and which was now used as a receptacle for all the tattered and tarnished finery which had decked out the nuptial feast, he would stand for a moment, and muse, and then kick over with his foot some of the dust-laden roses and lilies of the London artist, and walk away sighing, and rattling the few shillings which lay in his breeches-pocket.

Things at the academy, however, had not reached this point before Lady Brashleigh's departure ; yet since her marriage Sir Frederick had written but once to Rodney, and that, merely requiring a certificate of Fanny's age, for some legal purpose ; and Mrs. Rodney was absolutely affronted with her daughter for entreating her not to continue sending presents to them at the hotel ; which, when the packages had been opened by his Excellency's servants, proved to be, at one time perhaps " a sucking pig," at another " a chine and sausages," the annunciation of which arrivals regularly produced an accession of rage in the General, until at length Lady Brashleigh was obliged, for her own quiet's sake, to implore her kind mother to be more sparing of her gifts ; which so much increased the unsophisticated lady's anger, that the following day, without saying a word to Rodney, she transmitted half a dozen larks, and a nice cream cheese which she had made, to

the General himself, directed by one of the boys specially
employed by her on that occasion, in a dreadfully large
legible hand, which, being very nicely packed up and
sealed pacquet-wise, was brought to, and actually opened
by 's Excellency in the drawing-room of Mivart's hotel,
in the presence of two East India directors, his own staff,
and Lady Brashleigh ;—in the parcel was the following
note :

  " DEAR SIR,

    " Fanny has got so proud that she will not ac-
cept of presents, so I send them to you, because I know
you don't mind taking things which are no cost whatever to
us, but which may make a nice dish to keep down London
bills ;—I only gave three-halfpence apiece for the larks,
yesterday, and the cheese I made myself; please to turn
it every day, and if you keep it up in the cupboard in your
own room (which is the best way to keep it safe), you had
better set the cupboard-door a-jar after the servants are
gone to bed.
  " We shall have a nice small pig fit for killing next
week, which I shall send you. Give my affectionate love
to Fanny, and believe me,

      " Yours, &c.,

        " CORDELIA RODNEY.

  " P.S. Will you tell Fanny that she has left two hair-
brushes and a small bottle of salts in her dressing-table
drawer, and please to ask her if I shall send them up next
week—don't tell her of the pig, but they can all go together in the same parcel."

  This was a death-blow to his Excellency, who in a rage
desired the contents of the parcel to be thrown into the
street ; and having read the letter he threw it to his Lady,
exclaiming, ' Ma'am, the old woman is mad, Ma'am, mad
as a March hare ;" observing, however, at the same time
the delicacy of not mentioning the name of his mother-in-
law, from no respect for his wife's feelings, but because he

was afraid that his own consequence would suffer in the
estimation of his associates, if it could be imagined that
larks and cheese could possibly come from her Ladyship's
mother.

I shall I hope be pardoned for this episodaical anecdote,
which has brought me, unwittingly, back to the Rodneys,
because it displays the consequences of Mr. Rodney's
scheming, and prepares the reader for the fact, that all
correspondence ceased, before their departure, betwe n the
young couple, and the parents.   Mrs. Rodney finding her
delicate attentions were ill received, appealed to her husband, who, angered at being despised in his own person,
or that of his wife, by the child to whom they had given
birth ; and being as ignorant of the ways of the world as
infants, wrote a violent letter to Sir Frederick, reproach-
ing him, in the most poetical language, with the horrible
crime of exciting their daughter to ingratitude, and load-
ing him with reproaches for having made a rebel of the
fondest creature that ever drew breath.

To this Fanny, at her husband's desire, replied ; and
being now a little initiated into the customs and manners
of society, vindicated Sir Frederick from the charges exhibited against him, and explained in mild, but proper
terms, the total difference of the sphere in which she now
moved from that which she had left ; and endeavoured to
show that what were amongst equals very satisfactory
marks of friendship and affection, became, when offered
under different circumstances, irksome on the one hand,
and ridiculous on the other.   Indeed, with unaltered feelings of affection for her parents, Fanny saw the absolute
absurdity of continuing such a system ; and although she
was bitterly wounded, in the first instance, when the objectionable basket of sandwiches was ejected from the carriage, she had reverted in her mind to that occurrence
with subdued feelings, now that she knew the world better : and upon the same principle solicited her parents to
avoid any repetition of the unintentional offence, or at
least, undesired civility.

To this letter, written in affectionate language, and
which concluded by again impressing upon the minds of

her parents the difference of her present station from that in which she had been formerly placed ; the poor girl received the most violent answer from her father, whose temper, soured by the evils which he saw threatening him, charged her with pride, and every base feeling which could inhabit the breast of a fiend—every allusion to her change of situation was met by the question, whether she had forgotten who qualified her for such a change, who fed and educated her (as if feeding and educating one's children was a meritorious performance, instead of a parental duty), and calling upon her to remember her father and mother, who were, in fact, every bit as good as Sir Frederick, although they had not enriched themselves by either cajoling right heirs out of their property, or cutting the throats of poor innocent Indians.

One letter led to another, one reproach to another, until Sir Frederick felt, and properly too—that it was quite time to put a stop to the correspondence, and stopped it was ; but so deeply and bitterly had the old couple been wounded by the neglect, or refusal of their misplaced attentions, that Fanny was doomed to receive the malediction of her father,—to avoid which, and save him from ruin, she had sacrificed every hope of happiness on earth.

In this dreadful family contest, Fanny acted purely from principle, she would have given worlds, had it been possible, to throw down her pen and rush to the arms of her parents, and explain to them verbally why their conduct was offensive ; she would rather still have fallen back into the society where their kindnesses would have been acceptable, and, as the partner of Welsted, have joyously received the same humble well-meant marks of maternal affection ; but it was now too late to think of this :—the choice had been her father's, not her own ; she had been forced into a sphere which was adapted neither to her taste nor inclinations, but it was done, and it was now her duty to conform herself to *him* to whom she owed obedience, and to whose habits and will it was a matter of principle to adapt herself: she therefore did that which was right, but being unhappily misunderstood, caused that feud which raged so violently, that it was not until the ship was actually under way, and therefore impossible to receive any answer or insult, that Sir Frederick would allow her to write a letter of adieu to her parents ; which, such was the inveteracy of Rodney, was, after all, returned unopened to the hotel in London : nor did the once fond parents know any thing of their beloved child's departure from England, until they read it in the weekly county paper, then two days old.

Whatever hopes Rodney might have had of Welsted's return, which he ardently desired, they were entirely frustrated by the offer which the Earl had made, and which he had accepted ; and bitter and dark were the prospects before him.   For the present we must leave him repining over his fate, correcting themes and dictating nonsense verses, as usual, and return to the drawing-room in Grosvenor-square, to which, after a lengthened conversation in the library, Feversham and his accredited tutor had returned.

To the well-regulated minds of people of tact and good taste, the moment a gentleman, under any circumstances, is placed relatively to them in a dependent situation, it is a pleasure to render him as much as possible unconscious of the position in which he actually stands ; and nothing is stronger evidence of littleness and a bad disposition, than the exaction of respect and attention from inferiors thus peculiarly situated ;—indeed, it is a mark of folly into the bargain, because to a man of any feeling, the very concession of the superior excites the attention and respect which haughtiness and importance would fail to extort.   When Welsted joined the ladies, it seemed as if he were actually one of the family ; and again fascinated and delighted by their society, it was with no agreeable sensation he heard the carriage announced which was to take him back to Hackney ; where he was unfortunately involved in another affair, of which the reader is at present ignorant, but with which he shall be made acquainted in due time.

When the Earl and Countess parted from the overwhelmed young man, it was with every possible expression of kindness ; and her Ladyship was pleased to avow, that his acceptance of the tutelage of her son was to her the most gratifying event which could have taken place, as although Feversham was a very different sort of a person from the generality of young men, still to have a companion who, while he was personally agreeable and pleasant to him, would act upon emergencies as his mentor and guide, could not fail to afford her the greatest possible satisfaction ; in short, whether by the Earl or the Countess, the Viscount or his lovely sisters, Welsted was loaded with praises and kindness ; and elated and delighted, as he well might be, with the bright prospect before him, he stepped into the chariot which was destined to take him back to his home.

When left alone, his feelings overcame him, and it was with tears of regret, amidst his grateful joy for what had occurred, that he recollected how happy he might have been had he been blessed with his present good fortune a little earlier ; he was not, however, able long to dwell upon the dark side of the picture, for the short space of time occupied by the drive, was divided between all the feelings connected with this part of his career, and another, of which further particulars will be found in the next chapter.

CHAPTER XIV.

Canst thou so easily pronounce Farewell,
When that farewell may be perhaps—for ever ?
Oh ! can you leave me thus ?

HAVARD.

THAT a person so prudent and well-principled as Mr. Francis Welsted should have involved himself in a quarrel, in the midst of his successes in better society, might perhaps never strike the reader ; and therefore it becomes me duty (part of which consists in concealing nothing from his knowledge which it is important he should know, let

who may be compromised) to enlighten him on this point
of the story.

Nobody, except a parent, would have imagined that an
attachment so ardent and strong, as that of Miss Elizabeth
Tickle and Mr. Stevens, could be broken off at the bidding
of superior authority : or doubt, unless some paramount
principle militated against it, that the sudden separation
of two fond hearts would be the most certain incitement
to some more violent measures on the part of the lovers ;
—certain it is, that at the moment in which Mr. Tickle
was at the supper-table, consigning his late usher safely
to the bosom of his family in the country, the said usher
was walking up and down before the academy, whistling
"Soger Laddie," in hopes of attracting the ear and notice
of Miss Elizabeth, but in vain. She was, as we have
already seen, most unsentimentally employed in swallowing a very hearty supper; and all the satisfaction Mr.
Stevens obtained, in return for paddling up and down in
a muddy road for two hours, eyed suspiciously by the
watchmen, and saluted disagreeably by the patrol, was
the sight of lights beaming through the crevices of the
parlour window-shutters, and the sound of an occasional
horse-laugh, ill enough calculated to gratify an " outside
passenger," under his circumstances.

Every class of people has of course its peculiar mode of
love-making, and indeed the many disclosures which are
made in the course of law proceedings upon amatory subjects, prove the vast variety of methods adopted to attain
the same object. Mr. Stevens was placed in that sphere,
of which the inhabitants delight in moonlight walks in the
vicinity of the metropolis ; going to see a new tragedy ;
weeping during the performance into white pocket-handkerchiefs, and eating oranges or munching apples between
the acts ; making perhaps a Sunday excursion to Rich-
mond in a steam-boat, or a party to the great oak at Fair-
lop Fair in a glass-coach : and it must be confessed that
Elizabeth Tickle's taste was wonderfully accommodating
to this system. She delighted in little dances, and *walks
home* after them, and what are called walks out in the

morning, to be met somewhere and joined by her beloved, and then to come in, hungry, and eat a hearty dinner of roasted mutton or a hot round of boiled beef, with huge carrots and greasy greens, and then have some nice toast or muffins with tea, and play Pope Joan with *fiche* at sixpence per dozen by way of an exciting wind-up: always remembering to make sundry waggish allusions to matrimony, which that elegant diversion so fortunately favours, and never forgetting those gentle pressures of feet under the table, which are the most decided and general evidences of mutual affection in that class of society.

Now, it so happened that Stevens determined, when he quitted Tickle, to keep up a correspondence, with his daughter, and marry her eventually in spite of him. The twopenny-post was liable to interruption; Dixon warned him that he could not be privy to any clandestine intercourse; Ronfleur was sure to have made some blunder, had he been trusted; and as for the servants, they valued their places too much to risk stratagems without higher bribes than it suited an ex-usher like Mr. Stevens to supply them with.

In the dreadful dilemma, in which Mr. Stevens found himself placed, he bethought him of addressing a pathetic appeal to his successor in office, imagining that the least Welsted could do, having got his place, would be to forward his views upon the girl; for which purpose, he actually wrote Frank a letter, enclosing one to Elizabeth, and begging him to deliver it and secure her answer; or failing of that, as a gentleman, not to betray him.

The situation was an awkward one for Francis. He had no desire to take part in a rebellion against the existing government of Montgomery-place, nor could he make up his mind to return the letter to the lover, of whose feelings he made a most flattering estimate, by a comparison with his own: to betray him was farthest from his thoughts; but he felt that to give the letter to the girl, in open defiance and contravention of her father's authority, whose servant in fact he was, would be equally improper; and therefore, after a short deliberation with himself, he enclosed the letters to Mr. Stevens, directed, as he desired, to No. 14, Little Phœnix-row, Upper Caroline-street, Bethnal Green, stating his regret that he could not, consistently with his principles, make himself a party to such a concealment, in the family which he had so recently entered, and in which he was so delicately situated.

This letter produced an abusive, vulgar, and ungentlemanly answer : which was as cowardly as it was ill-principled, because the writer knew that the feeling which had induced Welsted to keep his former address secret would actuate him at present; and it was while this was pending, and Welsted debating what step he should take, that the Sunday arrived on which he was destined to dine at the Earl's. This naturally stopped any active measures, but he determined, on the following morning, to visit the residence or hiding-place of his antagonist, and argue the point with him amicably, so long as it might be possible, and then resort to other measures if he found him unreasonably violent, and entitled to any other mode of proceeding.

A circumstance, however, wholly unexpected on the part of the elders of the family, brought matters to a crisis, and rendered all doubt or discussion needless. Elizabeth had invited herself to old Mrs. Biddle's at dinner after church, on that very Sunday, and thus secured permission to quit the Academy unsuspected and unmolested ; to which peaceful home, however, she did not think proper to return; and when search was made for her at the house to which she had professed to go, no intelligence could be obtained either of herself or her place of destination. Harriet, who was in her confidence, never breathed a syllable of suspicion ; and not until the following morning discovered, *by accident,* a letter in her sister's room, announcing that she had taken the decisive step of eloping with Stevens; and, moreover, that she should be his wife before they next heard from her.

" 'Tis an ill wind that blows nobody good," says a proverb, which hereafter I intend to illustrate ; and Tickle and his wife having communed together upon the indiscretion of their daughter, and either of them having pacified the other, by the consoling reflections that " it was well it was no worse; and that " what was done could not be undone;" and that " it was too late to shut the stable-door when the steed was stolen ;" and sundry other equally conclusive adages, the father softened and the mother melted, and agreed that it would be perfectly ridiculous to maintain any thing like hostility towards the young couple, as the affair *had* happened; suddenly discovering that at all events, Stevens was really a very respectable young man, and had been always very civil and attentive in his office.

This is quite natural,—for, in fact, their existed no earthly objection to the *ci-devant* usher, who was a perfectly suitable husband for Miss Tickle; and the only ground upon which the democratic parent had expelled him his house was the inferiority of *his birth*, relatively to his daughter's rank in society. This anomaly was of a piece with all the rest of the consistency, by which political feeling in such persons is regulated; and indeed the whole affair was one which, as it caused no surprise in the neighbourhood of Hackney, would not be very likely to excite any interest in my readers, had it not afforded Welsted an opportunity of pleading favourably for the person who had vilified and injured him ; and, moreover, of resigning his office in favour of the Benedict ; thus bringing back into the bosom of her family the blushing bride, relieving himself from the trammels, of which he was now so eager to be divested, and freeing the head of the house from an engagement with a new usher, whose services, if Stevens were to return, would of course be superfluous and useless.

Never, indeed, did coincidence more happily occur, and every body seemed pleased with the new arrangement, except Harriet Tickle and poor old Ronfleur. Harriet was tinderly tender, and so susceptible to the approaches of sparks, that she had drunk love's poison even in the short stay of Welsted, —a fact which she took no pains to conceal, if one might judge by the expression of her eloquent eyes. Ronfleur heard of Frank s departure with sorrow, because, of all the persons with whom he had associated under that roof, no other human being had sympathized with his sorrows, no other being had listened to his story without occasionally smiling, or perhaps laughing outright at his mistakes and bad English. To Francis it seemed the language of the heart, regulated by no set forms, constructed on no given principles ; it was eloquent because it was true ; and if, in the course of the narrative, a self-confessed fault had been developed, the tear which trickled down the old man's cheek was quite sufficient, in Welsted's mind, to blot it out eternally. When Frank parted from him, the grateful Frenchman pressed his hand to his lips with fervour and sincerity, and when he turned from him to quit the apartment, raised his eyes to heaven, and shrugging up his shoulders, sighed deeply, as if he had lost his only friend on earth.

Mrs. Tickle, when she was made acquainted with the bright prospects of Mr. Welsted, seemed anxious to redouble her assiduities and expressions of gratitude ; and when Frank earnestly and decidedly delined any remuneration for his brief services, Mr. Tickle insisted upon presenting him with a shirt-pin, made of jewellers' gold wire, with a small bit of mock cornelian on its head, as a mark of his respect and regard.

Welsted's object was, if possible, to quit Montgomery-place before the return of the new-married couple, not wishing more than necessary to be brought into contact with Stevens, who clearly never could be induced to view him in any other light than the cause of his marriage, —an event which Frank thought it extremely probable the said Mr. Stevens might, without attaining to any extra-ordinary longevity, live to repent.

Welsted, however, having taken leave of the family, and thus unexpectedly ridded himself of his engagement at the school, was yet doomed to undergo a scene.—Miss Harriet, who had not appeared in the parlour during the leave-taking, surprised him in the passage leading to the side gate by which he was about to make his egress ; she was absolutely in tears, and affected to be so much affected, that she could not speak ; she took his hand and bathed it with briny drops of sorrow, and uttered, much to his surprise and mortification, a fervent blessing upon what she called, " Is ead, from eaven." A burst of across the yard luckily cut short the performance, and thus parted the susceptible Miss and the astonished usher.

It is necessary now (for I have gone on detailing scenes and circumstances, which I considered illustrative of character and society so minutely, that I am warned to condense and bring to a close the narrative, in which we have been perhaps too long engaged), to describe somewhat more cursorily the proceedings of the next three years, years full of interest to Francis, and not less so to Fanny, who, by the force of habit, had, during that period, become almost callous to the ingenious barbarities of Sir Frederick, and who looked forward to nothing but death for a release from sufferings which every body said she was undergoing, and which lost none of their acuteness from that very circumstance.

To say that she was, during that period, subjected to those advances to which a girl so situated is liable, is only to say truth ; but that rigid principle of duty, which first induced her to sacrifice herself for her father, imperiously governed her conduct as a wife ; and, although driven, by suspicion and almost insult from Sir Frederick, almost to madness, she trod the even tenour of her way the placid martyr to her own excellence. From all the allurements of wit, and gaicty, and pleasantry, and wealth, and valour, and personal attractions, Fanny was secured by the inherent feeling of right. The only sentiment she cherished. was her natural love for Francis ; this, it is true, she *did* retain in all its early warmth and purity ; but it was, as she justly called it herself, " unearthly,"—it was devotion to a lost, though living object. The only difference between her feelings and those of pious recollection of one buried in the grave, consisted in the deep existing interest which she could not cease to feel for one so dear ; and this she nursed, and loved to cherish in her heart of hearts, and did so with the less restraint, because it was improbable, indeed, almost impossible, that she should ever see her Welsted more. How such a meeting would affect her, if it could take place, she did not stop to calculate. She had heard from her father of her mother's death ; she had heard from her father of the legal proceedings of the

holder of his securities; she had heard from that father
in prison, and in poverty, she had heard that Frank had
saved him from perdition, and placed him beyond the
reach of want.

She had even heard her stern husband praise the conduct
of Welsted, whom he remembered as having seen in the
Opera-house: nor did Sir Frederick himself withhold that
portion of aid to his father-in-law, which was what the
world would call right and proper: but think what a pang
must his cold and formal bounty have inflicted upon
Fanny—most especially when it was accompanied by a
desire, on the part of his Excellency, that she would abstain, in conversation, from alluding to her parents, of
whom his Excellency was pleased to say that nothing
satisfactory could be told, and whose misfortunes, unde-
served as they might be, could not be amended by discussion; and most assuredly would not, under any circumstances, add to the *éclat* or respectability of his Excellency or her Ladyship, in their present station.

Welsted's benevolence and kindness, however, did not
alone show themselves in his conduct towards poor Rodney during the remnant of his wretched life;—the old
man's mind was totally subdued by misfortunes, and he
lived hardly long enough to be conscious of his aristocratic son-in-law's liberality. He died in lodgings in the
neighbourhood of London, whither Welsted hastened from
Oxford, to follow his old master's coffin to the grave;
nor was he alone in the performance of his duty; the
amiable and excellent Feversham accompanied his tutor
to town, and joined in the melancholy office, which the
grateful young man had imposed upon himself.

Who was now to communicate the death of the poor old
man to his daughter—who *could* do so? There was but
one who had a right to perform this task. Welsted took
counsel of the Viscount, who decided him at once upon
assuming it, and forwarding the melancholy detail to India; but Welsted, scrupulously tender of his beloved
Fanny's comfort, and religiously adhering to his determination to do nothing which even *she* might innocently
misconstrue into an endeavour to awaken past remem-

brances, and rekindle the smothered, perhaps extinguished, passion of her heart, wrote an account of all that had happened (save his own exemplary conduct in the business) to Sir Frederick ; alleging as a reason for *his* presuming to address his Excellency, the fact, that Rodney had left no friend or relation to record his departure from this transitory world ; and explaining to him his situation relative to the old gentleman, lest he might have forgotten his name ; and, above all, explaining how necessary he felt it to be, that Lady Brashleigh should hear the sad tidings with less abruptness than would be the necessary consequence of a letter addressed directly to herself.

It must be confessed that the melancholy intelligence which reached Lady Brashleigh in due course, lost none of its bitterness by the evidence which the details of her father's utter ruin gave of the uselessness of the sacrifice she herself had made in her marriage ; nor could she well command her feelings, when she discovered from her husband, that his nephew had been actuated to the hostilities which first ruined, and then killed her parent, by the very measure which that short-sighted and unworldly being had pressed upon her, as his only means of extrication from embarrassment.

Altogether, Fanny's situation might be considered truly miserable ; and, as if to force her into the most extraordinary trials, and submit her principle and virtue to the most powerful tests, she found, in the midst of her sorrow, that Welsted was the supporter of her aged father in his distress ; the only being on earth to close his tear-fraught eyes in solitude and grief, the last protector of his waning life, the mourning follower of his loved remains. It was fortunate, perhaps, at the moment that seas unbounded rolled between them—contrasted as his conduct was, with the stubborn, cold, and calculating charity of her husband ; added as was the warmest gratitude, to the thousand tender feelings of affection which before had thrilled her heart—a meeting might have been too much for human fallibility.

Welsted felt that he had done his duty and no more; and his grief at the loss of an old friend and master, from

whose society he had been long estranged by circumstances, was greatly qualified by the reflection that the
poor old man was emancipated from the sorrows of this
life, by the only means which now remained for his relief
—the happy transition to " another and a better world,"
from the blessings of which, weak and ambitious as he had
been, no faults of his were, it was to be hoped. sufficient
to exclude him.   Francis returned with the Viscount to
Oxford, and shortly after, according to annual custom,
paid his second, and, as it proved, his last visit to Paris,
where the Earl still remained our minister.

It was at the period of this visit decided, that the Viscount, after a tour through Europe, in company with his
reverend tutor (for Francis had now been ordained),
should commence public life by representing that select
community to which I have before referred, and in
whose society his exemplary father had, three seasons
before, indulged in the sublime sport of gudgeon-catch-
ing, in the western part of England ; and it was on the
return of the young men from this tour, that Welsted
was informed by his patron, that he had obtained for
him an appointment, which he would advise him not
to refuse, although it required his absence from England ;
adding, that it had, ever since he had known him, been
his intention to offer him the only piece of church preferment in his own gift, whenever the then present incumbent
should die,—and that he thought the appointment which
he had secured, would most seasonably and agreeably
occupy his time and talents, until the event. to which he
had alluded should enable him to provide for him at
home.

The situation now proposed was a chaplaincy in the
island of Ceylon,—and it was pressed upon Welsted with
an earnestness which he could not but perceive, and which
induced him instantly to accept it.   I may perhaps appear to make my hero somewhat too much of a lady-
killer, by repeating facts ; but true it is, that his talents,
manners, and accomplishments, joined to a fine temper
and sweet disposition, had made a sensation in a quarter,
where, of all others, no sensation ought to have been

made, and which, if encouraged, or admitted for a moment, must have entailed ruin and wretchedness on a being as full of gentleness and kindness as ever breathed : and who, apparently unaware of her own excellence, the extent of her accomplishments, and the influence of her rank and beauty, was evidently disposed to sacrifice all worldly considerations for him, for whom, if she did feel what the world calls love, she at least owned a sentiment perfectly new to her young and unsophisticated heart.

Welsted had for some time felt conscious that the conduct of the Lady Maria Rutherford towards him, had been latterly marked with a devotion and attention which pained him beyond measure ;—delighted in his society, she was never lively or gay but when *he* was present ; he saw her eyes fixed on his, when he accidentally looked towards her, and felt assured that the Earl and Countess must have seen the same symptoms of her growing affec tion ; and he had determined to quit Paris, at all events, before her noble father made him the offer of the chaplaincy. It was true Lord Farnborough had observed the evidence of his daughter's partiality, but such was his respect for Welsted, such his confidence in his honour, such his admiration of his talents, that he actually felt himself unable to censure the preference evinced by his child ; besides, his Lordship knew that the strongest measures are not always the wisest, and meaning to provide for Frank eventually at home, judged that the middle course by which he might offer him, for the present, a really desirable piece of preferment, and at the same time separate him from his daughter (not as if purposely, would be the advisable one ; and by using his interest accordingly, he procured the situation which he now tendered him.

It is strange that if his Lordship had delayed this offer but one day, Welsted, as I have said before. intended to have withdrawn himself, upon some imaginary plea, from the family : as it was, when he accepted the offer (which he did instantly), the Earl could not fail to observe, that he had anticipated his wishes, and that he more readily gave in to the arrangement, because it involved the accomplishment of a double object.

In truth, Lord Farnborough was too much a man of the world to believe for a moment that Welsted was blind to the evident partiality of his Lordship's second daughter; indeed, he had spoken to the Countess, who admitted the suspicious appearance of the case: but it became too clear for concealment, when an excuse was brought down by the Lady Anne, for her sister's absence from dinner, on the evening of the day in which Welsted had accepted the appointment.

Welsted's conduct and determination were not lost upon Lord Farnborough, and he saw in his present acquiescence in his views, a fresh example of that high principle and immovable rectitude which had invariably characterized the intercourse between them during the last three years; indeed the restlessness and anxiety of the young man to remove himself from the ambassador's hotel were most satisfactorily indicative to the Earl of the propriety of his conduct, the delicacy of his feelings, and the genuineness of his views and intentions.

The last day's dinner at his Lordship's was very like what all last days of such an intimacy must be,—full o nervous, worrying anxiety, a desire to be gay, and ai unconquerable disposition to be miserable. The young ladies on that day both dined at table, and Welsted, who had purposely occupied himself in the different shops o Paris during the morning, was placed on the same side a the Lady Maria, but not near her: thus no conversation no look even passed between them; but there were two guests at the board, who were specially invited on the occasion, who were able to express their feelings toward him without fear or impropriety.

Those guests were M. the Marquis de Ronfleur, and his son, Henri. By the solicitation and interference o the Earl, at the request of Welsted, the poor old emi grant had been forgiven his political defection, and re stored by Louis XVIII. to his rank and title in his bell France. His son, who, as it turned out, had escaped th death which his father supposed him to have suffered

had, under another name, been living for many years in
Switzerland, where he had married and settled; and it
was not until the newspapers had announced the restoration of his brother, and his subsequent reception at the
Tuileries, that he disclosed to his amiable wife the secret of his birth, or ventured to declare himself publicly.
The necessary preliminaries having then been arranged,
and the requisite prudential measures taken, he proceeded to Paris, identified himself satisfactorily, and was
received with rapture by his wondering parent!

As for M. the Marquis de Ronfleur himself, full of gratitude as he was to Welsted, and anxious to convince
every body how much he felt his obligations, he had lost
all his interest, and had become neither more nor less
than the old fripon of the vieille Cour;—full of grimace,
affectation, and unmeaning levity, he seemed, in the
decline of life, to forget that there was such a thing in
the world as adversity, or such a resting-place from its
afflictions as the grave; and at seventy-two danced quadrilles, and sang les petites chansons amoureuses, with all
the airs of a boy of twenty;—in short, he was an average
French gentleman: and when Welsted beheld him playing
fancifully with some of the ornaments with which the
Countess's dress was decorated, making his little calem-
bourg's, and dealing out now and then a *double entente,*
he could not but marvel at the constitution of his mind,
when he recollected that he was just as gay, just as
childish, and just as good-humoured in the dinner parlour of Mr. Tickle, at Hackney, where he was the play-
fellow of the schoolboys and the butt of the family,
while labouring under the united afflictions of poverty
and exile:—in short, all the change perceptible in the
manners of the Marquis was disadvantageous to him.

Welsted, however, had exercised his influence upon
the best possible principle, and admitting, since I believe
I must admit, that he was a little disappointed in the way
in which his great man had "come out," he could not
but feel an honest pride in seeing the poor old nobleman
restored to his belle France, where his son was restored to
him.

Time, however, which flew rapidly with Welsted, flies with equal rapidity here, and again I am warned to close my little history: I must therefore hurry the departure of my hero, as I verily believe, for all our sakes, it is best I should ; and passing over the affecting separation between the nobleman and his family, from whom he had received so much liberal and nobly-exerted patronage, drive him along the Place Louis Quinze, the Rue Rivoli, the Rue Castiglione, the Rue de la Paix, the Boulevards, the Chaussée d'Antin, and so out of the gayest city in the world ; hurry him in the midst of his reflections and re-collections over the Pavé to Calais; and on the third day from his quitting the French metropolis, put him down with the greatest safety at Long's; whence he was the next morning to proceed, according to the directions of Lord Farnborough, to secure and assume the office to which he had been appointed.

The life of Welsted was an eventful one, but this last event was, perhaps, the most striking which had occurred. He felt cheered and exhilarated by the prospect of the voyage and change ; for devoted as he was to Fanny, the constant association with the Lady Maria Rutherford was a continuous source of excitement and trial; he still fervently and ardently loved the one dear object,—but *she* was Lady Brashleigh, and he dared not carry his hopes so far as to anticipate her release from what he was assured must be thraldom of mind and body. In *his* situation there was an indelicacy, almost an impiety, in looking forward to the event, which, in the common course of nature, ought to emancipate her from bondage, and leave her, after years of misery, free to choose a husband for herself, whose taste and habits might assimilate with her own, and towards whom she might feel a sentiment with which Sir Frederick Brashleigh, it was quite clear, never yet had agitated her gentle heart.

Besides, a regular domestication with a creature like Lady Maria Rutherford is, under all circumstances, perilous in the extreme. Who can resist the tender, yet almost unconscious advances of approving woman ? She, innocent as a child, and lovely as angels are painted, feeling no guile, no necessity for concealing what *she* considered her " *likings*," pursued an artless, undisguised line of conduct, which wounded while it charmed ; and I defy the most phlegmatic thing that ever was made to look like man, to be constantly " paired off" with such a being as the second daughter of the Earl of Farnborough, admitted to all the privileges of a brother, and not being imbued with the natural and instinctive feelings of fraternity, without becoming more deeply interested in her fate than any individual ought to feel for a girl, in whose power it was not, to put the only period to such an acquaintance which could possibly justify its existence.

I have no time to moralize upon all this---the ship was waiting to sail, which was to bear Welsted to his destination—the different departments were all on the alert to give fresh impetus to his flight ; and in less than three weeks from the present period of my narrative, Francis Welsted was ploughing the salt sea on his way to Ceylon.

CHAPTER XV.

Which ends this strange eventful history.
SHAKSPEARE.

THE description of a pleasant voyage, through fine weather and smooth water, is as devoid of interest as the details of an every-day life, or the journal of a man confined to his room ; an uniformity and regularity characterize its course unbroken and unvaried, save by accidental differences in the quality of dinner or the quantity of wine consumed. Every thing goes on with the precision of clock-work, and one day is only the shadow and echo of another; suffice it then to say--and I hope I may escape the imputation of abruptness, for I am warned by my printer that I have already exceeded the prescribed length of a volume—that Francis luckily escaped all the perils of wind and weather, and at the close of the second month from the day of his departure, saw clear and distinct on the horizon, the Table Land of the Cape of Good Hope, at which place the master of the merchant ship in which he had secured his passage, had engaged to touch.

Like enjoyment from the sanguine expectant, the land seemed to fly from pursuit, and night closed upon them while still it was far distant; but when the following day dawned, they found themselves close to True Cape (for their destination was Symond's Bay); and before noon they were within False Bay; by ship dinner-time close to Seal Island, and at six o'clock in the evening, let go the anchor in sixteen fathom water. The Block House bearing one mile and three quarters south-east.

The sun was just casting its parting light behind the abrupt and lofty hills, at the back of the picturesque village, called Symond's Town; and the waving flags on the highest pinnacle of the signal mountain, upon which the reddened rays still played, announced to Cape Town, the arrival of a ship from England. Francis gazed on the new and interesting scene before him, with perfect delight.

The snow-white houses, with their spiral chimneys, contrasted with the deep tint of the high ground immediately behind them, appeared neat and comfortable; groups of soldiers leaning on the steps of the elevated barracks, watching the progress of the vessel to her anchorage, varied the scene upon what might be called the second ground of the picture; while others, either on the lengthened wharf of the dock yard, or on the road which runs along the cliff, some with glasses, and others trusting to their eyes, endeavouring to catch a glimpse of some returning resident, or some expected friend, gave to the whole an air of joyousness and snugness, not exactly in unison with Frank's preconceived ideas of the allurements of a small town in Southern Africa.

The natural anxiety of passengers to get on shore, was speedily gratified : the necessary forms having been complied with, the master of the ship, accompanied by Welsted and the only other passenger (a returning Indian), proceeded to the landing place, and thence to Baumaun's Hotel, at which they were accommodated with sitting and sleeping-rooms, and the privilege (if desired) of the billiard table, which occupied the centre of the room below. Welsted, who had been provided with a letter to the resident clergyman, having thus secured a *pied à terre*, next questioned the master of his vessel, as to how long he proposed remaining at the Cape, and having ascertained that three or four days would be the extent of his stay, resolved to visit Cape Town during that period, and then proceeded to deliver his note of introduction to the reverend gentleman before mentioned.

He was kindly and warmly received by the person in question; but, as it turned out, he came upon him at a moment of distress and affliction; his infant child, who had accompanied his wife to Cape Town, had there been taken dangerously ill : his duty for the following day (Sunday), would prevent his proceeding immediately to visit his infant; and the agitation and irritation, consequent upon such affliction, prevented the full display or that hospitality which the English resident in distant colonies loves to exercise towards his countrymen, whenever they chance to be brought in contact with him; but, as if Frank had been doomed always to benefit those with whom he was ever so slightly connected, his arrival relieved the anxiety of the fond parent, and enabled him to start instantly to his afflicted wife and sick child. Welsted, upon hearing the circumstances, volunteered to take his new acquaintance's duty for the next day ; and, although not perhaps extremely well prepared, was delighted to set the mind of a father and husband at rest, by inconveniencing himself in so trifling a degree.

It will be needless to describe the gratitude which the clergyman endeavoured, indeed vainly, to express, and the arrangement was made, that since Welsted wished to visit Cape Town as speedily as possible, his host should proceed forthwith to that place ; and, as there were no conveyances in Symond's Town, send down from Dixon's Livery Stables, at Cape Town, a light curricle-waggon, to bring him up on the Monday morning, where Frampton (such was the resident clergyman's name) might, should his child be convalescent, show the lions to the stranger, and endeavour, by his attentions, to repay the civility which he so warmly felt and gratefully acknowledged.

Accordingly, having given the necessary directions, he hurried his departure for Cape Town, whither also had gone direct, on horseback, the master of the ship, anxious to have a speedy conference with some of the Winkle-keepers at Capstadt, to whom he might probably dispose of part of his present investment.   Thus was Frank abandoned, as it were, to the alternative of a solitary second dinner, for which he felt a wholesome appetite; or the society of the returning Indian before named, with whom he had quarrelled three times every day for the last seven weeks : he preferred the former, and at nine o'clock sat down, in the dexter-parlour of M. Bauman's British Hotel, to a Roman fish, a boiled fowl, part of a porcupine, and as good a beef-steak as ever was dished at Dolly's, with a regular half-quartern loaf of Cockney-looking bread, which one would have sworn could not possibly have been made out of " the bills of mortality."

To claret he was driven at once, by a threat of native wine.   Having tasted the superior sorts of Cape physic at Miss Wilkinson's rural routs in his younger days, he most carefully eschewed that unpleasant exhibition of grape juice, and, as Port in Africa is at once rare, dear, and disagreeable, he had no choice; besides he had to prepare himself for the morning's service, and select from his trunk (which luckily was ashore) one of some half dozen sermons, which he had brought with him; and read, and re-read, so as to give himself courage to address a congregation of course wholly new and utterly strange to him.

This reading, however, was speedily interrupted by the arrival of several midshipmen, and masters' mates, and eke lieutenants of his Majesty's ships in the Bay, who summoned the markers and lamp-lighters, and proceeded forthwith to illuminate and occupy the billiard-table, refreshing themselves periodically with cigars, and glasses of grog, punch, or negus, according to their several tastes and propensities.

It was a moonlight evening, and after Frank had finished

his repast, and discovered that any attempt at study would be unavailing, either in his sitting-room, or bed-room, until the hotel should be closed for the night (for the plafond of the apartments was merely planked, so that the ascending noise of the mirthful party below, was even louder above stairs than in the next room), he left the house, strolled along towards the turnpike on the Cape-Town road, and saw by the bright beams of the orb of night, the hospitable mansion of King Osmond (as he is called), one of the most striking instances of successful industry perhaps on record. This excellent man, from an humble station in the British navy, has become the founder and proprietor of the greatest portion of the town which he inhabits, and whose doors would have flown open to receive Welsted, could their master have instinctively known that an English traveller was so near them.

In a remote part of the world like that which I am now attempting to describe, the settlement of our countrymen produces the strangest possible anomalies;—for instance, the man at the *turnpike-gate* seeing a stranger, warned Welsted not to turn into the *orange-grove*, opposite the commissioner's *street*-door, for fear of *snakes*—this struck the unaccustomed ear of Welsted as particularly odd, and he felt deeply interested in his exploration of the town, and took the whole range of it, from the toll-gate at the one end, to the naval hospital at the other, and was perfectly astonished at the neatness, regularity, and comfortable appearance of every thing he saw.

When he returned, or shortly after, the youngsters were dispersing, and although they were succeeded by some young Dutchmen, the games were concluded by eleven o'clock, and Welsted was at his table, "reading up," for the morning's exhibition.

The clerk, who was moreover post-master, and ci-devant beater of the long-drum, in the Cape corps, was at his door betimes, although Frank was up before his arrival: even the school-mistress, resembling much in shape a fillet of veal on castors, thought it right to pay her devoirs to the new minister, and inform his reverence how it was

customary to place her tender charges at chapel, so that
my hero had a sort of clerical levee at his breakfast-table.

It was extremely gratifying to see the neatness and regularity with which the lower orders repaired at the proper
time to divine service ; the dock-yard men, and the schoolboys and the girls, and the troops from the barracks, all in
their best array, associated with the officers and respectable inhabitants, and under the mild, yet pious *surveillance* of the gallant Baroi et, who has distinguished himself not more by intrepidity in his splendid naval career,
than by excellence in private life, mingled in one equal
undistinguished body, to raise the voice of supplication
and of gratitude, to HIM who made and who supported
them.

The hour of service at length arrived, and Welsted, who
had but seldom appeared in a reading-desk, and not much
oftener in a pulpit, experienced that nervous trepidation
which was perfectly natural, on presenting himself in the
midst of strangers ; he was cold, and almost trembled ;
and church oratory, from its nature, not admitting of any
of those marks of approbation which cheer and encourage
the senator, the pleader, or the player, he felt, as he
almost unconsciously ascended the steps of the desk, the
most sensitive dread of hearing his own voice sounding
alone through the silence of the chapel—for one might
have heard a pin drop, as the old women say,—so still and
orderly were the congregation.

Feeling, however, that retreat was impossible, and that
it was imperative upon him to fulfil the duty he had undertaken, he arranged his books, and commenced the beautiful service of our church:—his voice was tremulous at
first, but deep and melodious; and though the general
silence was unbroken, except when the people made the
responses ; as he proceeded he gained fresh confidence, and
felt himself warm with energy and pleased and supported
by the attention which at first he had so much dreaded.

At length he dared to look around him : it was as he
was about to commence the first lesson for the day, and
his eyes naturally fell upon those nearest to him.   At the

same juncture, a female in a pew immediately under him in front of the reading-desk, raised her head from the inclined posture in which she had devoutly kept it during the prayers : her cheek was pale as death, and her eyes were filled with tears ;—her look met his—it was Lady Brashleigh.

Those who know what treasured love is—those who know the pangs, unseen, unmarked, which hearts are doomed to feel when sorrow must be mute ; those who know what the sight of a loved object, after years of bitter separation, can effect ; those who know, in short, what human nature is, when excited to the last stretch of feeling ; may, if they can, imagine the horrors of Welsted's situation at this moment.

In the fulfilment of his pious office, he suddenly beheld, as it were in a vision, her, to love whom was sin. Conscious of his own fallibility, words damnatory of worldly weakness quivered on his lips, while his heart thrilled with a fervent and unholy passion ; he read, but the lines seemed to dance before his eyes ; his thoughts were not on the Divine Being, whose minister he was, and to whom he was addressing himself. He felt all this, and dared not trust himself to look again upon the object of his agitation, even hoping, as he did, that he might yet undeceive himself, and that after all it was but a likeness of his Fanny.

At length a pause in the service allowed him again to cast a glance towards her ; again did she raise her pale countenance. It was all too true—he saw her tremble—she was in mourning—what were his thoughts ?—what, in that holy place, and in that reverend garb his *hopes ?*—must I say it ?—no—they must be guessed. The agonies he felt, the self-conviction of his fault, were enough to weigh him down, without the accusing voice of his historian.

The sermon commenced—it had been written by him, not in bitterness, but in the warmth of personal feeling, against ambition and the love of worldly gain. Every line seemed as he read it, to apply pointedly to his own circumstances, and those of Fanny , to his self-devotion, and her father's thirst for wealth and title, as if he had endeavoured expressly to wound her, and harrow up the recollection of her parents' weaknesses and follies. A picture even of a contented home in humble life, drawn (as it naturally would be) from that in which he had himself enjoyed *her* society, illustrated his doctrines ; what could all this appear, but pointed cruelty to wound the heart that loved him.

His doubts (for Fanny was so much altered, that he *did* doubt the identity) were cleared up by the clerk, when he retired to change his vestments—it *was* Lady Brashleigh, who had come with Sir Frederick for the benefit of his health from Bombay, and who now, being restored, was on the eve of returnng to India.

When the sermon was concluded, there appeared a wilful delay on the part of the congregation, until Welsted should leave the pulpit and come amongst them. He felt that he would give the world to quit his place and join the group below, in which stood Lady Brashleigh herself: he even thought she cast a wistful look towards the spot where he stood, but he felt convinced that he ought not—that he could not approach her. The congregation moved onwards, and the chapel was cleared ; he *then* felt he would have given the world that he *had* spoken to her, but it was then too late, and he proceeded to the hotel, half mad with contending miseries, convinced that Fanny was dearer to him than ever; and conscious, that in the execution of his holy functions that day, his lips had belied the feelings of his heart, even in the presence of his Maker.

His first inquiries at Bauman's were relative to the Brashleighs ; and he found the account which he had received from the clerk to be perfectly true : he found also, that His Excellency had been for some time residing at an extremely pretty house in the neighbourhood of Symond's Town; and that his health was so wonderfully restored, that he was " quite another man." He inquired of the waiter the situation of their residence (which was described to him as being mid-way between the town and race-course), determined when night should come, to bend his steps that way; for though worlds would not have tempted him to an interview, still he thought he might gaze on the house where she dwelt, the casket which contained the jewel; and accordingly, after he had gone through the forms of another dinner (for with all his anxiety to meet Lady Brashleigh, he was confined to the house during the day by an inexplicable dread of a *rencontre* with her), he prepared himself for his evening's stroll, it having been first announced to him that one of Dixon's curricle-waggons had arrived from Cape Town in readiness for the following morning, and that the messenger had brought a note from his new friend Frampton, informing him that his child was out of danger, and that he should be delighted to introduce him to his wife, and show him every civility in his power during his stay.

Welsted felt greatly relieved by the anticipation of a journey and a visit to Cape Town; in short, by any excitement which could divert his thoughts from the object upon which they were rivetted, and which could now rest no where else, at all events, while he remained in that neighbourhood. Following the directions of the waiter, he proceeded in his ramble, and very soon came in sight of the house so accurately described by his informant. He stood and gazed upon the lights which glittered in the apartments; he saw figures moving to and fro; in his imagination distinguished that of Fanny from the others, at a distance, whence any difference in persons was wholly undiscernible. But tired of the melancholy pleasure of gazing, he crossed the road, and lighted by the bright moon, proceeded down the heath-studded cliff towards the spot where the strange rock, called Noah's Ark, seems floating on the waves, and as he stepped from point to point down the precipitous path, a huge eagle, pale as the orb which beamed upon her broad wings, roused from her nest, rose swiftly and loudly as it were from under his feet; he was startled at the unexpected sight; in a moment he heard voices near him—they were of females: in another moment they were close to him; by the clear moon's light he saw Fanny and another person unknown to him, followed at a few paces distance by Major Mims (without whom Sir Frederick could not live), carrying a huge bundle of heaths and water-lilies, which the ladies had been collecting. Welsted saw her as plainly as I see this paper, and *she* saw *him;* but they spake not. She seemed to hurry past him; and he felt spell-bound, as they say men are who see spectres. They passed on their different ways: the Major, half enveloped by his botanical burden, civilly made way for the descending stranger, and even favoured him with half a bow, evidently recognising him as the preacher of the morning; and *that* was all that passed; lucky it was, that it was so.

The morning came, and with it, at least to the door of the hotel, Dixon's curricle-waggon, and a pair of as nice horses as ever trotted under a bar. Welsted stepped into the snug vehicle, and was whisked along at an extremely pretty pace, the driver being wholly unaffected by the loose stones which had rolled into the ruts of the road, and as little mindful of the heaviness of the sands, while following the curvatures of the different bays, in which the sea rolled over the naves of the wheels, and threatened the footing of the steeds—this precaution of keeping so near the water's edge being taken to avoid the more perilous depths of sand farther in-shore. Along, however, went the waggon, thumping and bumping up this hill and down that, till sundry indications were given of their approach to the whale-fishery, the whole of which sport I would stop to describe, as Welsted stopped to see it, but that I am circumscribed for room. The pass of Mussenburg, the Thermopylæ of the Cape, next presented itself, and the road by degrees grew better, until at length the far-spreading valley of Constantia gave to the eye of the traveller, not only a beautiful and extensive prospect, but a road as excellent as Mr. Macadam himself could make in a moment of enthusiasm.

At this period of the journey, the driver suggested a short halt at the half-way house; and upon receiving an affirmative to his application, from Welsted, he dashed out of the high road, across a sort of ditch, waggon and all, and took across the country right on end towards the inn, scorning the beaten paths of former travellers, and, miraculous as it seemed, to the uninitiated passenger, reached the court-yard of Mr. Green's caravansary in perfect safety.

Here again some colonial anomalies startled the traveller : a Caffre was paid with three penny pieces for carrying a bundle, and a Hottentot driver was regaling himself with ale out of a pewter pot, while mine host of the halfway house was telling the driver of a *glass* coach, that *the wolves* had been down into the *inn-yard* the night before, and carried off one of his pigs. " nolus bolus " (so Mr. Green expressed himself). This, and the contrast afforded by the neat English-looking house, with fireplaces in the sitting-rooms, and pipes and punch-bowls in the bar, to the wild scenery of the valley bounded by the stupendous Table Land, the farms of great and little Constantia in the distance on one side ; and on the other, by the mountains in Hottentot's Holland, or that inaccessible range known as the " back-bone of the earth," excited the strangest sensations in Walsted's mind, but as he proceeded towards the colonial metropolis, the houses on either side the road presented the appearance of comfort and civilization : and when Newlands, the country-seat of the governor, and Van Rienen's beautiful place, the " Brewery." with the residences of many wealthy official and mercantile persons developed themselves, the surprise and strangeness of the first approach wore off ; and by the time he reached the castle of Cape Town, he fancied himself again in England.

He was not, however, prepared to see such a town as that which he then entered, nor do I think that any of my readers who have not visited it, have formed a clearer idea of it than Welsted. The streets, which are broad and magnificent in their appearance, run parallel to each other, and occasionally diversified by large open squares, give a bold and splendid appearance to the South-African capital, which no writer, I think, has led one to expect.

The parade, which separates the town from the castle, planted with trees, and laid out in walks, is one of the most spacious perhaps extant ; in the castle are the apartments of the military commandant and other officers ; to the north, is a range of fine private houses ; and the barracks, which are vastly extensive, form one side of a square, called Caledon-square, in which stands the custom-house, an elegant and convenient building.

I have no space to describe the localities, but it is only justice to give a fair impression of one of our most interesting possessions ; and it may therefore be right to endeavour to express Welsted's surprise, when he found Laugstreet, a mile in length—stretching from Strand-street to the Tuinwick ; Brae-street, of equal length, upwards of one hundred and fifty feet in width ; and Loop Street and Berg-street of equal pretension, replete with every attribute of comfort and occupation ; the Heer-Graat boasting its club-houses, and loungers ; the Company's Gardens (in which stands the Government House), beautifully laid out, and ornamented, and the environs reminding him strongly of Bath, supposing it were possible to remove that picturesque city from the sink of vapour and steam in which it stands, to the edge of a magnificent bay, whose shores are studded with farms, and villas, and villages, skirted by cloud-clapped mountains, and splendidly characterized by the stupendous Table Land, whence it derives its name.

Welsted was speedily set down at the door of Frampton's residence, where he found that worthy personage so changed in manner and conduct, by the favourable alteration in the health of his child, that he would hardly have recognised him ; he completely succeeded with my hero in doing away every doubt of his cordiality, by the earnest expression of thankfulness for his kindness, and the most assiduous attentions during his stay in the capital ; at the close of which, he joined Frank in returning to Symond's Town, leaving his lady there, until the infant should be sufficiently recovered to undertake the journey.

When Welsted reached Bauman's hotel, the waiter told him that his Excellency Sir Frederick Brashleigh had called upon him twice during his absence, and the last time had left a letter. Frank's astonishment was great at this announcement, but his surprise was indescribable when he read the following billet ·

" Dear Sir,

" I almost scolded Lady Brashleigh when she told me,
on my return hither from Newlands, that you had arrived
in this colony, and even preached at Symond's Town on
Sunday, because she had not immediately invited you to
our bungalow, where she ought to have known I should be
most happy to see you.   Indeed, your conduct towards
Lady B's unfortunate parents has given me the greatest
satisfaction ; and I confess that her Ladyship's conduct
towards you evinces a coldness of which I did not suspect
her ; and so I have taken the liberty of telling her.   I
trust she will be able to give an account of herself, which
may be satisfactory to *you*, when we have the pleasure of
seeing you here.

" The people at the inn do not seem to know exactly
when you return, but I leave this to request you will dine
with us, whatever day you come back, at seven o'clock.

" Meanwhile believe me yours obediently,

" FRED. BRASHLEIGH "

This letter, so contrary in spirit to the general conduct
of Sir Frederick, so widely different in its character from
the manner he assumed when speaking to Welsted, at the
Opera-house, staggered my hero, who did not at first perceive, that although a basilisk would have been almost as
welcome to his Excellency as himself, his Excellency felt
it politic to play the " Liberal," and by soothing and
pleasing the friend and protégé of his late father-in-law,
obtain his good opinion, and consequently good report, in
order that he might not, under a feeling of disappointment or neglect, be induced to give circulation to anecdotes of Lady Brashleigh's early days, or conjure up the
ghost of her departed sire, to mar the splendour of his
Excellency's reign.

To refuse the invitation, was of course impossible—to
accept it, terrible—and yet was Frank not prepared for the
importance of the trial to which he and Fanny were destined to be exposed.   I have no space to detail the proceedings of this important day, nor paint the dreadfully

agitating embarrassment of both parties ; every allusion to
past events, every remark of his Excellency upon her
Ladyship's coldness, overwhelmed Welsted ; every cross
word or angry look of his Excellency's, went to his heart ;
and while his Excellency seemed over anxious to load him
with civilities and attention, he shrank from him, as the
being who had marred his earthly happiness, and reduced
by continual irritation and overbearing tyranny, the blooming, lovely Fanny Rodney, to the pale, melancholy, woe-
begone creature, who now stood before his eyes, the faded
vision of her former self.

But imagine what must have been Frank's sensations
when, after due preparation, his Excellency announced
the fact that he had secured a passage for himself, Lady
Brashleigh and his family, in the ship in which he (Welsted) was a passenger, and which, after landing him at
Ceylon, was to carry them on to Bombay.

What was to be done ? Had Frank previously known of
this plan, he would have made some excuse to quit the
vessel ; but now his doing so would be so marked, and so
evidently a measure founded on the intelligence he had just
received, that it would be impossible. And yet he felt bewildered by the prospect before him : to be domesticated
day by day, hour by hour, with the being nearest and dearest
to his heart, the witness of her sorrows, perhaps the deposi-
tary of her confidence.—What then ?—They might still be
friends—was it not natural ?—They had been playmates,
brought up together ; might not their intimate association
continue with equal security and innocence ? Welsted
hoped it might, yet trembled at the consideration of the
subject. Strong and inflexible as was his principle, excellent and pure as was his Fanny's heart, the trial seemed
almost too much for human fallibility.

It was no common case ; the lover who had relinquished
her to secure her happiness at the expense of his own, was
to be brought, not only into constant contact with her, not
only was she to enjoy the society which she loved best in
the world, not only were the recollections of their youth
to be refreshed by his presence, but all these harrowing,
agitating combinations were to acquire new force, new

strength, by taking place in the actual presence of him whom, had she never known, she would in all human probability have never been unhappy. And then for her to endure the constant dread of that ferocious jealousy which characterized Sir Frederick's conduct; and which, smooth and smiling as was the expression of countenance which he had chosen to assume towards Frank, she knew would burst into a flame on the first appearance of even common cordiality between them: was it not altogether fearful? It was a dreadful struggle for the unhappy creature, to maintain the dignified demeanour, the cold and placid indifference of manner towards Francis, which she knew it was expected she should exhibit, even during the four hours of his first visit; what would be the effect of the continued effort during weeks, perhaps months, of a voyage in his society; and what the effect upon her own conscious mind, of the reflection, that even if she succeeded, it *was* after all an effort. For the first time, perhaps, in their lives, Francis and Fanny wished that they were not destined to be together; a wish which, like many others they had sympathetically felt, not destined to be fulfilled; the preparations for the voyage went on rapidly, to suit the arrangements of the master of the ship; and in ten days (during which the long disunited pair had never been alone together, nor exchanged one syllable upon their almost marvellous meeting), every thing was in readiness for sailing.

Sir Frederick and her Ladyship proceeded, the day previous to their departure, to Newlands, to bid farewell to the Governor and his family, whence they were to return and embark direct; all the persons of his Excellency's suite, except Major Mims, being on board, as well as the other two passengers. On that day it occurred at one time to Welsted to absent himself, and allow his passage to be lost; such was the dread with which he anticipated the eventful voyage with Fanny. But, finding from the master, that his disappearance would only delay the ship until he appeared again, he relinquished his scheme, and was on board ready to receive the party on the following morning.

The day came, and a little after noon, the *cortège* of the Governor was seen traversing the various bays, on its way to Symond's Town ; and Welsted, with his glass traced the party in their progress ;—he saw but Fanny—she sat pale and motionless as ever ; no word moved her lips—no object seemed to attract her eyes : no—she was considering in her mind the importance of the duty she had to perform, the overwhelming conflict she had to sustain.

At length, the carriages were hidden from the sight ; nor did they reappear until they drew up at the gates of the dock-yard, at the stairs of which, one or two boats belonging to the men-of-war in the bay, and the Commissioner's barge, were ready to convey the important passengers on board the vessel destined to transport them to their splendid exile.   A gay crowd hovered round the steps, and in a few minutes the guns from the block-house announced that dignity was afloat.   The barge, however, instead of proceeding direct to the merchantman, steered a course towards the frigate which was at anchor, led by the captain in his gig, who " gave way," and was at the gangway ready to receive the party, who by pre-arrangement were to go " all over the ship," and partake of a cold collation on board.

When there are two great men afloat together, it becomes extremely difficult properly to apportion the salutes and other honours.   The governor at the Cape wished to compliment his visiter, and the captain of the frigate wished to compliment the governor at the Cape ; and although his Excellency gave precedence to the other Excellency, the moment his Excellency the Governor Regnant stepped on board, the salute was begun, and his Excellency's Vice-Admiral's red flag run up to the foretopgallant-masthead ; poor Fanny was whipped up smartly, and landed safely, but more dead than alive, on the quarter-deck, and in the midst of the roaring of guns and the smoke which gracefully darted from their muzzles, her Ladyship was conducted by the gallant captain to his cabin, where a superb *déjeuner à la fourchette*, graced the board.

During this imposing ceremony, Welsted was watching the proceedings with all a lover's interest, and saw clearly her Ladyship leaning on the arm of the captain as they stood by the tafferil, where the gallant officer was pointing out to her Ladyship the singular and colossal natural likeness of the late king, formed by a mountain at the back of one of the smaller bays, and which constitutes one of the lions of those parts. Welsted saw the attentive manner of the captain, and saw her Ladyship smile at some remark he made, and his heart palpitated more rapidly than usual ; but the moment afterwards he observed Sir Frederick approach and invite her Ladyship, in action not to be misunderstood, to change her position ; for although courtesy demanded that the captain should take charge of the lady on board his own frigate, his Excellency saw no necessity for the geological discussion into which he appeared to be entering. and which seemed to his Excellency to have been already sufficiently protracted.

The master of the merchant-ship, who was anxious to get away, bestowed, as persons of that class under similar circumstances are not unapt to do, divers and sundry imprecations upon the heads of all the parties concerned in this breakfasting affair, and proceeded to make ready for starting as far as he was able ; he therefore " upped with his anchor," and " out topsails," and began clumsily to disport about, tacking and wearing, and laying-to by turns, until six bells, when, just as his patience was exhausted, another salute from the frigate announced his Excellency again afloat, and in a few moments the Commissioner's barge was seen shooting from under the lee of his Majesty's ship, and the well-trained crew pulling steadily towards the trader.

Lady Brashleigh was doomed to be yet more annoyed and alarmed ; for the schipper, determined not to be *out-done* by a frigate, had all his guns ready ; and no sooner had his Excellency ascended the side, than away went his ricketty carronades and long sixes promiscuously, helter-skelter, both sides, at once,—the great beauty of the performance being its graceful irregularity.

The moment the party were on board, the topgallant sails were shaken out, down went the foresail, and the heavy trader was under way ; at which juncture another salute, intended to perform the double duty of a return

18

to that of the schipper and a compliment to the Cape Governor at the same time, was fired; his Excellency was
seen returning to the dock-yard, his Honorary bunting
having been duly dowsed from the mast-head of His Majesty's ship.

To Fanny, the morning had been miserably oppressive;
forced to appear to take an interest in the minutest details of naval regulations, poking about, half double, into
dark holes to look at three links of a chain cable, fitte l
upon the last new principle! indulged with a dissertation
upon the merits of a double capstan : and gratified before
luncheon with the sight of soup for five hundred, in a
sort of tank, and the smell of rum served out to the crew
in watering-pots; suffocated with the closeness of the at
mosphere, invited into the gun-room, where two lieutenants were playing drafts, the purser reading Paul and Vir-
ginia, and the surgeon and master, arguing in a loud tone
on the merits of a captain with whom they both had sailed
(all the said personages wishing the party at old Scratch,
who were thus brought to their quarters); and subsequently placed at table, sick with sorrow and fatigue, next
the gallant captain, afraid of receiving coldly the marked
attentions which he paid her, indifferent to them herself,
and conscious that every civil word he uttered, would cost
her an hour of scolding from her magnificent spouse; her
thoughts being at the moment precisely as far from the
scene of action, as the merchant-ship chanced to be from
the frigate.

When she reached the former, there was a soothing
quietude in her own cabin, which pleased her; and having, by pleading a violent headach (which his Excellency
considering the travelling, and boating, and breakfasting,
and saluting, considered only natural), excluded the partner of her existence from her *sanctum*, she found relief
from her agitation in a flood of tears.

The inconvenience which ladies inevitably feel on their
first embarkation, the many absolutely essential arrangements to be made, superadded to a secret dread of encountering Francis, kept poor Fanny in her cabin, until
the clumsy merchantman had passed (which she did in a

squall) the Anvil and Bellows ; the wind whistled through
the shrouds and rigging, and a dense fog came over her,
so that the latter rock was hardly seen before the whirl of
waters announced it near, and they passed it within half-
a-mile's distance to the N.N.W of them. It now blew
pretty fresh, the topsails were close-reefed, the jib and
driver stowed, and just before dusk they saw True Cape
Point, N.E. and by N. about three miles ; wind still fresh
at N.W. and by W

At the usual hour of supper on board Sir Frederick
made his appearance and conversed with Welsted with
much affability and complacency, to the utter astonishment of Major Mims, who stood peering his small face
over the windward bulwarks, lost in wonder. The
breeze almost stopping his breath, and the spray which
broke about her quarter, sousing him, every five minutes.
He was evidently lost in a revery, and chilled not more
by wonder and the water, than by the absence of Lady
Brashleigh : for although her Ladyship had been properly
drilled into silence and obedience, still, having a fellow-
sufferer in slavery was something ; and the Major, who
was as affectionate as a poodle, had got such a habit of
trotting about after her Ladyship, that he felt quite unhappy that on board her Ladyship wanted none of his assistance and care, and felt even jealous of the waiting-
women, whose services she actually required.

One thing tended amazingly to improve his Excellency's
temper ; the small yellow personage, with the patent countenance of invalid Indians, who was now returning with
very little of his liver left (quite satisfied that he was entirely cured of any complaint in that region), to work his
way into council ; turned out to be a very old friend of
Sir Frederick, and it was quite edifying to hear the worthies comparing the merits of the presidencies (for the ci-
vilian was a Bengalee), and infinitely amusing to listen to
the details of tours, travelling by dawk through the jow
jungle, wetting their whiskers in nullahs, tiffing in topes,
punkah'd by Ranees and salamed by Shaws ; and then
the aqueous delights in which they had both indulged ;
the budgerowing and pinnacing, the mhangees and the

naar's, the goleahs and the dandies, and the stories how
the Howah acted upon the Paul and the Lungur on the
pankah, and the minute and elaborate calculations of how
many koss it actually was, from Ochra to Dalmow, with
a history of all the quicksands and pullings and pushings,
till it was time to legow somewhere about Kutterah.   In
such stories as these did the time of these companions
pass, and Sir Frederick smoked his chilum, his hookah
cleeted to the deek, and whiffed and " wobbled," and
wore away the evening, until six bells proclaimed it at a
proper hour to turn in.

The wind blew fresh, and the bulk-heads creaked ; and
besides the usual quantum of disturbance in a merchantman, the guns, two of which had long been used as props
to the filtering-stones (two more having served to keep a
scuttle-butt in its place), got adrift upon the quarter-deck,
and produced a most awful disturbance.   A bulk-head
only divided the round-house (Lady Brashleigh's cabin),
from the cabin of Welsted ; and in the momentary lulls of
the tremendous noise, he could hear her sobs of alarm at
what really sounded very frightful, replied to by the harsh
and angry scoldings of her irritable husband, who, elated
by the pleasures of a friend and chilum, if not by the frequent libations of grog, in which his Excellency had indulged, was actively alive to carry on a discussion, which,
if it partook not of the character of civil war, sounded at
all events, very like domestic contention.

The morrow came, but the weather mended not ; indeed, the wind had freshened considerably in the night,
and its effects, conspired with the positive dread Fanny
felt of recommencing her intimacy with Welsted, to con-
fine her to her cabin ; nor did she regret the inconvenience
which she suffered, as it afforded a plausible pretext for
absenting herself from the cuddy ; and would, she hoped,
afford her time to compose her spirits and subdue her
feelings, so as to meet and converse more calmly with the
beloved object of her affections.

During the day, the breeze freshened to a gale, and
there was a great deal of sea on ; the master of the ship
himself looked anxiously towards some flashes of light-

ning in the N.W., and gave practical proof of his apprehensions, by getting down his topgallant masts and yards,
and in his jib-boom. After a considerable delay and
search, the dead-lights were gradually found and fitted,
and darkness in the after-cabin was added to the comforts
which it already afforded. The unsoundness of the dead-
lights, however, permitted a certain degree of light to
penetrate through sundry cracks and fissures which most
certainly should not have appeared in them, but which it
was equally certain could not now be repaired.

At midnight it blew tremendously, and the ship was
under two close-reefed topsails, straining and labouring
dreadfully; about one A. M. she shipped a heavy sea,
which washed away all the starboard bulwarks and wash-
boards, and deluged the cabins, which were near the companion; and yet, in the midst of the hurly-burly of the
elements, the rattling of chairs and tables adrift, which
swept the cuddy from right to left, as the huge helpless
ship rolled about in the mountainous sea, Welsted could
still hear the sobbing of Lady Brashleigh, and the inces-
sant reproaches of her husband, for absurd timidity, when
there was not the smallest danger.

At daylight, the gale blew, if possible, still harder;
the men were constantly at the pumps; at eight A. M.
another tremendous sea struck her, and stove in the larboard quarter-boat, the davits were unshipped, and the
boat cut away; in a moment after, the iron-work of the
dead of the main rigging went, and three following seas
swept her fore and aft; before noon, another sea, equally
awful with the former, struck her on the starboard quarter, and stove the quarter-boat, which was cut away,
as that on the larboard side had been before, and the
night closed in, with awful presages of even yet worse
weather.

All these prognostics were verified; a little after midnight (the darkness unmitigated, except by a faint, un-
frequent, distant flash of forked lightning, which seemed
itself baffled and driven about by the wind), a huge sea
rolling onwards, like a black mountain topped by snow,
broke directly on board, to windward, and swept away the

launch, the live stock, and the cabooce; the staunchicns, and ring-bolts, tearing up the decks along with them, and leaving them open to the rolling waves, which made regular way over her.

In the middle of the night, all the starboard main-chain-plates gave way; the forerunners and tackle were got to secure the mast, but the worst misfortune was yet to occur; a leak was discovered under her sternpost, through which, as she rose to meet the coming waves, rushed in at every pitch an awful quantity of water

All hands were at the pumps, and it was clear, that unless the ship were lightened, the leak would gain upon them; before daylight the men were fainting from fatigue, and cold, and wet, and sank from their labour; the ship seemed rapidly settling, and the waist was ankle deep in water, yet no one dared to sound the well, lest those who already had begun to despair, should, if the report were bad, give themselves up for lost, and, by abandoning themselves to their fate, involve the fate of others.

In the midst of this tremendous storm, there gleamed a pale flickering light upon the topmast head: it seemed to burn unmoved by the contending gusts around it,—in a moment it shifted to the fore-topmast—then darted back to its old position, having in its rapid flight touched the iron ring at the mainyard-arm; the undisturbed serenity of the flame, the striking contrast it afforded to the surrounding darkness, coupled with the sad time at which they beheld it, rendered this natural phenomenon deeply interesting, if not positively awful.

Out of her cabin, and out of her bed, was dragged the half lifeless Fanny, by her husband, contrary to her inclination, and in opposition to her earnest prayers, to look on this; his Excellency carried his point, as he was wont to do—and called to Welsted to support her Ladyship as she stood on the companion ladder, in obedience to his Excellency's command.

In the horrors of this night, in the midst of hurricanes and tempests, now lifted to the mountain's top, now buried in the fathomless valley of waters below, the ill-fated Fanny leaned once more for support upon the companion of her youth, the beloved of her heart; again did she experience the gentle solicitude which ever marked his conduct towards her; again did she feel the pressure of that hand which she had so often clasped in friendship and affection; he spoke soothingly to her, and though the words he uttered were lost to her ear in the general din, she felt his breath upon her cheek—her feelings overcame her—she fainted in his arms—in the arms of Welsted, who thus was driven, in conjunction with her husband, to carry her into her cabin. The dangers and difficulties of such a proceeding in such a time, trifling as they may seem to landsmen, will be duly appreciated by those who have ever been partakers of them.—She was at length, however, safely placed on her couch, although insensible to every thing around her.

" She is a bad passenger in a storm, Mr. Welsted," said his Excellency.

A storm, indeed !—not the wild roarings of the mighty waters, not the rude elemental strife, at whose mercy she was, not the forked lightning that glared, nor the pealing thunder that roared over their heads, was half so potent as the storm that agitated her own mind—there raged the dreadful conflict of PASSION WITH PRINCIPLE.

As soon as day dawned, and the wretched state of the ship, then almost a wreck, was evident, the master gave orders to commence lightening her; all hands were turned up; the bulk-heads forward were knocked down, and every one set to work to heave cargo overboard; the difficulty of getting at it, as she was then rolling and pitching, was great; but, after half an hour, a chain of hands was formed aft; and bales, and chests, and barrels, and cases, were promiscuously hoisted upon deck, where the foaming waves took them, and swept them into the bosom of the deep.

All exertions, however, appeared unavailing, and though the day had been expended in alternately heaving overboard and pumping, the ship laboured just as much, the leaks continued to gain, the men grew fainter, and the storm, if possible, increased ;—Birds flocked for shelter to the rigging, and the bravest sailor there, held on, and trembled.

At eight at night, without consulting or communing with a human being, the master resolved, if possible, to wear ship, conscious as he was, that the experiment was perilous in the extreme, and would in all probability be fatal; having made all ready, he gave the word, and in a momentary lull, she went about, without straining a rope-yarn.   Hope beamed on his mind then; those who knew not his thoughts felt increased apprehensions; for, after wearing, she lay in the trough of the sea rolling gunnel under; no sail set, for none could stand the weather; the small one, used to bring her round, was blown into ribands from the stay; till just at midnight, a crash on deck announced the main-mast gone; at one blow, like the stricken deer, she fell toppling with her yards and top-mast over the starboard side; she went about ten feet above the deck, just above the mizen-stay; and the mizen-mast itself trembled like a reed, as Welsted clung to it, to watch the work of havoc going on above.

It was a scene for a painter : the noise was inconceivable, the night inky black, the waves were dashing over every part of the vessel; the women battened down forward, were screaming for mercy; their cries were mingled with the clashing of axes cutting away the rigging, by the gleaming light of lanterns, disposed in the most advantageous points; the stern bawling of those in command were heard through the tumult, with the faint replies of others who were in the main-chains, in the midst of the stupendous waves, endeavouring to clear the ship of wreck; for the mast clung as it were to the quarter, and the counter beat so heavily upon the main-top, which lay close beneath it, that every moment they expected she would be stove in.

At this instant, three following seas again swept her fore and aft, and a shriek of horror, which overtopped the howlings of the tempest itself, announced some dreadful calamity.   All those who were forward were washed at one " fell swoop" from off the bows, and plunged into imevitable destruction. Even Fanny was conscious of the increase of noise, and of a change of motion in the ship; she rushed from her cabin, and caught the arm of her husband, who was holding on by the top of the companion-ladder, encouraging by his presence the hardy sailors in their duty.

" Sir Frederick," said she, " what is it?—let me——"

" Nothing, ma'am, nothing!" said the General, harshly and angrily; " go to bed, Lady Brashleigh; there is no danger, ma'am—all will be well soon."

Another following sea struck her—and another—it was the last!—the dead lights were shivered into splinters—the stern-frame itself yielded to the shock—the water deluged the decks below, and carrying every thing before it, burst upwards through the deck itself, driving those who were on the companion forward.

Fanny was caught, as she was whirled forward, by Welsted, who seized firmly hold of the binnacle, which broke away from its cleets; Sir Frederick was hurried onward in the mass of waters, and the master of the ship, having uttered an exclamation too clearly indicative that all was over, was seen endeavouring for a moment to " hold on" by the foremast, but in another instant the overwhelmed ungovernable ship met a tremendous coming wave, and rose not to meet it—unresisted and unopposed the huge mountain burst directly upon her; the contending sea rushing forward from the stern, met the advancing torrent; the ship plunged forward for a moment, as if struggling with destruction, but the effort was vain, and forging ahead, she sank at once into the fathomless deep.

Welsted, who had never let go his precious charge, during the important period in which all this was transacting, had lashed his beloved to the binnacle; himself holding on firmly, and when the whirl of waters, in which the ship seemed to suck down every thing around it, had a little subsided, he awoke to a consciousness of his situation; the binnacle floated beyond the confines of the horrid abyss, and upon the surface of the mountainous waves still floated the fond devoted pair.

The power of endurance with which humanity is gifted

is hardly credible to th)se who have not suffered ; here
was the delicate Lady Brashleigh, nurtured with the
fondest care, and couched on downy beds, the evening
breeze itself too rude to blow upon her, exposed to the
tempestuous wind and constant drenching of a raging sea
through a night of awful misery.   She was unconscious of
her situation ; and it was with the greatest care and toil
that Welsted could sustain her in a position which alone
secured her from almost entire immersion in the waves.
The sickening and dreadful sameness of mounting rapidly
on one high billow, followed by the dreadful and impetuous
fall from it, only to rise upon another, and that perhaps
the last, had worn her out, and it is doubtful whether at
the time, she was even conscious whose arm it was, that
held her in safety, or upon whose bosom her aching head
reclined.

   The day had just begun to dawn, when the sound of a
gun, deadened by the storm, as if it were muffled, broke
upon Welsted's ear. He raised himself to look, but could
see nothing except water—water—water ! He thought he
had been deceived—he spoke to Fanny—she answered,
but evidently unconscious of her situation.   Again the
sound struck him ; and the day brightening for a moment, as he mounted on the edge of a high-rolling wave,
he caught a glimpse of a vessel near them.

   It was a sloop of war returning to the Cape from India

   The doubt, the danger, and the difficulty of their situation now aro e from the minuteness of the object upon
which they floated, and the almost impossibility of ren-
dering them aid even if they were discovered, in so tempestuous a sea ; but it was doomed to be otherwise.   The
man-of-war had seen the distressed merchantman on
the preceding night, and missing her in the morning, when
it was evident she could not have outsailed her, the guns
were fired for the purpose of attracting those who might
be (as indeed Fanny and Welsted were) still survivors of
the fatal catastrophe which the captain of the brig concluded had occurred.

   It was certain, by the increased loudness of the report
of the next gun heard, that the vessel was nearing them.

Welsted waved, as well as he was able, the shawl in which Fanny had been enveloped, and which he disengaged from her for the purpose : but it was almost hopeless to expect so small an object to attract the eye through such a space or at such a distance. It was not seen ; yet Providence guided the brig towards the place where the unhappy creatures still existed ; they were actually caught sight of—the weather was somewhat more moderate—the gallant bark ploughed the foaming waves, and neared the sufferers.

Now was the difficult part of the task to do ; no boat could live ; and even if a rope could be thrown to Welsted, in all probability the moment the floating wreck came in contact with the larger object, it would be dashed to atoms along with those upon it. The brig got to windward, and after many fruitless efforts, at length the rope was hove towards Francis—he caught it—every eye now beamed—every heart beat. " Stand by !" was the word. —" Fend off !—Fend off !"—" easy !"—" now !"— " now !"—" now !"

The moment came ; the wreck touched the quarter of the brig ;—four or five good men, and true boatswain's mates and captains of tops, were ready in the main chains to seize it—the grasp was firm—the hold was certain— —the rope was aboard—all was right,—" Ease off !"— " Ease off !" was the cry. " Avast !"—" avast there !" sounded at the gangway. Fanny was safe on deck—the brig gave a sudden heel to windward—the wreck rose sharply under the chains, and Welsted received a mortal blow on his head at the instant of Fanny's preservation.

She was senseless. She heard not his death-scream— it was momentary—lost in the gush and rush of waters— he was seen but for an instant. In his agony he raised his hands, and a huge wave bursting over him, buried him in its black and relentless bosom——

* * * * * *

* * * * * *

It is now some time since I saw the widowed Lady Brashleigh ; she resides in a small picturesque cottage in Devonshire ; her life is one continued round of persevering piety and charity : the poor of the village in which she lives bless her name; and the aged and the sick find in *her*, the prop of their declining years, the ministering comforter of their afflictions !

In the excellent family of Lord Farnborough she passes much of her time during their residence in the west of England. Her sole consolation is derived from conversations of which her lost Welsted is the subject; and the affection which his Lordship's family so unequivocally express for him, and the grateful recollection, which they cherish of his merits and his virtues, sooth her wounded spirit.

I confess, after having heard the story of her sorrows, I felt surprised that she should survive them ; but the fond, faithful servant who knew her as a child, and who had left her native village (that in which Fanny first saw light), at her young mistress's desire, to live with and serve her; told me that her Lady seldom wept; at least before witnesses : much of her time was spent in solitude and prayer, for she was a Christian, and looked forward to a world to come, as the certain resting-place from all earthly afflictions. " And, Sir," said the poor woman, " my Lady is right; we should all have faith, and bear up against misfortune; for the proverb says " THAT WHICH CANNOT BE CURED, MUST BE ENDURED.'"

THE END

MARTHA, THE GYPSY.

————These midnight hags
By force of potent spells, of bloody characters
And conjurations horrible to hear,
Call fiends and spectres from the yawning deep,
And set the ministers of hell at work.

LONDON may appear an unbefitting scene for a story so romantic as that which I have here set down : but strange and wild as is the tale I have to tell, *it is true;* and therefore the scene of action shall not be changed; nor will I alter nor vary from the truth, save that the names of the personages in my domestic drama shall be fictitious.

To say that I am superstitious would be, in the minds of many wise personages, to write myself down as an ass ; but to say that I do not believe *that* which follows, as I am sure it was believed by *him* who related it to me, would be to discredit the testimony of a friend, as honourable and brave as ever trod the earth. He has been snatched from the world, of which he was a bright ornament, and has left more than his sweet suffering widow and orphan children affectionately to deplore his loss.

It is, I find, right and judicious most carefully and publicly to disavow a belief in supernatural visitings : but it will be long before I become either so wise or so bold as to make any such unqualified declaration. I am not weak enough to imagine myself surrounded by spirits and phantoms, or jostling through a crowd of spectres, as I walk the streets; neither do I give credence to all the idle tales of ancient dames, or frightened children, touching such matters : but when I breathe the air, and see the grass grow under my feet, I cannot but feel that *He* who gives me ability to inhale the one, and stand erect upon the other, has also the power to use, for special purposes, such means and agency as in his wisdom he may see fit; and which, in point of fact, are not more in-comprehensible to us than the very simplest effects which we every day witness, arising from unknown causes.

Philosophers may pore, and in the might of their little-ness, and the erudition of their ignorance, develope and disclose, argue and discuss; but when the sage, who sneers at the possibility of ghosts, will explain to me the doctrines of attraction and gravitation, or tell me why the wind blows, why the tides ebb and flow, or why the light shines—effects perceptible by all men—then will I admit the justice of his incredulity—then will I join the ranks of the incredulous.—However, a truce with *my* views and reflections : proceed we to the narrative.

In the vicinity of Bedford-square lived a respectable and honest man, whose name the reader will be pleased to consider Harding. He had married early : his wife was an exemplary woman, and his son and daughter were grown into that companionable age at which children repay, with their society and accomplishments, the tender cares which parents bestow upon their offspring in their early infancy.

Mr. Harding held a responsible and respectable situation under the government, in Somerset House. His income was adequate to his wants and wishes; his family a family of love : and, perhaps, taking into consideration the limited desires of what may be fairly called middling life, no man was ever more contented, or better satisfied with his lot than he.

Maria Harding, his daughter, was a modest, unassum-ing, and interesting girl, full of feeling and gentleness. She was timid and retiring; but the modesty which cast down her fine black eyes could not veil the intellect which beamed in them. Her health was by no means strong; and the paleness of her cheek — too frequently, alas ! lighted by the hectic flush of our indigenous complaint— gave a deep interest to her countenance. She was watched and reared by her tender mother, with all the care and attention which a being so delicate and so ill-suited to the perils and troubles of the world demanded.

George, her brother, was a bold and intelligent lad, full of rude health and fearless independence. His character was frequently the subject of his father's contemplation; and he saw in his disposition, his mind, his pursuits, and propensities, the promise of future success in active life.

With these children, possessing as they did the most enviable characteristics of their respective sexes, Mr. and Mrs. Harding, with thankfulness to Providence, acknowledged their happiness and perfect satisfaction with the portion assigned them in this transitory world.

Maria was about nineteen, and had, as was natural, attracted the regards, and thence gradually chained the affections of a distant relative, whose ample fortune, added to his personal and mental qualities, rendered him a most acceptable suitor to her parents, which Maria's heart silently acknowledged he would have been to *her* had he even been poor and pennyless.

The father of this intended husband of Maria was a man of importance, possessing much personal interest, through which George, the brother of his intended daughter-in-law, was to be placed in that diplomatic seminary in Downing-street whence, in due time, he was to rise through all the grades of office (which, with his peculiar talents, his friends, and especially his mother, were convinced he would so ably fill), and at last turn out an ambassador, as mighty and mysterious as my Lord Belmont, of whom I have had occasion to speak in another part of this collection of narratives.

The parents, however, of young Langdale and of Maria Harding were agreed that there was no necessity for hastening the alliance between their families, seeing that the united ages of the couple did not exceed thirty-nine years: seeing, moreover, that the elder Mr Langdale, for private reasons of his own, wished his son to attain to the age of twenty-one before he married; and seeing, moreover, still, that Mrs. Langdale, who was little more than six-and-thirty years of age herself, had reasons, which she also meant to keep entirely to herself, for seeking to delay as long as possible a ceremony, the results of which in all probability, would confer upon her, somewhat too early in

life to be agreeable to a lady of her habits and propensities, the formidable title of grandmamma.

How curious it is, when one takes up a *little bit* of
society (as a geologist crumbles and twists a bit of earth
in his hand, to ascertain its character and quality), to look
into the motives and manœuvrings of all the persons connected with it; the various workings, the indefatigable
labours, which all their little minds are undergoing to
bring about divers and sundry little points, perfectly unconnected with the great end in view, but which, for
private and hidden objects, each of them is toiling to
carry. Nobody, but those who really understood Mrs.
Langdale, could possibly have understood why she so
readily acquiesced in the desire of her husband to postpone the marriage for another twelvemonth. A stranger
would have seen in this amiable compliance only the
dutiful wife, according with the sensible husband; but I
knew her, and knew that there must be something more
than met the eye, or the ear, in that sympathy of feeling
between her and her spouse, which was not upon ordinary
occasions so evidently displayed.

Like the waterman who pulls one way and looks another,
Mrs. Langdale aided the entreaties and seconded the
commands of her loving partner, touching the seasonable
delay of which I am speaking; and it was eventually
agreed that, immediately after the coming of age of
Frederick Langdale, and not before, he was to lead
to the hymeneal altar the delicate and timid Maria
Harding.

The affair got whispered about; George's fortune in
life was highly extolled—Maria's excessive happiness prophesied by all their acquaintance; and already had sundry
younger ladies, daughters and nieces of those who discussed
these matters in divan after dinner, begun to look upon
poor Miss Harding with envy and maliciousness, and
wonder what on earth Mr. Frederick Langdale could see
in her to make him marry her. She was proclaimed
insipid, inanimate, shy, bashful, and awkward; nay, some
of her female friends went so far as to discover that she
was absolutely awry.

Still, however, Frederick and Maria went loving on;

and their hearts grew as one; so truly, so fondly, were
they attached to each other.   George, who was somewhat of a plague to the pair of lovers, was luckily at
Oxford, reading away till his head ached, to qualify himself for a degree, and the distant duties of the office
whence he was to cull his bunches of diplomatic laurels,
whence were to issue rank and title, and ribands and crosses
innumerable.

Things were in this prosperous state, the bark of life
rolling gaily along before the breeze, when, as Mr. Harding
was one day proceeding from his residence to his
office in Somerset-place, through Charlotte-street, Blooms-
bury, he was accosted by one of those female gypsies who
are found begging in the metropolis, and especially in
the particular part of it in question.   "Pray remember
Martha the Gypsy," said the woman: "give me a halfpenny for charity, Sir, pray do!"

Mr. Harding was a subscriber to the Mendicity Society,
an institution which proposes to check beggary by the
novel mode of giving nothing to the poor: moreover he
was a magistrate—moreover, he had no change; and he
sowewhat sternly desired the woman to go about her
business.

All availed him nothing; she still followed him, and
reiterated the piteous cry, "Pray remember Martha the
Gypsy!"

At length, irritated by the perseverance of the woman—
for even subordinates in government hate to be solicited
importunately—Mr. Harding, contrary to his usual custom,
and contrary to the customary usages of modern society,
turned hastily round, and fulminated an oath against the
supplicating vagrant.

"Curse!" said Martha; "have I lived to be cursed?
Hark ye, man—poor, weak, haughty man!   Mark me,
Sir—look at me."

He did look at her; and beheld a countenance on fire
with rage.   A pair of eyes blacker than jet, and brighter
than diamonds, glared like stars upon him; her black hair
dishevelled, hung over her olive cheeks; and a row of
teeth whiter than the driven snow displayed themselves
from between a pair of coral lips, in a dreadful smile, a

ghastly sneer of contempt which mingled in her passion. Harding was rivetted to the spot; and, affected partly by the powerful fascination of her superhuman countenance, and partly by the dread of a disturbance in the street, he paused to listen to her.

" Mark me, Sir," said Martha; " you and I shall meet again. Thrice shall you see me before you die. My visitings will be dreadful; but the third will be the last!"

There was a solemnity in this declaration which struck to his very heart, coming too, as it did, only from a vagrant outcast. Passengers were approaching; and wishing, he knew not why, to soothe the ire of the angry woman, he mechanically drew from his pocket some silver, which he tendered to her.

" There, my good woman—there," said he, stretching forth his hand.

" Good woman!" retorted the hag, pushing back the proferred alms, " Money now? I—I that have been cursed? 'tis all too late, proud gentleman—the deed is done, the curse is on you!" Saying which, she huddled her ragged red cloak about her shoulders, and hurried from his sight, into the deep and dreary recesses of St. Giles's.

Harding experienced, as she vanished from his eye, a most extraordinary sensation: he felt grieved that he had spoken so harshly to the poor creature, and returned his shillings to his pocket with regret. Of course fear of the fulfilment of her predictions did not mingle with any of his feelings on the occasion; and he proceeded to his office in Somerset-place, and performed all the arduous official duties of reading the opposition newspapers, discussing the leading politics of the day with the head of another department, and signing his name three times before four o'clock.

Martha the Gypsy, however, although he had *poohpoohed* her out of his memory, would ever and anon flash across his mind; her figure was indelibly stamped upon his recollection; and though, of course, as I before said, a man of his firmness and intellect could care nothing, one way or another, for the malediction of an ignorant, illiterate

gypsy, still his feelings—whence arising I know not—
prompted him to call a hackney-coach, and proceed *en
voiture* to his house, rather than run the risk of again
encountering the metropolitan sybil, under whose forcible
denunciation he was actually labouring.

There is a period in each day of the lives of married
people, at which, I am given to understand, a more than
ordinarily unreserved communication of facts and feelings
takes place; when all the world is shut out, and the two
beings, who are in truth " but only one," commune together freely and fully upon the occurrences of the past day.
At this period, the else sacred secrets of the drawing-room
coterie, and the *tellable* jokes of the after-dinner con-
vivialists, are mutually interchanged by the fond pair, who,
by the barbarous customs of uncivilized Britain, have been
separated during part of the preceding evening.

Then it is that the husband informs his anxious consort
how he has forwarded his worldly views with such a man—
how he has carried his point in such a quarter—what he
thinks of the talents of one, of the character of another; while
the communicative wife gives *her* view of the same subjects,
founded upon what she has gathered from the individuals
composing the female cabinet, and explains why she thinks
he must have been deceived upon this point, or misled
upon that. And thus, in recounting, in arguing, in discussing, and descanting, the blended interests of the happy
pair are strengthened, their best hopes nourished, and,
perhaps, eventually realized.

A few friends at dinner, and some refreshers in the evening, had prevented Harding from saying a word to his
beloved Eliza about the Gypsy ; and perhaps, till the
" witching time" which I have attempted to define, he
would not have mentioned the occurrence, even had they
been alone. Most certainly he did not think the less of the
horrible vision ; and when the company had dispersed, and
the affectionate couple had retired to rest, he stated the
circumstance exactly as it had occurred, and received from
his fair lady just such an answer as a prudent, intelligent,
and discreet woman of sense would give to such a communication. She vindicated his original determination not
to be imposed upon—wondered at his subsequent willing-

ness to give to such an undeserving object, particularly
while he had three or four soup-tickets in his pocket—was
somewhat surprised that he had not consigned the bold
intruder to the hands of the beadle—and, ridiculing the
impression which the hag's appearance seemed to have made
upon her husband's mind, narrated a tour performed by
herself with some friends to Norwood, when she was a girl,
and when one of those very women had told her fortune,
not one word of which ever came true—and, in a discussion
of some length, animadverting strongly upon the weakness
and impiety of noticing the sayings and doings of such idle
creatures, she fell fast asleep.

Not so Harding: he was restless and worried, and felt
that he would give the world to be able to recal the curse
which he had rashly uttered against the poor woman.
Helpless as she was, and in distress, why did his passion
conquer his judgment? Why did he add to the bitterness
of refusal the sting of malediction? However, it was useless
to regret *that* which was past—and, wearied and mortified
with his reflections, he at length followed his better half
into that profound slumber, which the length and subject
of his harangue had so comfortably ensured her.

The morning came, and brightly beamed the sun—that
is, as brightly as it ever beams in London. The office hour
arrived; and Mr. Harding proceeded, *not* by Charlotte-
street, to Somerset House, such was his dread of seeing
the ominous woman. It is impossible to describe the effect
produced upon him by the apprehension of encountering
her: if he heard a female voice behind him in the street, he
trembled, and feared to look round, lest he should behold
Martha. In turning a corner he proceeded carefully and
cautiously, lest he should come upon her unexpectedly;—
in short, wherever he went, whatever he did, his actions,
his movements, his very words, were controlled and constrained by the horror of beholding her again.

The anathema she had uttered rang incessantly in his
ears: nay, such possession had it taken of him that he had
written her words down, and sealed the document which
contained them. " Thrice shall you see me before you
die. My visitings will be dreadful; but the third will be
the last !"

" Calais " was not more deeply imprinted on our Queen's
heart, than were these lines upon that of Harding; but he
was ashamed of the strength of his feelings, and placed
the paper wherein he had recorded them at the very bottom
of his writing desk.

Meanwhile Frederick Langdale was unremitting in his
attentions to Maria; but, as is too often the case, the
bright sunshine of their loves was clouded. Her health,
always delicate, now appeared still more so, and at times
her anxious parents felt a solicitude upon her account, new
to them; for decided symptoms of consumption began to
shew themselves, which the faculty, although they spoke of
them lightly to the fond mother and to the gentle patient,
treated with such care and caution as gave alarm to those
who could see the progress of the fatal disease, which was
unnoticed by Maria herself, who anticipated parties, and
pleasure, and gaieties, in the coming spring, which the
doctors thought it but too probable she might never enjoy.

That Mr. Langdale's *punctilio*, or Mrs. Langdale's excessive desire for apparent juvenility should have induced
the postponement of Maria's marriage, was indeed a melancholy circumstance. The agitation, the surprise, the
hope deferred, which weighed upon the sweet girl's mind,
and that doubting dread of something unexpected, which
lovers always feel, bore down her spirits and injured her
health: whereas, had the marriage been celebrated, the
relief she would have experienced from all her apprehensions, added to the tour of France and Italy, which the
happy couple were to take immediately after their union,
and a thousand little incidental occurrences consequent
thereupon would have restored her to health, while it ensured her happiness.

It was now some three months since poor Mr. Harding's
rencontre with Martha; and habit, and time, and constant
avocation, had conspired to free his mind from the dread
she at first inspired. Again he smiled and joked, again he
enjoyed society, and again dared to take the nearest road
to Somerset House; nay, he had so far recovered from the
unaccountable terror he had originally felt that he went to
his desk, and, selecting the paper wherein he had set down
the awful denunciation of the hag. d·· ··· ··· ··· ·· into

bits, and witnessed its entire destruction in the fire, with something like real satisfaction, and a determination never more to think upon so silly an affair.

Frederick Langdale was, as usual, with his betrothed, and Mrs. Harding enjoying the egotism of the lovers (for, as I said before, lovers think their conversation the most charming in the world, because they talk of nothing but themselves), when his curricle was driven to the door to convey him to Tattersall's, where his father had commissioned him to look at a horse, or horses, which he intended to purchase; for Frederick was, of all things in the world, the best possible judge of a horse.

To this sweeping dictum, pronounced by the young gentleman himself, Mr. Harding, however, was not willing altogether to assent; and therefore, in order to have the full advantage of two heads, which, as the proverb says, are better than one, the worthy father-in-law elect proposed accompanying the youth to the auctioneers' yard at Hyde-Park Corner, it being one of those few privileged days when the labourers in our public offices make holiday. The proposal was hailed with delight by the young man, who, in order to shew due deference to Mr. Harding, gave him the reins, and bowing their adieux to the ladies at the window, away they went, the splendid cattle of Mr. Langdale prancing and curvetting, fire flaming from their eyes, and smoke breathing from their nostrils.

The charioteer, however, soon found that the horses were somewhat beyond his strength, even putting his skill wholly out of the question, and, in turning into Russell-street proposed surrendering the reins to Frederick. By some misunderstanding of words, in the alarm which the adventurous middle-aged phaeton felt, Frederick did not take the reins which Harding (perfectly confounded) tendered to him in great agitation. They consequently slipped over the dashing iron on to the pole directly between the horses, which, thus freed from all restraint, reared wildly in the air, and, plunging forward, dashed the vehicle against a post, and precipitated Frederick and his respectable and respected father-in-law on to the curb-stone; the off-horse kicked desperately as the carriage became entangled and impeded, and struck Frederick a desperate blow on the head

Harding, whose right arm and collar-bone were simultaneously broken, raised himself on his left hand, and saw Frederick weltering in blood apparently lifeless before him. The infuriated animals again plunged onwards with the shattered remnant of the carriage, and, as this object was removed from his sight, the wretched father-in law beheld, standing on the opposite side of the street, watching the dreadful scene with a fixed and unruffled countenance—MARTHA, THE GYPSY.

It was doubtful whether the appearance of this horrible vision, coupled as it was with the first verification of her prophecy, had not a more striking effect upon Mr. Harding than the sad reality before him. He trembled, sickened, and fell senseless on the pavement.

Assistance was promptly procured, and the wounded sufferers were carefully removed to their respective dwellings. Frederick Langdale's sufferings were much greater than those of his companion, and, in addition to severe fractures of two of his limbs, the wound upon his head presented a most terrible appearance, and excited the greatest alarm in his medical attendants.

Mr. Harding, whose temperate course of life was greatly advantageous to his case, had suffered comparatively little . a fracture of the arm and collar-bone (which was the extent of his misfortune,) was, by skilful treatment and implicit obedience to professional commands, soon pronounced in a state of improvement; but a wound had been inflicted upon his mind which no doctor could heal. The conviction that the woman, whose anger he had incurred, had, if not the power of producing evil, at least the power of foretelling it, and that he had twice again to see her before the fulfilment of her prophecy. struck deep into his heart : and, although he felt himself more at ease when he had communicated to Mrs. Harding the fact of having seen the Gypsy at the moment of the accident, it was impossible for him to rally from the shock which his nerves had received. It was in vain he tried to shake off the perpetual apprehension of again beholding her.

Frederick Langdale remained for some time in a very precarious state. All visiters were excluded from his room, and a wretched space of two months passed, during which his affectionate Maria had never been allowed to see him nor to write to, nor to hear from, him; while her constitution, like that of my poor Fanny Meadows, was gradually giving way to the continuous operation of solicitude and sorrow.

Mr. Harding meanwhile recovered rapidly, but his spirits did not keep pace with his mending health : the dread he felt of quitting his house, the tremour excited in his breast even by a knocking at his door, or the approach of a footstep from the street, lest the intruder should be the basilisk Martha, were not to be described ; and the appearance* of his poor child did not tend to cheer the gloom which hung over him.

When at length Frederick was sufficiently recovered to receive visiters, Maria was not sufficiently well to visit him ; she was too rapidly sinking into an early grave, and even the physicians themselves began to feel desirous of preparing her parents for the worst, while she, full of the symptomatic prospectiveness of the insidious disease, still talked anticipatingly of future happiness, when Frederick would be sufficiently re-established to visit her.

At length, however, her doctors suggested a change of air—a suggestion instantly attended to, but alas !—too late—the weakness of the poor girl was such that, upon a trial of her strength, it was found inexpedient even to attempt her removal.

In this terrible state, separated from *him* whose all she was, did the exemplary patient linger, while life seemed flickering in her flushing cheek ; her eye was sunken, and her parched lip quivered with pain.

It was at length agreed that, on the following day, Frederick Langdale might be permitted to visit her :—his varied fractures were reduced, his wounds had assumed a favourable appearance. The carriage was ordered to convey him to the Hardings' at one, and the physicians advised by all means that Maria should be fully apprized of, and prepared for, the meeting, at least one day previous to its taking place. Those who are parents, and those alone, will be able to understand the tender solicitude, the wary caution with which both her father and mother proceeded in a disclosure so important as the medical men thought, to her eventual recovery—so careful that the coming joy should be imparted gradually to their suffering child, and that all the mischiefs resulting from an abrupt announcement should be avoided.

They sat down by her—spoke of Frederick—the anxious girl joined in the conversation—raised herself in bed—by degrees hope was excited that she might soon again see him—this hope was gradually improved into certainty—the period at which it might occur was next spoken of—that period again progressively diminished; the devoted girl at length caught the whole truth—she became conscious that she should behold him on the morrow—it was admitted—confessed—promised; she burst into a flood of tears, and sank upon her pillow.

At that moment the bright sun, which was shining in all its splendour, beamed into the room, and fell strongly upon her flushed countenance.

" Draw down the blind, my love," said Mrs. Harding to her husband. Harding rose and proceeded to do so.

A shriek of horror burst from him—" She is there !" exclaimed the agonized man, pointing through the window with a look of terror and dismay, almost unearthly.

" Who ?" cried his astonished wife.

" She—she—the horrid she !"

Mrs. Harding ran to her husband, and beheld, standing on the opposite side of the street, with her bright black eyes fixed attentively on the house—MARTHA, THE GYPSY.

" Draw down the blind, my love, and come away ; pray come away." said Mrs. Harding.

Harding drew down the blind.

" What evil is at hand ? What misery is impending ?' sobbed Harding.

A loud scream from his wife, who had returned to the bed-side, was the dreadful answer to his painful question.

MARIA WAS DEAD !

Twice of the thrice had he seen this dreadful fiend in human shape ; each visitation was (as she had foretold) to surpass the preceding one, in its importance of horror.—What could surpass this ?

There, before the afflicted parents, lay their innocent child stretched in the still sleep of death ; neither of them could believe it true—it seemed like a dreadful dream. Harding was overpowered, and turned fainting from the corpse of his beloved to the window he had just left. Martha was gone—and he heard her singing a wild and joyous air at the other end of the street.

The servants were summoned—medical aid was called in—but it was all too late! and the wretched parents were doomed to mourn their loved, their lost, Maria. George, her fond and affectionate brother, who was at Oxford, hastened from all the academic honors which were waiting him, to follow to the grave his beloved sister.

The effect upon Frederick Langdale was most dreadful: it was supposed that he would never recover from a shock so great, and at a moment so unexpected; for, although the delicacy of her constitution was a perpetual source of uneasiness and solicitude to her tender parents and her devoted lover, still the immediate symptoms had taken rather a favourable turn during the last few days of her life, and had re-invigorated the hopes which those who so dearly loved her entertained of her eventual recovery. Of this distressed young man I never indeed heard any thing, till about three years after, when I saw it announced in the papers that he was married to the only daughter of a rich west-country baronet; which event, if I wanted to work out another proverb here, would afford me a most admirable opportunity of doing so

The death of poor Maria, and the dread which her father entertained of the third visitation of Martha, made a complete change in the affairs of the family By the exertion of powerful interest, he obtained an appointment for his son, to act as his deputy in the office which he held; and, having achieved this desired object, resolved on leaving England tor a time, and quitting a neighbourhood in which he must be perpetually exposed to the danger which he was now perfectly convinced was inseparable from his next interview with the weird woman

George, of course, thus checked in his classical pursuits, left Oxford, and, at the early age of nineteen, commenced active official life, not certainly in the particular department which his mother had selected for his *début*; and it was somewhat observable that the Langdales, after the death of Maria, not only abstained from frequent intercourse with the Hardings during their stay in England, but that the mighty professions of the purse-proud citizen dwindled by degrees into an absolute forgetfulness of any promise, even conditional, to exert an interest for their son.

Seeing this, Mr. Harding felt that he should act prudentially, by endeavouring to place the young man where, in the course of time, he might prehaps attain to that situation, from whose honourable revenue he could live like a gentleman, and " settle comfortably."

All the arrangements, which the kind father had proposed being made, the mourning couple proceeded on a lengthened tour of the Continent : and it was evident that Harding's spirits mended rapidly when he felt conscious that his liability to encounter Martha had decreased. The sorrow of mourning was soothed and softened in the common course of nature, and the domesticated couple sat themselves quietly down at Lausanne, " the world forgetting, by the world forgot," except by their excellent and exemplary son, whose good qualities, it seems, had captivated a remarkably pretty girl, a neighbour of his, whose mother, he wrote them word, appeared equally charmed with the goodness of his income, and the consequent reasonableness of a marriage between them.

There appeared, strange to say, in this love affair, no difficulties to be surmounted, no obstacles to be overcome; and the consent of the Hardings (requested in a letter, which also begged them to be present at the ceremony, if they were willing it should take place), was presently obtained by George ; and, at the close of the second year, which had passed since their departure, the parents and son were again assembled in that house the sight of which could not fail to recal to their recollection their unhappy daughter and her melancholy fate, and which never could cease to be associated most painfully in the mind of Mr. Harding with the hated Gypsy.

The charm however had, no doubt, been broken. In the two past years Martha was probably either dead or gone from the neighbourhood. Gypsies were a wandering tribe—and why should she be an exception to a general rule ? and thus Mrs. Harding checked the rising ap-

prehensions and renewed uneasiness of her husband ; **and
so well did she succeed that, when the wedding-day came
and the bells rang and the favours fluttered in the air, his**
countenance was lighted up with smiles, and he kissed the
glowing cheek of his new daughter-in-law with warmth,
and something like happiness.

The wedding took place at that season of the year when
friends and families meet jovially and harmoniously, when
all little bickerings are forgotten, and when, by a general
feeling founded upon religion, and perpetuated by the
memory of the blessing vouchsafed to the world by the Almighty, an universal amnesty is proclaimed ; when the
cheerful fire and the teeming board announce that Christ-
mas is come, and mirth and gratulation are the order of
the day.

It unfortunately happened, however, that to the account
of Miss Wilkinson's marriage with George Harding, I am
not permitted, in truth, to add that they left town in a
travelling carriage and four, to spend the honey-moon, in
some shady blest retreat, either of their own, or lent to them
for the occasion. Three or four days of permitted absence
from his office alone were devoted to the celebration of the
nuptials, and it was agreed that the whole party, together
with the younger branches of the Wilkinsons, their cousins
and second cousins, &c., should meet on Twelfth-night to
celebrate in a juvenile party the return of the bride and
bridegroom to their home.

When that night came, it was delightful to see the happy
faces of the smiling youngsters : it was a pleasure to behold
them pleased—a participation in which, since the highest
amongst us, and the most accomplished Prince in Europe,
annually evinces the gratification he feels in such sights, I
am by no means disposed to disclaim. And merry was the
jest, and gaily did the evening pass ; and Mr. Harding,
surrounded by his youthful guests, smiled, and for a season forgot his care ; yet, as he glanced round the room, he
could not suppress a sigh, when he recollected that in that
very room his darling Maria had entertained *her* little parties on the anniversary of the same day in former years.

Supper was announced early, and the gay throng bounded
down stairs to the parlour, where an abundance of **the
luxuries of middling life crowded the board. In the centre**

appeared the great object of the feast—a huge Twelfth-cake; and gilded kings and queens stood lingering over circles of scarlet sweetmeats, and hearts of sugar lay en-shrined with warlike trophies of the same material.

Many and deep were the wounds the mighty heap re-ceived, and every guest watched with a deep anxiety the coming portion, relatively to the glittering splendour with which its frosted surface was adorned. Character-cards, illustrated with pithy mottoes and smart sayings, were dis-tributed; and, by one of those little frauds which, in such societies, are always tolerated, Mr. Harding was announced as king, and the new bride as queen; and there was such charming joking, and such harmless merriment abounding, that he looked to his wife with an expression of content, which she had often but vainly sought to find upon his countenance since the death of his dear child.

Supper concluded, the clock struck twelve, and the elders looked as if it were time for the young ones to de-part. One half hour's grace was begged for by the " King," and granted; and Mrs. George Harding on this night was to sing them a song about " poor old maidens" — an ancient quaintness, which by custom and usage, ever since she was a little child. she had annually *performed* upon this anniversary; and, accordingly, the promise be-ing claimed, silence was obtained, and she, with all that show of tucker-heaving diffidence which is so particularly becoming in a pretty plump downy-cheeked girl, prepared to commence the venerable chaunt, when a noise resem-bling that produceable by the falling of an eight-and-forty pound shot, echoed through the house. It appeared to descend from the very top of the building down each flight of stairs, rapidly and violently. It passed the room in which they were sitting, and rolled its impetuous course downwards to the basement. As it seemed to leave the hall, the parlour door was forced open, as if by a rude gust of wind, and stood ajar.

All the children were in a moment on their feet, huddled close to their respective mothers in groups. Mrs. Harding rose and rang the bell to inquire the meaning of the up-roar. Her daughter-in-law, pale as ashes, looked at George; but there was one of the party who moved not, who stirred not—That one was the elder Harding, whose eyes, first fixed steadfastly on the half-opened door, slowly followed the course of the wall of the apartment to the fire-place—there they rested.

When the servants came, they said they had heard the noise, but thought that it proceeded from above. Harding looked at his wife; and then, turning to the servant, observed carelessly that it must have been some noise in the street, and, desiring him to withdraw, entreated the bride to pursue her song. She did so; but the children had been too much alarmed to enjoy it, and the noise had in its character something so strange and unearthly that even the elders of the party, although bound not to admit anything like apprehension before their offspring, felt extremely well pleased when they found themselves at home.

When the guests were gone, and George's wife lighted her candle to retire to rest, her father-in-law kissed her affectionately, and prayed God to bless her. He then took a kind leave of his son, and, putting up a fervent prayer for his happiness, pressed him to his heart and bade him adieu with an earnestness which, under the common-place circumstances of a temporary separation, was inexplicable to the young man.

When Harding reached his bed-room he spoke to his wife, and entreated her to prepare her mind for some great calamity.

" What it is to be," said Harding, "where the blow is to fall, I know not; but it is over us this night!"

" My life!" exclaimed Mrs. Harding, " what new fancy is this?"

" Eliza, ove!" answered her husband, in a tone of unspeakable agony, " I have seen her for the third and last time !'

" Who?"

" Martha, the Gypsy."

" Impossible!" said Mrs. Harding; " you have not left the house to-day!"

" True, my beloved," replied the husband; " but I have seen her. When that tremendous noise was heard at supper, as the door was supernaturally opened, I saw her. She fixed those dreadful eyes of her's upon me; she proceeded to the fire-place, and stood in the midst of the children, and there she remained till the servant came in."

" My dearest husband," said Mrs. Harding, " this is but a disorder of the imagination !"

" Be it what it may," said he, " I have seen her. Human or superhuman—natural or supernatural—there she was. I will not strive to argue a point where I am likely to meet with little credit : all I ask is, pray fervently, have faith, and let us hope the misfortune, whatever it is, may be averted."

He kissed his wife's cheek tenderly, and, after a fitful feverish hour or two, fell into a slumber.

From that slumber never woke he more.—HE WAS FOUND DEAD IN HIS BED IN THE MORNING.

" Whether the force of imagination, coupled with the unexpected noise, produced such an alarm as to rob him of life, I know not," said my communicant; " but he was dead."

This story was told me by my friend Ellis in walking from the City to Harley-street late in the evening ; and when we came to this part of the history we were in Bedford-square at the dark and dreary corner of it where Caroline-street joins it.

" And there," said Ellis, pointing downwards, " is the street where the circumstance occurred !"

" Come, come," said I, " you tell the story well, but I suppose you do not expect it to be received as gospel ?"

" 'Faith," said he, " I know so much of it that I was one of the Twelfth-night party, and heard the noise.'

" But you did not see the spectre ?" cried I.

" No," replied Ellis, " I certainly did not."

" Nor any body else," said I, " I'll be sworn." A quick footstep was just then heard behind us.—I turned half round to let the person pass, and saw a woman enveloped in a red cloak, whose sparkling black eyes, shone upon by the dim lustre of a lamp above her head, dazzled me.—I was startled —" Pray remember old MARTHA, THE GYPSY !" said the hag.

It was like a thunder-stroke—I instantly slipped my hand into my pocket, and hastily gave her therefrom a five-shilling piece.

"Thanks, my bonny one," said the woman, and setting up a shout of contemptuous laughter, as if preternaturally aware of the motive for my bounty, she bounded down Caroline-street, towards Russell-street, singing, or rather yelling, a wild air.

Ellis did not speak during this brief scene—he pressed my arm tightly, and we quickened our pace. We said nothing to each other till we turned into Bedford-street, and the lights and passengers of Tottenham-court-road reassured us.

"What do you think of *that?*" said Ellis to me.

"Seeing is believing," was my reply.

I have never passed that dark corner of Bedford-square in the evening since.

THE END

www.ingramcontent.com/pod-product-compliance
Lightning Source LLC
Chambersburg PA
CBHW031405270326
41929CB00010BA/1339